Optimisation in Economic Analysis

Optimisation in Economic Analysis

GORDON MILLS

Professor of Economics, University of Sydney

London
GEORGE ALLEN & UNWIN

Boston   Sydney

George Allen & Unwin (Publishers) Ltd,
40 Museum Street, London WC1A 1LU, UK

George Allen & Unwin (Publishers) Ltd,
Park Lane, Hemel Hempstead, Herts HP2 4TE, UK

Allen & Unwin Inc.,
9 Winchester Terrace, Winchester, Mass 01890, USA

George Allen & Unwin Australia Pty Ltd,
8 Napier Street, North Sydney, NSW 2060, Australia

First published in 1984

HB
143.7
.M54
1984

British Library Cataloguing in Publication Data

Mills, Gordon
    Optimisation in economic analysis.
1. Economics, Mathematical   2. Mathematical
optimization
I. Title
330.01'515   HB135
ISBN 0–04–311001–0
ISBN 0–04–311002–9 Pbk

Library of Congress Cataloging in Publication Data

Mills, Gordon.
    Optimisation in economic analysis.
Includes bibliographies and index.
1. Mathematical optimization. 2. Economics,
Mathematical.   I. Title.
HB143.7.M54 1984   330'.01'51   84–359
ISBN 0–04–311001–0
ISBN 0–04–311002–9 (pbk.)

Set in 10 on 12 point Times by Mathematical Composition Setters Ltd.,
7 Ivy St. Salisbury, Wilts.
and printed in Great Britain by
Mackays of Chatham

Contents

Preface

This book is well travelled. My teaching of optimisation techniques began at the University of Bristol in 1962, when Ronald Tress (then head of the Department of Economics) and my other colleagues there were so kind (rash?) as to agree to my proposal for an undergraduate course in optimisation. In consequence, a first draft of Chapters 1–4 was written in 1970.

In 1971–2, my appointment as visiting professor in the Department of Economics of the University of Virginia resulted in my teaching a mathematical economics course in which I included non-linear optimisation, with some emphasis on the Kuhn–Tucker conditions; this yielded a first draft of Chapter 7. From 1977 onwards, a course assignment in the Department of Economics of the University of Sydney renewed my interest in the teaching of optimisation, and eventually led to rough drafts of most of the remaining chapters.

The first draft of the complete text was prepared in Sydney in 1980 and 1981, with the able help of Swee Kuen Pan, who has outstanding skill in the typing of mathematical work.

Much of the final revision was done during the later part of the academic year 1982–3, while I was a visiting scholar at the University of Virginia, on sabbatical leave from the University of Sydney. The work was completed during the (northern) summer of 1983, while I was a visitor at the London Business School. The generous and friendly nature of my two hosts is greatly appreciated.

Most of the final draft was typed by Swee Kuen Pan. Some later chapters were typed by Sarah Harrod at the London Business School.

The publisher's (anonymous) readers provided a helpful blend of encouraging praise and trenchant criticism; and Nicholas Brealey of Allen & Unwin insisted on careful and extensive revision.

My wife Pauline suffered the usual pains associated with having a husband working on a book; she also proof read the typescript, prepared the index and claims to have improved the grammatical quality of the text.

To all these people go my thanks. Of course, I take sole responsibility for the book's remaining imperfections.

Sydney
September 1983   GORDON MILLS

Introduction

THE ROLES FOR OPTIMISATION IN ECONOMIC ANALYSIS

Because the fundamental economic problem is one of making the best use of limited resources, mathematical optimisation methods have an important position in the economist's tool-kit. Indeed, various different kinds of economic study employ models of optimising behaviour, and hence use such methods.

One major field in which optimisation methods are widely used is neoclassical economic theory, which perceives all economic agents as optimisers. Or, to be more specific, the theory postulates that an economic agent chooses values for decision variables (e.g. consumption quantities, prices charged by manufacturers) so as to optimise the value taken by the target or objective function (e.g. profit, utility). The choice of values for the decision variables is, of course, circumscribed by various limitations inherent in the situation being modelled (e.g. the restricted availability of some resources), and these limitations are expressed as constraints in the mathematical model. The optimising analysis is then used to explain or predict behaviour. In recent decades, economists have attempted to come to grips more effectively with the complexities of the real world by building more detailed models, and this in turn has led to the deployment (and, on occasion, even the invention and development) of more powerful mathematical methods.

Of course, the applicability of optimisation techniques is not restricted to the particular view of the world that is implicit in such neoclassical theory. This proposition is most amply demonstrated by the use of these techniques in economic planning. Here the aim of the study is explicitly *prescriptive:* given the target of the economic agent, what investments should be made, what output levels should be set, what purchases should be made, so as to meet this target to the greatest degree possible? The use of such planning techniques transcends geographical and political boundaries, as may be seen readily by considering some examples.

The transnational oil company pursues its capitalistic goals with the help of planning tools such as mathematical programming procedures which help it to decide (*inter alia*) what pattern of purchases of crude oils of differing specifications will enable it to meet stated market demands at minimum cost. Equally, similar optimisation techniques are used (albeit with different goals) at a variety of levels in the planning bureaucracies of the centrally planned economies of Eastern Europe.

The universality of interest in the use of optimisation techniques to guide planning decisions may be illustrated also from the history of what has come to be called 'linear programming', one of the most widely used planning techniques. When consulted in 1938 about a practical problem concerning the most economical utilisation of resources in a local enterprise a Russian mathematician, L. V. Kantorovich, came to realise that there was an entire class of such problems that could be formulated in terms of a linear optimising model; he also realised that the development of an effective mathematical procedure to find the optimal solution to such a problem would be a far from trivial task. In 1947, an American mathematician, G. B. Dantzig, independently came to the same understanding (while considering some planning problems occurring in large military enterprises), and discovered the first effective general-purpose mathematical procedure for computing optimal solutions to such problems.

Since then, development of linear programming and related mathematical optimisation techniques has gone on apace in these two and many other countries. Some of the purely mathematical research, and most of the development of skills in the practical use of these planning techniques, has taken place in planning agencies and in the planning sections of productive enterprises, government departments and so forth. This work has contributed to the growth of an entire profession of people who specialise in model-building for planning decisions, who practise what is now often called management science or operational research, and for whom mathematical optimisation techniques are an important tool.

Much the same set of mathematical optimisation methods is used in the two areas of economic theory and applied planning (prescriptive) analysis. However the style of use differs. Traditionally the economic theorist has been concerned primarily with so-called *comparative statics* analysis: this postulates a change in some exogenous factor (e.g. an increase in taxation, a discovery of a new oil field, an increase in pay in an industry) and studies the behaviour of the relevant economic agents before and after the change; each of the 'before' and 'after' situations is analysed in a static way, i.e. as if it had prevailed for a long time and all agents had adjusted fully to it; the analysis is not concerned with the process of transition, in which the agents move from the old to the new situation. Thus the study requires only a double application of a static, single-period model; and hence the analysis may not be at all complex.

In contrast, a proportion of the more recent work in economic theory deals with *dynamic* situations, in which a principal focus is the way in which economic agents adjust their behaviour over time. These studies address questions such as: what is the optimal consumption pattern for an individual over a lifetime, given that the individual's income rate first increases, and then (later in life) decreases? and how and at what rates will society use up stocks of an exhaustible natural resource? In such dynamic analysis, the distinctive feature is not merely that time passes; rather it is that some underlying features necessarily change with the passage of time. For example, the individual grows older; the resource stock is diminished. And in such analyses, the transitions matter: the rates of change (per unit of time) of the various economic magnitudes are an essential feature of the situation being studied.

For such studies in *economic dynamics,* the optimising models are necessarily more complex. Because the values of the economic variables can change over time, all variables must be identified by time – i.e. for each variable, a distinction must be made between the value at time t and the value at each other time. If time is divided into discrete periods (as is often the practice), then a dynamic model necessarily deals with a significant number of such periods, and this makes the model larger than that for a (corresponding) analysis in comparative statics, where the model represents only a single time-period.

Most prescriptive studies for policy decisions also require dynamic formulations, and hence here too multi-period models are commonly used. In many such contexts, the stylised representations often used in economic theory are inappropriate; instead, the specific history of the situation must be included in the model. Where the entity is not newly begun (as, for example, where the model represents production opportunities open to a long-established firm), it is usually necessary to include the history of past investment decisions, at least where these lead to a heterogeneous collection of productive capacities. Such studies are termed exercises in *historical dynamics.* Because of the need to include historical detail, the models tend to be even more complex than those used in dynamic studies in economic theory.

A further reason for the additional complexity of applied prescriptive models is the empirical need to define commodities very narrowly, a practice that can lead to very large dimensionality. Models with thousands of commodity variables are by no means uncommon, and the number of resource and other constraints can also be very considerable. In much economic theory, on the other hand, it is often sufficient to postulate only two commodities; where the model contains more than two, the stylisation may permit all or many products to be regarded as having similar general properties, and hence not requiring individual treatment.

Thus developments in the use of optimisation methods in economic analysis (a term used here to embrace both theory and prescriptive policy studies) have depended not only on the research of mathematicians (and economists, and others) who have developed the new mathematical techniques, but also on the astounding growth in computational power afforded by the advances in micro-electronics, and needed to handle the great dimensionality required in many models.

Nevertheless the dazzling results stemming from these conceptual and engineering advances must not be allowed to hide the fact that the building of the mathematical model is still an art that requires good judgement and sense. No matter how great the intellectual prowess in developing optimising procedures, and no matter how striking our ability to make enormous optimising calculations in remarkably small time-spans, if the model is a foolish, or merely a poor, representation of the problem in hand, then the (nominally) 'optimal' results will not bring benefits; indeed, if they are misleading, they can be positively dangerous in the hands of a susceptible and enthusiastic innocent.

Although there can be significant problems in modelling the technology and in ascertaining the resource or other constraints, the greatest difficulty is often found in establishing an acceptable maximand (or minimand, as the case may be). Does the firm really want to go the whole way in maximising profits? If the individual is to be regarded as maximising utility, how is utility to be conceptualised and measured? It seems that it is doubts on this aspect, above all, that lead some to criticise and reject formal optimisation in economic analysis.

Although such wholesale rejection is usually no more than an act of nihilism, those who favour and practise formal optimisation must never forget that model-formulation is usually the weakest link in the whole business. In empirical prescriptive work (though not in economic theory), some consolation is to be had from the fact that, with the great computational power now at our disposal, it is often possible to use a maximand (which is admitted to be an unsatisfactory formulation) simply to lead the calculations to an initial solution, which (it is hoped) is at least 'sensible', and perhaps even 'good'. Further calculations can then be used to explore other good solutions in the neighbourhood of the first. The choice among these alternative policies is then made directly by the decision-makers, who first use the formal optimising calculations to guide them to the more promising outcomes in the realm of the possible, and then use their judgements about what is preferable to select among alternatives, even when those preferences can not be made sufficiently explicit for formalisation in a maximand.

THE ORGANISATION OF THE BOOK

The style of the book is informal, and I have attempted to present arguments in a detailed step-by-step manner, often with intuitive explanations, in order to facilitate understanding by readers who do not consider themselves specialists in mathematical work. In general, computational procedures are not considered; mathematical proofs are rarely given, but I do try to convince the reader of the plausibility of the results. At the same time, such informality is no excuse for lack of rigour. My aim is to state theorems with precision, and to demonstrate the great care that is needed for safe and successful application of the mathematical tools.

Although the greater part of the book is devoted to explanation of mathematical tools, there are some parts dealing with the art of model formulation; and, throughout the book, there is discussion of economic uses and interpretations.

The first four chapters deal with linear models, that is to say models where the maximand is a linear function of the decision variables, and where the constraints are also linear in those variables. Chapter 1 introduces in some detail the components of the linear model; the discussion also serves to illustrate the elements of the general problem in constrained optimisation. Chapter 2 identifies the nature of the optimal solution in a linear model and gives a very brief introduction to linear programming, i.e. to the basic ideas underlying the computational procedures used to calculate the optimum in a linear model. This mathematical analysis is continued in Chapter 3, which defines and interprets the so-called 'duality' properties of the optimum solution, properties that are of crucial significance in many economic applications. Chapter 4 provides more examples of the formulation of linear models; it considers the possibility of alternative formulations, and discusses the equivalence between optimisation and competitive equilibrium.

These linear models may be used to represent static or single-period situations, and the illustrations in the first four chapters are all of this kind. However, a great strength of such modelling is that it may be extended to multi-period situations; it is used in this way both in economic theory and in prescriptive policy studies. Chapter 6 treats such optimisation over time: the first few sections deploy linear models in this new context; the later parts deal with the concept of the planning horizon, and consider the question of consistency in decision-making over time, i.e. where the agent can change later parts of a plan before they have been implemented.

Neoclassical economic theory supposes that, at the outset of the optimisation, a list of the efficient solutions is available; the economist's task is then to apply the relevant economic criterion in order to select the most desirable of these efficient solutions. This view supposes (in effect) that some engineers or other generous souls have carried out some prior optimisation in order to produce the list of efficient points. For work in economic theory, this approach *may* be entirely satisfactory, since the objective is to establish the *qualitative* nature of the optimum. For *empirical* work in prescriptive policy studies (or elsewhere), no such short-cut is ever possible. Instead, the analysis must begin with the fundamental building blocks. This is what the linear (programming) model does, and thus it is no surprise to find programming models much used in empirical work. This theme, in which traditional neoclassical theory is contrasted with programming analyses, is explored in detail in Chapter 5, in the context of production theory.

A further comparison between neoclassical theory and programming models relates to the nature of the optimal solution. The traditional theory uses calculus-based models, in which it is supposed that non-negativity (and similar) requirements are met automatically. Programming methods in contrast (and more realistically) give explicit recognition to such requirements, and the optimal solution is not uncommonly a 'boundary' solution, i.e. at a point where the non-negativity (or other) requirement is an effective constraint. Indeed, it is one of the particular strengths of linear programming that it recognises this point, and uses the property to guide efficient methods of calculation.

For non-linear problems, the traditional calculus approach has been extended in recent years. The crucial innovation is the development of the Kuhn–Tucker conditions; these characterise an optimum when the problem has *inequality* constraints, which is of course the norm in economic models. These developments are treated in Chapter 7.

The Kuhn–Tucker conditions may be used in (qualitative) inquiries in economic theory, and also to guide explicit numerical calculations for small-scale models. But the conditions themselves do not comprise a computational procedure and hence are not applicable, as they stand, to large-scale numerical cases. The first section of Chapter 8 considers the nature of the non-linear optimum, to show why computation is difficult in the general case, and briefly describes some general computational procedures. The next two sections deal with relatively powerful computational procedures for *separable* and *quadratic programming,* two special cases that are important in economic analysis. The related topics of *indivisibilities* and *diseconomies of scale* (and the problems they create for competitive markets) are considered in the remaining parts of the chapter.

Multi-period situations can be regarded as merely one (important) class of multi-stage decision processes, in which a number of decisions are taken sequentially (or may be so regarded). Often, there are a number of alternative computational procedures that may be used for such a problem. However, the conceptual approach known as *dynamic programming* commonly leads to the most effective computational procedure; this is the subject of Chapter 9.

Chapter 10 presents detailed accounts of some further economic applications using formal optimising methods. The aim of the chapter is to convey to the student something of the practicalities of using such methods in economic analysis. In the same spirit, the chapter ends with some advice on reading such research in the journals and research monographs.

Finally it must be noted that the book does not discuss uncertainty. Recent years have seen very important developments in the modelling of uncertainty (mainly by using probabilistic concepts), and in consequence significant methods and results have been established, both in economic theory and in prescriptive work. But these problems and methods generally require models that are even more complex than those noted earlier in this introduction, and it seems best not to include them in a book intended for the student's first approach to the field of optimisation.

To help the student with limited mathematical background, Appendix A identifies the mathematical prerequisites, and offers advice on reading for any student who wishes to undertake some revision of these topics. Some students (especially those with a business orientation) may come to the book with a limited knowledge of the fundamental concepts of economic theory. Although some such concepts are sketched briefly when first used in the text, fuller and more formal definitions of some of the terms are given in a glossary (Appendix B).

Traditionally the student of economic theory has not been led to pay sufficient attention to the practicalities of applying the analytical models. As should be clear already, this book seeks to avoid that shortcoming, and it is hoped that such a student will wish to read the whole book. However, any student of theoretical inclination who insists on a narrow specialisation may omit, without significant loss of continuity, a few 'very applied' sections, such as: 1.10, 2.5, 4.1, 4.2, 5.10, 8.2, 8.3 and 8.8.

Similarly the business-oriented student should read the whole book to obtain the widest perspective. But lack of economic background may encourage such a student to omit, again without significant loss of continuity, sections 4.4, 4.5, 4.6 and 8.7.

Some chapters need not be studied in the order in which they are presented. The first three chapters must be read at the outset. Thereafter, for an initial reading, the student may pass over any or all of Chapters 4, 5 and 6 if it is desired to come quickly to the non-linear optimisation of Chapter 7. On the other hand, the student with business and management interests might read the first three sections of Chapter 4, include or pass over Chapter 5 according to taste, and then read Chapters 6 and 9 before turning to the non-linear and related topics discussed in Chapters 7 and 8. But all students are urged to return later to the omitted chapters, in order to get a balanced and full picture of economic optimisation.

1

The Formulation of
Linear Models

1.1 PROGRAMMING PROBLEMS

Many decision problems facing economic agents can be represented by *programming* models. The word 'programming' seems to have been used initially to denote that the aim of the economic calculation is to find a programme, or set of decisions. The mathematical techniques for performing such calculations have become known as 'mathematical programming'. A distinctive feature of these techniques is that they are directed towards *finding* numerical solutions (as distinct from merely describing the general properties of solutions); hence the emphasis is on computational efficiency.

The programme or solution that is sought is the one that optimises some function; depending on the context, the aim is to maximise something desirable (e.g. profits, utility, output of steel, balance-of-payments surplus) or to minimise something undesirable (e.g. costs, the time it takes to complete a set of tasks). As in all optimisation problems in economics, resources are scarce, and hence the programming model has constraints to reflect this. The model may also need to include constraints to represent other requirements that the decision variables must meet.

This and the following three chapters deal with *linear* programming problems; in other words, the models optimise linear functions, subject to linear constraints. This might turn out to be a serious restriction on our field of interest. But as will be seen, a wide variety of problems can be represented satisfactorily by linear models. In many cases, the problem naturally takes a linear form; in *some* of the cases where this is not so, the problem may be represented approximately by a linear model, with results that are a sufficiently good approximation to be worth using. However, there are many cases where a linear model will not serve, and some of these are considered in later chapters.

Until further notice, it is supposed that the commodities involved in the models are continuously divisible, i.e. they may be measured in fractions of a unit if necessary. On many occasions, this will be conceptually precise (e.g. tons of steel); on other occasions it will be a good approximation (e.g. if weekly production is of the order of 2,000 cars, it will be permissible to round to the nearest car any fractional result that comes out of the programming model). In yet other cases, the divisibility assumption is not tenable. For example, if a model solution proposes that 1.42 aircraft be flown from A to B, the answer clearly will not do as it stands. Furthermore, it is by no means obvious what rounding would be best, since the change made by rounding will be a large proportion of the original answer. In these 'awkward' cases, a rather different approach is necessary; this too is discussed later.

This chapter introduces three examples of problems that may be represented by linear models. It shows how the models may be formulated (although the task of finding solutions is postponed until the next chapter) and goes on to discuss some general features of such linear models.

1.2   A FIRST LINEAR MODEL: EXAMPLE A

For a first example (Example A), suppose that a manufacturer of a homogeneous commodity has stocks of 100 tons of the commodity at depot A and 250 tons at depot B; he has agreed to supply customers C, D and E (each at different locations) with 50, 120 and 180 tons respectively, as indicated in Table 1.1. The total stock (of 350 tons) exactly matches the total tonnage to be delivered to the customers, and thus all the stocks must be used up; all that the manufacturer has to decide is how many tons should be sent from each depot to each customer. Suppose that the manufacturer's aim is to arrange delivery at minimum transport cost, and that he finds that the cost of transport on any particular route is constant *per ton* irrespective of how many tons are sent along that route from a particular depot to a particular customer. Specific cost assumptions for each route are indicated in Table 1.1, and these complete the specification of the problem.

Model-building is begun by defining algebraic variables for the unknowns: let x_1 represent the number of tons to be sent from depot A to customer C, x_2 the number of tons from depot A to customer D, and so

Table 1.1   *The data for Example A – a transportation problem*

	Depot A	Depot B	
No. of tons available:	100	250	
	Customer C	Customer D	Customer E
No. of tons required:	50	120	180
Route	*Transport cost ($ per ton)*	*Variables (number of tons along each route)*	
A to C	5	x_1	
A to D	10	x_2	
A to E	12	x_3	
B to C	3	x_4	
B to D	4	x_5	
B to E	9	x_6	

forth, as listed in Table 1.1. (Note that the task of identifying the variables of the problem, and inventing the notation for them, is part of the job of building the model; it is convenient here to list the variables in Table 1.1 even though they do *not* form part of the given data.)

If x_1 tons are sent from A to C, the cost of doing so (at \$5 per ton) is obviously \$$5x_1$; similar expressions apply for the other routes. Thus the total cost (in \$) of all the transport to be arranged may be expressed as a linear function of the variables, namely

$$5x_1 + 10x_2 + 12x_3 + 3x_4 + 4x_5 + 9x_6.$$

(Note that the linearity of this function follows from the assumption that, for any given route, the cost per ton is constant.) This cost function is to be minimised by appropriate choice of values for the variables, and this part of the model is summarised in the upper part of Table 1.2.

It is also necessary to identify the requirements that the solution must meet and to write down the constraints that represent these requirements. Because the total stock just matches the total quantity demanded, the stock at *each* depot will be fully used. At depot A, for example, the solution requires that the quantity dispatched (which is the sum of x_1, x_2 and x_3, the amounts sent to C, D and E respectively) must equal the amount in stock (100 tons). This gives the first constraint in Table 1.2, while the second constraint represents the corresponding requirement for depot B.

Similar considerations apply to customers. For customer C, for example, the total amount delivered (x_1 tons from A plus x_4 tons from B) must equal the amount demanded (50 tons). This gives the third constraint.

Finally, negative values for the variables would have no acceptable meaning within the framework of the model; thus non-negativity requirements must be specified, as noted in Table 1.2. That table summarises the complete model; it is however only a summary, and in building a model it is wise to write down in plain words each element of the model before moving to the algebraic representation.

The aim here is simply to formulate the model and not to solve it. However, it may be noted that, although the choice of values for the six

Table 1.2   *The model for Example A*

Find values for $\quad\quad x_1, x_2, x_3, x_4, x_5$ and x_6 so as to
minimise $\quad\quad\quad\quad 5x_1 + 10x_2 + 12x_3 + 3x_4 + 4x_5 + 9x_6$
subject to the following constraints

$$
\begin{aligned}
x_1 + x_2 + x_3 \quad\quad\quad\quad &= 100 \\
x_4 + x_5 + x_6 &= 250 \\
x_1 \quad\quad + x_4 \quad\quad\quad &= 50 \\
x_2 \quad\quad + x_5 \quad\quad &= 120 \\
x_3 \quad\quad + x_6 &= 180 \\
x_1, x_2, \ldots, x_6 &\geq 0
\end{aligned}
$$

variables is significantly restricted by the presence of the five equality constraints and the non-negativity requirements, there is still considerable freeedom of action in choosing *feasible solutions,* i.e. values that satisfy these constraints but do not necessarily minimise the cost function. One such feasible solution is to send 50 tons from A to C, 50 tons from A to D, 70 tons from B to D and 180 tons from B to E, at a total transport cost of $2,650. Another feasible solution is to send 50 tons from A to C, 50 tons from A to E, 120 tons from B to D and 130 tons from B to E, at a total transport cost of $2,500. (Check these solutions for yourself and calculate some other feasible solutions.) Among all the feasible solutions to a programming model, one (or sometimes several) will be an *optimal solution,* i.e. will minimise the cost, or maximise the profit, or whatever the objective is. In the present case, it may be shown that the second of the feasible solutions quoted above is indeed an optimal solution, and thus that $2,500 is the lowest transport cost that can be achieved. In fact, no other feasible solution is as good, and so on this occasion the optimal solution is unique.

1.3 A FURTHER MODEL: EXAMPLE B

Example B is a heavily simplified production situation in which two goods (product 1 and product 2) are made by using three inputs that are in scarce supply (while any other inputs used are available in unlimited quantities). The production data are given in Table 1.3, where it is also noted that there are constant prices for each of the three inputs and for each of the two outputs. The firm wishes to choose output levels so as to maximise total net revenue.

As indicated in Table 1.3, each unit of product 1 requires 2 manhours of labour, 1 semi-finished unit, and 2 machine-hours of machine capacity; product 2 also requires constant amounts (per unit of output) of each of

Table 1.3 *The data for Example B – a production problem*

Input	Units	Amount available	Price per unit ($)	No. of input units required per unit of product 1	product 2
Labour	man-hours	700	4	2	1
Semi-finished units		400	5	1	1
Machine capacity	machine-hours	1050	3	2	3

Each product 1 sells for $24, each product 2 for $21. The firm's aim is to maximise total net revenue. Per unit of product 1, net revenue is $5 (being the gross revenue of $24 less the outlay $19 on inputs). For product 2, net revenue is $3 per unit.

Table 1.4   *The model for Example B*

Let numbers of units made of product 1 and product 2 be denoted x_1 and x_2 respectively.
Find values for x_1 and x_2 so as to

maximise	$5x_1 + 3x_2$
subject to	$2x_1 + x_2 \leq 700$ (labour supply)
	$x_1 + x_2 \leq 400$ (semi-finished units)
	$2x_1 + 3x_2 \leq 1050$ (machine capacity)
	$x_1 \geq 0 \; x_2 \geq 0$

these inputs. The model has three constraints, each of which says:

total amount of input used ≤ amount of input available.

The entire model is summarised in Table 1.4; check this derivation for yourself. Note again that the model is comprised entirely of linear functions; this follows from the supposed constancy of the input–output ratios, and from the constancy of input and output prices – which are supposed not to be affected by the scales of purchases or sales.

1.4   A THIRD MODEL: EXAMPLE C

In Example C, the problem is to determine the best mixture or recipe for the blending of individual agricultural products into a mixed feeding stuff to be consumed by dairy cows. Again, the problem is a very heavily simplified representation of reality.

Suppose that the blender considers the use of only six potential ingredients – oats, bran, etc. – as shown in Table 1.5. The (constant) prices

Table 1.5   *The data for Example C – a blending problem*

Ingredient	Price per 100 kg ($)	Nutrient content (kg of nutrient per 100 kg of ingredient)			
		Total digestible nutrients	Digestible protein	Calcium	Phosphorus
Oats	26.3	70	9	0.09	0.39
Bran	19.7	67	13	0.14	0.98
Flour middlings	24.1	78	16	0.09	0.73
Linseed meal	41.2	77	30	0.41	0.91
Soybean meal	35.0	78	37	0.26	0.65
Gluten feed	23.8	76	21	0.48	0.82
Minimum nutrient requirements (per 100 kg of mixed feed)		74	22	0.21	0.71

currently paid for these products are also shown in the table, together with an analysis of each ingredient showing the weight of each of four kinds of nutrient per 100 kg of ingredient. The blender has already set a product specification, shown in the bottom line of the table: each 100 kg of mixed feed he produces must have *at least* 74 kg of digestible nutrients, *at least* 0.21 kg of calcium, and so on. (The implicit assumption here is that if the mixture is particularly rich in, say, calcium, the cows do not suffer from any calcium excess.) The aim of the blender is to choose proportions (by weight) per 100 kg of mixed feed, of each of the six ingredients to ensure that the mixed feeding stuff meets these quality requirements, whilst at the same time minimising the outlay on the ingredients.

Variables for the model are defined at the top of Table 1.6, where the cost function is displayed next. (Check for yourself what money units are used in this function.) Each of the four nutrient requirements leads to a constraint of the form:

total amount of nutrient per 100 kg of mixed feed $\geq$ required nutrient amount

In Table 1.6, the left- and right-hand sides of each of the first two constraints have been scaled up by a factor of 100, as a matter of convenience; similarly, the third and fourth constraints have been scaled by a factor of 10,000. Of course, these scaled constraints are precisely equivalent to the originals; the scaling eliminates decimal points, and makes all the coefficients the same order. This last facilitates a neat layout, and (more importantly) helps with the control of rounding errors in those calculations that are needed to find the optimal solution.

Once the non-negativity requirements have been included, it may be thought that the model is complete. However, although the variables have been defined as quantities of ingredients per 100 kg of mixed feed, there is nothing in the model (so far) to ensure that the quantities $x_1, x_2, \ldots, x_6$ will total 100 kg. If the aim is indeed to minimise the cost per 100 kg of mixed

Table 1.6   *The model for Example C*

Let x_1 denote the number of kg of oats used per 100 kg of mixed feed, x_2 the similar weight of bran, and so forth.

Find values for $x_1, x_2, \ldots, x_6$ so as to

minimise $26.3x_1 + 19.7x_2 + 24.1x_3 + 41.2x_4 + 35.0x_5 + 23.8x_6$

subject to $70x_1 + \ 67x_2 + \ 78x_3 + \ 77x_4 + \ 78x_5 + \ 76x_6 \geq 7400$

$\qquad\qquad\quad 9x_1 + \ 13x_2 + \ 16x_3 + \ 30x_4 + \ 37x_5 + \ 21x_6 \geq 2200$

$\qquad\qquad\quad 9x_1 + \ 14x_2 + \ \ 9x_3 + \ 41x_4 + \ 26x_5 + \ 48x_6 \geq 2100$

$\qquad\qquad\ 39x_1 + \ 98x_2 + \ 73x_3 + \ 91x_4 + \ 65x_5 + \ 82x_6 \geq 7100$

$\qquad\qquad\quad\ x_1 + \quad x_2 + \quad x_3 + \quad x_4 + \quad x_5 + \quad x_6 = \ 100$

$\qquad\qquad\ x_1 \geq 0, \quad x_2 \geq 0, \quad \ldots, \quad x_6 \geq 0$

feed (rather than the cost of providing the stated nutrient amounts), then this requirement must be included in the model, giving the fifth constraint in Table 1.6.

1.5 EXERCISES

Formulate a model for each of the following situations:

(1) To make threaded nuts, an engineering department carries out two operations on specially prepared blanks: first one kind of machine is used to drill a hole in a blank, and then a second type of machine taps the thread in the hole. The department has five identical drilling machines, and twenty identical machines that tap threads. Only two types of nut are manufactured: for type A, it takes 2 seconds of machine-time to drill the hole and then 10 seconds on the other kind of machine to tap the thread; for nuts of type B, the respective amounts of machine-time are 3 seconds and 8 seconds. The manufacturer can sell as many as he wants of each type of nut, and makes a profit per nut of 3 cents for type A, and 4 cents for type B. How many nuts of each type should be manufactured in an eight-hour shift, in order to maximise total profit?

(2) In Example A, suppose some additional considerations now arise. Depot A and customers C and D are located in country I, while depot B and customers E are in country II. The government of country I will not allow imports to exceed 100 tons. Furthermore, the transport route from depot A to customer C passes over difficult ground, and no more than 40 tons can be sent along that route.

(3) A retailer has stocks (shown in the table below) of three models of a consumer durable good that happens to be in short supply. Model A is a de luxe version, Model B a standard version and Model C an economy type. He has two shops D and E located, respectively, in rich and poor suburbs of a city. His policy is to charge higher prices in shop D; the resulting unit profits are as shown in the table. He reckons that he can sell 100 units in shop D and 80 in shop E and that, because of the shortage, the customers will be prepared to take whatever model is offered, though only at the prices already established. The retailer wants to assign stocks to shops so as to maximise his total profit.

Model	No. of units in stock	Profit per unit for sales in shop D ($)	shop E ($)
A	40	15	8
B	70	7	6
C	50	6	4

1.6 THE COMPONENTS OF THE LINEAR MODEL

The fundamental building block is the *process* or *activity*. In Example A, a process comprises the transporting of a commodity along a particular route; in Example C, it is the inclusion of an ingredient in the blend; in Example B, a manufacturing process. Each process is characterised by the ratios between the input and output amounts; in the first process of

Example B, for instance, *2* man-hours, *1* semi-finished unit, and *2* machine-hours are combined to yield *1* unit of model 1, and *0* units of model 2. This set of ratios, namely $2:1:2:1:0$ identifies this process, and distinguishes it from the other technological process, which yields model 2 as output and has ratios $1:1:3:0:1$.

One of the distinctive features of the linear model is the assumption that these ratios are unchanging as the scale of the process is altered. In Example B, for instance, it is supposed that a doubling of the output of product 1 requires a doubling of each of the input quantities; in particular, this requires that all inputs vary in the same proportion. If some industrial or other process does not have this property, it may nevertheless be possible to adapt the linear model to give an approximate but adequate representation. Failing that, a linear model should not be used at all. The activity often carries an input–output interpretation, as in Example B; for Example A, however, this is not a natural interpretation. Thus the common feature of all activities is not their interpretation, but the mathematical property of fixed ratios.

As already seen, it is assumed that the scale of the activity may be varied continuously. It is necessary to define a *unit level* for each process; any convenient definition may be adopted. In Example A, a natural choice is to define x_1 as the number of tons sent from A to C, so that unit level is the transportation of *1* ton; but it would be equally valid to define x_1 as the number of *hundreds* of tons transported, thus giving as unit level the transportation of 100 tons.

A further assumption made in building a linear model is that activities are *additive*. In Example A, if x_1 tons are carried from A to C, x_2 tons from A to D and x_3 tons from A to E, then, in establishing the first constraint, it is supposed that the total number of tons carried from A is simply the sum of the parts: $x_1 + x_2 + x_3$. This may seem so obvious as not to require comment. Nevertheless the assumption is less obvious in other contexts; in Example C, for instance, the total weight of calcium in 100 lb. of the mix is assumed to be simply the sum of the amounts in the constituents. But of course this is an assumption about how the blending works. There are some chemical blending problems where additivity (which is essentially a kind of linearity assumption) does not apply. Although the assumption of additivity does generally hold, it should not be employed without pause for thought (and for empirical enquiry, if that seems necessary).

This additivity assumption enables construction of the *constraints* of the model. As the examples indicate, these may arise as equalities or inequalities. The economic context usually requires that the decision variables take non-negative values; these *non-negativity requirements* can be thought of as special kinds of constraints.

The final element of the model is the target or *objective function* – here a *linear* function of the decision variables – to be maximised or minimised as the case may be. There are many circumstances where it is not valid to suppose this function is linear (e.g. when a unit price varies with the scale of purchases); in such cases it may be possible to extend the linear model to cope with this — see section 8.1 below.

In conclusion, the linear model is a particular type of *constrained optimisation model,* in which a linear function of the decision variables is to be optimised subject to equality or inequality constraints on linear functions of the variables, and to non-negativity requirements on all the variables.

1.7 SLACK AND SURPLUS VARIABLES; STANDARD FORMS

All the variables introduced so far have represented process levels. In addition to these, a slightly different kind of variable, the so-called 'slack' or 'disposal' variable, is sometimes useful or necessary in model-building. In Example B, for instance, the first constraint was written:

number of man-hours used $\leq$ number of man-hours available.

It may be more convenient to have the constraint in the following form:

number of man-hours used + number of man-hours not used = number available.

Using x_3 to denote the number of man-hours not used, the algebraic representation of this first constraint becomes

$$2x_1 + x_2 + x_3 = 700.$$

The device of adding an appropriate slack variable to a 'less-than-or-equal-to' constraint converts that constraint to an equality; by definition, the slack variable is non-negative.

In Example B, the new variable x_3 will appear in the objective function with a zero coefficient (since the firm does not pay for labour not employed). Although a zero coefficient is common for slack variables, each case must be considered in context. Where, for example, the inequality form of a constraint signifies

amount of product sold $\leq$ amount produced,

the slack variable denotes literal disposal of excess product, and this may entail significant costs (perhaps to mitigate pollution problems); generally these costs would appear in the objective function.

Where an inequality constraint is of the opposite type (i.e. 'greater-than-

or-equal-to'), an equivalent equality form may be obtained by *subtraction* of a 'surplus' variable (which again is non-negative, by definition). In Example C, for instance, the second constraint may be reformulated:

actual weight of digestible protein *less* surplus weight = required weight.

With x_8 used to denote the surplus weight (in kg) of digestible protein (per 100 kg of mixed feed), the algebraic representation becomes

$$9x_1 + 13x_2 + 16x_3 + 30x_4 + 37x_5 + 21x_6 - 100x_8 = 2,200.$$

A surplus variable's coefficient in the objective function is again a matter for empirical consideration. (In this example, it is zero.)

It is sometimes convenient to convert an equality constraint into inequality form. For instance, the constraint $x_1 + x_3 = 8$ may be replaced by the requirement that *both* of the following be satisfied:

$$x_1 + x_3 \leqq 8$$
$$x_1 + x_3 \geqq 8$$

The above devices are sometimes required when the model is prepared for submission to a computer. Another use occurs when the model is to be transformed into the so-called *standard form* (a transformation that facilitates understanding of duality in linear models – see Chapter 4).

In the standard form for a *maximisation problem,* each of the constraints must be an inequality in which the (linear) function of the (non-negative) variables is required to be less than or equal to some numerical constant (which may be zero). For Example B, the model set out in Table 1.4 is already in such standard form.

For a *minimisation problem,* the standard form requires that each constraint be an inequality of the opposite type. In Example C, the first four constraints are already in the appropriate form. The fifth constraint may be replaced by

$$x_1 + x_2 + \ldots \quad + x_6 \geqq 100$$

and

$$x_1 + x_2 + \ldots \quad + x_6 \leqq 100$$

The second of these is multiplied by -1, to give

$$-x_1 - x_2 \ldots \quad - x_6 \geqq -100$$

and this completes the conversion to standard form.

Finally note that a maximisation problem may be converted to a minimisation problem (or vice versa) by multiplying the objective function by -1. In converting to standard form, it is sometimes simpler to do this to avoid the need to convert many (or all) of the constraints.

1.8 EXERCISES

(1) Convert the following model to the standard minimisation form:

find values for x_1, x_2 and x_3 so as to
minimise $\qquad\qquad\qquad x_1 + 2x_3$
subject to $\qquad\qquad\qquad x_1 + x_3 = 1$
$$2x_1 - x_2 + x_3 \leqq 2$$
$$x_1, x_2, x_3 \geqq 0$$

(2) Convert the above model to the standard maximisation form.
(3) In Exercise 1 of section 1.5, it was assumed implicitly that no variable cost was incurred for the time any machine stood idle. Now suppose that there is a variable cost of leaving any machine idle, namely $25 per hour for a drilling machine and $30 per hour for a threading machine.

Reformulate the model accordingly. How do the new constraints compare with the old?

1.9 THE GENERAL LINEAR MODEL: SOME NOTATION AND PROPERTIES

It is convenient to introduce here general notation that is widely but not universally used. For a general linear model in standard maximum form, let p represent the number of variables and m the number of constraints. The model may then be written:

find non-negative values for

$$x_1, x_2, \ldots, x_p \text{ so as to}$$

maximise $\quad c_1x_1 + c_2x_2 \ldots + c_mx_p$

subject to $\quad a_{11}x_1 + a_{12}x_2 + \ldots \qquad\qquad + a_{1p}x_p \leqq b_1$

$\qquad\qquad a_{21}x_1 + a_{22}x_2 + \ldots \qquad\qquad + a_{2p}x_p \leqq b_2$

$\qquad\qquad \vdots \qquad\qquad\qquad\qquad\qquad\qquad\qquad\qquad \vdots$

$\qquad\qquad a_{i1}x_1 + a_{i2}x_2 + \ldots + a_{ij}x_j + \ldots + a_{ip}x_p \leqq b_i$

$\qquad\qquad \vdots \qquad\qquad\qquad\qquad\qquad\qquad\qquad\qquad \vdots$

$\qquad\qquad a_{m1}x_1 + a_{m2}x_2 + \ldots \qquad\qquad + a_{mp}x_p \leqq b_m$

Note that subscript i is used to denote the typical constraint, and thus i runs from 1 to m; j represents the typical variable, and hence j runs from 1 to p. The double-subscripted coefficient a_{ij} is the coefficient associated with the jth variable when it appears in the ith constraint. (Of course, the general model in standard minimisation form may be written out similarly.)

This description can be abbreviated by the use of the summation sign, $\sum$. The objective function is then written

maximise
$$\sum_{j=1}^{p} c_j x_j$$

while the ith constraint becomes

$$\sum_{j=1}^{p} a_{ij} x_j \leq b_i.$$

Those familiar with matrix and vector notation will appreciate an even shorter rendering:

find values for elements of x so as to

maximise $\qquad\qquad\qquad c'x$

subject to $\qquad\qquad\qquad Ax \leq b$

$\qquad\qquad\qquad\qquad\qquad x \geq 0$

where x and c are column vectors of order p, b is a column vector of order m, and A is of order $m \times p$.

If the general (maximisation or minimisation) problem has been put into the form where all the constraints are equalities (by the addition of slack and surplus variables where necessary), a common convention is to use n to represent the number of variables (including any slack or surplus variables), while m still represents the number of constraints. For the maximisation problem, this version may be written:

find values for x_j so as to

maximise
$$\sum_{j=1}^{n} c_j x_j$$

subject to
$$\sum_{j=1}^{n} a_{ij} x_j = b_i \qquad (i = 1, \ldots, m)$$

$$x_j \geq 0 \qquad\qquad (j = 1, \ldots, n)$$

When the problem is in this form, i.e. with all constraints as equalities, it may be taken for granted that $n > m$. If this were not so, there would be at most one solution for the variables (provided there was no repetition or similar lack of independence among the constraint equalities, to put the point loosely). In other words, there would be no choice for the optimal values of the variables, and hence no programming problem.

1.10 SOME PRACTICAL ASPECTS OF MODEL-BUILDING

Of necessity, the examples and exercises considered so far are artificial and greatly simplified. This section discusses a few practical points relating to the more complex models found in empirical work. The first point relates to the size of such models: while a satisfactory analysis may require only a 'small' model with no more than (say) 100 variables and 20 constraints, some problems tackled today involve thousands of constraints and many thousands of variables. Even 'small' empirical problems require so much computation that it would not have been possible to solve them before the development of electronic computers. Most larger computers are furnished with elaborate programs for solving such linear programming models. Although computing costs have been greatly reduced as computer development has continued, the expense of solving a large linear programming problem can still be considerable.

Even quite small models may require a great deal of effort in the model-building stage. Apart from the need to identify the relevant activities and *all* the constraints of the situation, there is the task of estimating the empirical coefficients and then the mechanical labour of handling all the data and presenting them to the computer.

In practice, many of the coefficients a_{ij} appearing in the constraints of the model turn out to be zero. Although all six coefficients in Example B are non-zero, as are all thirty coefficients in Example C, a more typical pattern is found in Example A where there are only twelve non-zero coefficients out of a total of thirty. More formally, the *density* of the coefficients matrix is defined as the proportion of coefficients that are non-zero. For large problems, the density may be 1 per cent or even less. Other things equal, low density reduces the cost of preparing the model and computing the solution.

A related feature is the nature of the non-zero coefficients. In Example B, all have to be estimated from data. In Example A, on the other hand, each of the non-zero coefficients is $+1$, by definition. Example C has some of each type. Very large problems usually have a very high proportion of coefficients determined by the logic of the situation, and usually set at $+1$ or -1; again, this feature limits the cost of analysis.

2

Solving Linear Models

2.1 ALGORITHMS AND ELECTRONIC COMPUTERS

Although this book is not concerned with computational methods as such, this chapter gives some insight into the general style of linear programming calculations, and discusses some mathematical properties of the optimal solution. This is done to help the user of computer programs, and to facilitate subsequent economic interpretation of various properties of the linear model.

In many areas in traditional mathematics, there is a *general* analytical solution available for a class of problem, often a solution that can be expressed in terms of a simple formula. In the case of linear programming problems, however, all that the mathematician can provide is a numerical solution procedure or *algorithm,* in which the numerical coefficients of the specific problem are deployed at the outset. The algorithm must specify the steps of the calculation in great detail (for the benefit of the idiot-computer); and, because the calculations run through a sequence of feasible solutions before reaching the optimal solution, the algorithm is complex and the calculations very lengthy, even in the case of 'small' problems.

The computer program that embodies the algorithm sometimes requires that the model be presented in one of the standard forms described in section 1.7. Alternatively, the program may permit a constraint to be entered in *any* of the three forms ($\geq$, $\leq$ or = sign). For large problems, the user may never bring together, outside the computer, the whole collection of constraints; instead the data are prepared piece by piece, and a program known as a matrix generator is used to assemble all the data in the right order, in storage inside the computer.

Provided the users' manual describing the linear programming package has been written in a way that avoids too much technical jargon, the reader who has studied this and the previous chapter should find it relatively easy to instruct the computer to perform the required calculations.

2.2 A GRAPHICAL METHOD OF SOLUTION

Some very tiny problems can be solved by use of a graphical method. This is virtually useless for practical computation, but the approach does give a very helpful insight into some properties of the linear model and of the various computational algorithms.

Example B (introduced in section 1.3) will be used to illustrate. Because this problem has only two processes, the variables x_1 and x_2 can be plotted on the axes of a graph, as in Figure 2.1; the three constraints may then be drawn on this. (For an equality constraint, values of x_1 and x_2 satisfying the constraint lie *on* the straight line defined by the equation. In this example, each of the constraints is an inequality, and the values satisfying the constraint occupy the region on, and to *one* side of, the line; in this example, the origin is in this region; hence these regions are as indicated by the arrows shown in Figure 2.1.)

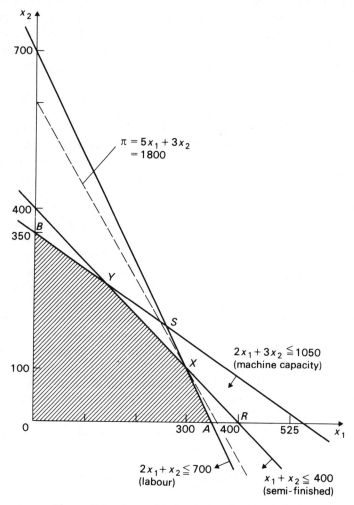

Figure 2.1 *A graphical solution for Example B*

Feasible solutions simultaneously satisfy all three constraints, together with the non-negativity requirements. The entire set of such solution points comprises the shaded area $0AXYB$, which is called the *feasible region*.

Among the points in the feasible region, the optimal solution is found at that point (or points) where the net revenue (or profit) function $5x_1 + 3x_2$ is maximised. For some arbitrary profit level π, the points that yield such profit lie on the (downward-sloping) line $5x_1 + 3x_2 = \pi$. As π is increased from zero, this line shifts sideways, moving out from the origin to the north east, keeping the same slope throughout. The largest feasible profit occurs at point X, where the iso-profit line $5x_1 + 3x_2 = 1,800$ (shown as a broken line in Figure 2.1) only just intersects the feasible region. (In other words, any further shift to the right would mean the line leaves the feasible region entirely.) Thus the maximum net revenue is $1,800, and this occurs at X, which is the intersection of the lines $x_1 + x_2 = 400$ and $2x_1 + x_2 = 700$. Solving these equations simultaneously yields the optimal policy, viz. $x_1 = 300$ and $x_2 = 100$.

This graphical approach works in much the same way for any problem that has only two variables. Of course the shape of the feasible region can differ markedly from one problem to another, and the region may not include the origin. The slope of the family of lines corresponding to different values of the objective function will also differ from case to case; and care must be taken to note whether the problem deals with maximisation or minimisation. The exercises in the next section illustrate a few of the possibilities.

2.3 EXERCISES

Solve each of the following problems by the graphical method.

(1) Find non-negative values for x_1 and x_2 so as to
maximise $\qquad\qquad\qquad\qquad x_1 + 2x_2$
subject to $\qquad\qquad\qquad\quad x_1 + x_2 \leq 4$
$\qquad\qquad\qquad\qquad\qquad x_1 \qquad\quad \leq 2$

(2) Find non-negative values for x_1 and x_2 so as to

maximise $\qquad\qquad\qquad\quad 2x_1 + x_2$
subject to $\qquad\qquad\qquad\quad x_1 + x_2 \leq 3$
$\qquad\qquad\qquad\qquad\qquad\qquad x_2 \geq 1$

(3) Find non-negative values for x_1 and x_2 so as to

minimise $\qquad\qquad\qquad\qquad x_1 + x_2$
subject to $\qquad\qquad\qquad\quad 2x_1 + x_2 \geq 6$
$\qquad\qquad\qquad\qquad\quad x_1 + 2x_2 \geq 4$

(4) Find non-negative values for x_1 and x_2 so as to

minimise $\qquad\qquad x_1 + 2x_2$

subject to $\qquad\qquad x_1 - \;\; x_2 \leqq 0$

$\qquad\qquad\qquad\quad x_1 + \;\; x_2 \geqq 2$

$\qquad\qquad\qquad 2x_1 + \;\; x_2 \geqq 2\frac{1}{2}$

2.4 EXTREME POINTS AND THE ITERATIVE NATURE OF LINEAR PROGRAMMING ALGORITHMS

As illustrated by Example B (and also by each of the problems in the exercises of section 2.3), the feasible region is always *convex*. Loosely speaking, this means that the boundary does not turn in on itself; a circular cake is convex (in plan, i.e. ignoring its thickness), but once a bite has been taken out, it is no longer convex. In Figure 2.1, the boundary of the region is composed of straight lines that meet at corners, or *extreme points*. (A precise mathematical definition of this term is given in Appendix A.) The optimal solution was found at one of these extreme points. Now if the unit profits are changed, the slope of the iso-profit line changes. For example, this slope might become less steep, in which case, with progressive change, the optimum point would eventually shift from X to Y. Generally, then, the optimum can always be found at an extreme point. The only qualification is that sometimes the optimum is not unique; for instance, if the iso-profit line took the same slope as the constraint $x_1 + x_2 \leqq 400$, then any point on the boundary from X to Y is optimal. Even in this case, however, the two extreme points X and Y are as good (by definition) as any of the other optimal solutions.

It may be proved that these qualitative results apply to any linear programming problem. Hence an optimal solution can always be found at one of the extreme points, and in searching for the optimum it is sufficient to examine the extreme points only. This result is exploited in the 'simplex method', which is the foundation of most linear programming algorithms. The method *iterates* by moving from one extreme point to another. It tests the current extreme point (feasible) solution to see if an adjacent extreme point gives a better solution (i.e. better value for the objective function). If one or more adjacent points are better, the calculation then moves to one such superior extreme point (usually choosing arbitrarily if there is more than one superior point). It then examines the extreme points that are adjacent to this new point, and so on. The iterative procedure stops as soon as the calculation reaches an extreme point that has no superior adjacent extreme point.

In Figure 2.1, for example, suppose that the calculation is started at 0. From the superior adjacent points A and B, suppose B is chosen. The calculation would next move from B to Y, and finally from Y to X. (Check the calculation for yourself.) Since X is superior to the adjacent extreme points, it gives what is called a 'local optimum'. Because the feasible region is convex, and the objective function is linear, it may be proved that such a local optimum is also a global optimum, i.e. the point is better than *all* other feasible points and not just the adjacent points. (However, if someone took a bite out of the feasible region, so that it was no longer convex, there may be more than one local optimum, and some of these local optima may be inferior to the best of them. Sketch some cases like this and experiment for yourself. Also use Figure 2.1 to see intuitively why X is also a global optimum; to do that, it helps to draw in a number of members of the family of parallel iso-profit lines. The general relationship between a local optimum and a global optimum is further explored in section 7.2.)

From Figure 2.1, it is clear how the simplex method is guaranteed to find the optimal point X, no matter which extreme point is used as the initial point. For the general linear programming problem, it may be proved that the computational procedure will always arrive at the optimal solution, and will do so in a finite number of steps. Indeed, in large problems, the method generally examines only a very small proportion of the extreme points.

Nevertheless, as the problem size grows, with more variables and more constraints, the number of extreme points grows; and hence, other things being equal, the program may be expected to work through a longer list of extreme points before reaching the optimal solution. Furthermore, the amount of computation involved in iterating from one extreme point to the next also tends to increase. Thus the total amount of computation, and hence the amount of computer time required, grows markedly with the problem size; with one large linear programming package, for example, the required time is roughly proportional to the third or fourth power of the number of constraints, and to somewhere between the first and second power of the number of variables, other things (such as the density of the matrix of coefficients) being held constant. Solution of very large problems should therefore not be attempted without prior reflection, preferably coupled with computing experience of smaller problems.

Computer programs generally do *not* require the user to specify an initial extreme point. However, if there is prior knowledge of a reasonably good extreme point solution, the program may permit this to be entered with the other initial data. Such knowledge may be available if, for example, similar problems have already been solved. With large problems, it is not generally a simple matter to identify a 'good' extreme point solution *ab initio;* but, if it can be done, it may enable the computing time to be very greatly reduced, as a result of a reduction in the number of iterations.

2.5 EXTREME POINTS AND THE ALGORITHMS: SOME FURTHER PROPERTIES

For the model of Example B, three slack variables may be defined, as in Table 2.1, where the consequent equality forms of the constraints are also recorded. Table 2.2 summarises the values taken on by the extended set of five variables at each of the extreme points. (These values may be calculated by noting from Figure 2.1 which constraint lines and non-negativity requirements (axes) pass through each extreme point.)

When the *optimal* extreme point lies *on* a constraint line (corresponding to an inequality constraint), that constraint is said to be binding; when the optimal point lies *inside* the region permitted by an inequality constraint, the constraint is said to be *non-binding*. Relative to the optimal point X in Example B, the labour and semi-finished unit supply constraints are binding (i.e. the supplies are fully used), while the machine-capacity constraint is non-binding (i.e. some capacity is left unused).

An important general result holds when a model has been put into the form in which all constraints are equalities (by introducing slack and surplus variables, if necessary). At any extreme point (including, of course, the optimal point), the number of variables taking on strictly positive values is generally equal to the number of constraints. (For Example B, this is illustrated by the results in Table 2.2.) The qualification is that occasionally a condition known as *degeneracy* can occur; in this case, an extreme point solution may have fewer strictly positive variables than there are constraints. (For an illustration, see Exercise 1 of section 2.6.)

Table 2.1   *The constraints of Example B in equality form*

Introduce three slack variables:
x_3 man-hours of labour left unused
x_4 number of semi-finished units not used
x_5 hours of machine capacity left unused

The constraints become
$$2x_1 + x_2 + x_3 \qquad\qquad = 700$$
$$x_1 + x_2 \qquad + x_4 \qquad = 400$$
$$2x_1 + 3x_2 \qquad\qquad + x_5 = 1{,}050$$

Table 2.2   *The extreme point feasible solutions for Example B*

Extreme point	Profit π	x_1	x_2	x_3	x_4	x_5
0	0	0	0	700	400	1,050
A	1,750	350	0	0	50	350
X	1,800	300	100	0	0	150
Y	1,500	150	250	150	0	0
B	1,050	0	350	350	50	0

In the absence of degeneracy, the general linear programming problem with n variables and m *equality* constraints (cf. section 1.9), where $n > m$, will have m strictly positive variables at an extreme point. Such a set of m variables is called a *basis* (and this term is often found in manuals describing linear programming computer packages). As the simplex method calculations move from one extreme point to an adjacent extreme point, one variable is dropped from the basis and another is brought in. For Example B, this phenomenon can be seen from the data in Table 2.2. (Some other computer algorithms, which are close cousins to the simplex method, seek to shorten the calculation by changing more than one basis variable at each iteration; but the fundamental idea is much the same as in the above account of the simplex method.)

2.6   EXERCISES

(1)   Solve each of the following two problems by using the graphical method. In each case, convert the constraints to equalities and hence note that the optimal solution is degenerate; study the graph to see what has happened.

(a)   Find values for x_1 and x_2 so as to

maximise $x_1 + x_2$

subject to $-x_1 + x_2 \leqq 0$

$x_1 \qquad \leqq 4$

$x_1 + x_2 \leqq 12$

$x_1, \ x_2 \geqq 0$

(b)   Find values for x_1 and x_2 so as to

minimise $2x_1 + x_2$

subject to $3x_1 + x_2 \leqq 18$

$x_2 \leqq 4$

$x_1 + x_2 \geqq 4$

$x_1, \ x_2 \geqq 0$

(2)   In the following two cases, portray the feasible region on a graph. What can be said of the third constraint in each case? What difference is there between these third constraints?

(a) $x_1 + x_2 \leqq 5$

$x_2 \leqq 4$

$2x_1 + 3x_2 \leqq 18$

$x_1, \quad x_2 \geqq 0$

(b) $x_1 + x_2 \geqq 4$

$2x_1 + x_2 \geqq 6$

$x_1 + 2x_2 \geqq 4$

$x_1, \quad x_2 \geqq 0$

2.7   FURTHER READING

The algebraic details of the simplex algorithm have not been given here because this book is not concerned with computational methods *per se*. However, any reader who wishes to study the algorithm will find the details in any one of a very large number of books. Some examples are Chapter 4 of Dorfman, Samuelson and Solow (1958), and Chapters 2 and 3 of Beale (1968).

3

Duality

3.1 A PRODUCTION EXAMPLE: THE VALUATION OF EXTRA SUPPLIES OF INPUTS

For the general linear model, this chapter explores the so-called 'duality' properties, which are of considerable importance both in theoretical analysis and in empirical applications. The fundamental mathematical point is that linear programming problems always occur in pairs. Whenever a linear model is formulated, it is possible also to formulate a non-identical twin model. Mathematical research has established some very close links between the models in the pair, and especially between their optimal solutions. The interpretation of the second model will depend on the context of the first, of course. However, in many economic applications, if the decision variables of the first model are commodity quantities, then the variables of the second are prices (of *other* commodities!), and vice versa.

In the case of a production situation such as that of Example B, the first model finds optimal output quantities in a situation where production is constrained by limits on input supplies. As will be shown later, the optimal solution for the second (or dual) model measures the values of *extra* supplies of these inputs, and provides a very simple way of finding these values.

Before turning to a formal duality analysis of Example B, however, the valuations of extra supplies will be calculated from a first-principles extension of the calculations in Chapter 2 of the optimal output quantities. The basic strategy to be deployed is this: suppose that there is a small increase in the available amount of *one* of the inputs; calculate the new set of optimal outputs; hence find the increase in net revenue and relate this to the input increment, to see how much extra revenue is earned per unit increase in the input supply.

First, consider changes in the labour supply relative to the initial limit of 700 man-hours, with the other two supply limits held fixed at their initial levels. In Figure 2.1, as the labour supply is increased (decreased), the constraint line $2x_1 + x_2 = 700$ shifts parallel to itself away from (towards) the origin. In the initial situation, the optimum is at X, the intersection of the labour constraint and the semi-finished units constraint. As the labour supply is increased, this intersection moves down the other line, towards R, and reaches R when the supply increases to 800 man-hours. (Check this from the graph.) Furthermore, the optimum is still at this intersection.

Similarly, when the labour supply is reduced, the intersection (and the optimum) moves up towards Y, and reaches Y when the labour supply is reduced to 550 man-hours. (Study of what happens outside the range of 550–800 man-hours is deferred until Chapter 5.)

For any specific labour supply in the range considered, the new optimal output and profit levels could be calculated directly from Figure 2.1. But a neater, general approach is the following: suppose that the labour supply is q man-hours, where $550 \leq q \leq 800$; the optimum is at the point where the constraint line $2x_1 + x_2 = q$ intersects the constraint line $x_1 + x_2 = 400$. Solving these two equations simultaneously gives

$$x_1 = q - 400$$
$$x_2 = 800 - q$$

while the optimal net revenue (measured in $) is

$$5x_1 + 3x_2 = 5(q - 400) + 3(800 - q) = 400 + 2q.$$

Thus, for variations in the labour supply within the specified range, each *extra* man-hour that becomes available leads (after re-optimisation) to the manufacture of one more unit of product 1 and one less unit of product 2, and to a consequent increase in net revenue of $2 (as indicated by the coefficients of q in the three expressions.) For the specified range of values for the labour supply, these rates of change are constant. Furthermore the valuation of $2 per man-hour of extra labour is a *net* valuation; it represents the extra profit to the producer *after* paying the standard wage of $4 per man-hour (cf. Table 1.3), a wage that is embedded in the net revenue function used in the optimisation.

For changes in the supply of semi-finished units (with labour supply and machine capacity held fixed at their initial levels – 700 man-hours and 1,050 machine-hours), a similar analysis yields optimal outputs of

$$x_1 = 700 - g$$
$$x_2 = 2g - 700$$

and net revenue (in $) of $1400 + g$, where the number of semi-finished units g lies in the range $350 \leq g \leq 437\frac{1}{2}$. Thus each extra semi-finished unit adds $1 (net) to the firm's profit, after the firm pays $5 for the extra unit.

For variations in the supply of machine capacity (again with the other supplies held at the initial levels), the story is a little different. From Figure 2.1, it is clear that some of the initial supply of machine capacity is not used in the initial optimal solution. As machine capacity changes, the optimum remains at X provided the capacity constraint cuts $2x_1 + x_2 = 700$ at a point above X. A little calculation shows that this applies provided the available machine-hours number not less than 900. For variations in this range, the rate of change of net revenue is zero.

Thus the (net) valuations of marginal supplies of the three inputs are $2, $1 and $0, respectively. One obvious use for this information occurs if an option arises to buy extra supplies. Suppose, for instance, the firm can buy up to 100 man-hours of *extra* labour at a (higher) wage of $5. Deployment of such extra labour would increase *gross* revenue by $6 per man-hour, and hence it would be profitable to employ all 100 extra man-hours.

3.2 SOME FURTHER PROPERTIES OF THESE VALUATIONS

Using y_1, y_2 and y_3 to denote these marginal valuations of (respectively) labour, semi-finished units and machine capacity, the calculations of the previous section may be summarised by noting that $y_1 = 2$, $y_2 = 1$ and $y_3 = 0$. For input j, y_j measures the increase in *net* revenue if an extra unit becomes available and is used optimally. Equally, if the supply of input j is *reduced* by one unit, y_j measures the reduction in (optimised) net revenue. If one unit of input j were taken away and used by the firm for some other purpose, the net revenue earned from products 1 and 2 would be reduced by y_j, and this measures the opportunity cost of the alternative deployment of that unit of input j.

Although these are *marginal* valuations, it is of interest to see what happens when they are used to value the total (initial) input supplies. This calculation gives a total value of

$$700y_1 + 400y_2 + 1,050y_3 = 1,800,$$

which is the same as the maximised net revenue obtainable if these input supplies are used optimally. As will be seen later, this result is not an accident. It means that if all inputs were paid sums equal to these marginal valuations (and this is over and above the market prices actually paid for the units), the total net revenue or profit of the firm would be exactly disbursed. (For those interested in the production theory of neoclassical economics, note that this result is related to Euler's Theorem applied to a situation of constant returns to scale; see, for example, Quirk, 1982, pp. 257–8 – or pp. 214–5 of the 1976 edition.)

Next consider the 'cost' of operating each process if the inputs are valued at these opportunity or imputed costs. For process 1 operated at unit level, the imputed cost is

$$2y_1 + y_2 + 2y_3 = 5,$$

which equals the net revenue earned. A similar result holds for the second process.

Are such equality relationships to be found for all processes in the optimum of any linear model? First consider a process used at positive level in the optimal solution. If the imputed cost were greater than the net revenue, the firm's total net revenue could be increased by deploying elsewhere some or all of the resources used in the process in question (because the value in the best alternative use is measured by the imputed cost); but this contradicts the assumption that the initial situation is optimal, and hence this case cannot occur. The opposite case can be similarly ruled out: if the imputed cost were less than the net revenue, it would mean that, for some other processes, the inputs were not very profitably employed and could with profit be transferred to the first process. Thus, in situations (like Example B) that can be interpreted in net revenue terms, for each process used in the optimal solution, the imputed cost must equal the net revenue. (A more general statement of this result is given later, in section 3.5.)

But what of processes that are not used in the optimal solution? Here, if the imputed cost were less than the net revenue, it would not be optimal to refrain from using the process. This contradiction again means that the case can be ruled out. However, imputed cost can exceed net revenue; this case indicates that the inputs can be used more profitably in other processes.

3.3   EXERCISES

(1)   A manufacturing firm operates two processes at levels x_1 and x_2, respectively. Each process uses three inputs (available in limited amounts, without variable cost). The input requirements and the input supplies are as indicated in the following linear model of the firm's profit-maximisation problem:

find non-negative values for x_1 and x_2 so as to
maximise $\qquad\qquad\quad 3x_1 + 2x_2$
subject to $\qquad\qquad\; 2x_1 + \;\; x_2 \leq \;\; 8$
$\qquad\qquad\qquad\quad\; x_1 + \;\; x_2 \leq \;\; 5$
$\qquad\qquad\qquad\quad\; x_1 + 3x_2 \leq 12$

For each of the three inputs, find the marginal valuation applicable to variation in the supply around the initial level, and state the range of variation for which the value holds. What is the economic interpretation of these values?

(2)   For the valuations of the previous exercise, test the relationships that are explored in section 3.2.

(3)   Suppose that the model introduced in Exercise 1 of section 2.3 is interpreted in terms of maximisation of net revenue subject to limits on the supplies of two inputs. For this model, repeat the analysis described in Exercises 1 and 2 above. What is the nature of the relationship between imputed cost and net revenue, per unit level of the first process? How does this result relate to the optimal solution to the maximisation problem?

3.4 THE DUAL PROBLEM FOR EXAMPLE B

The mathematical theory of duality is introduced by applying it to Example B. With the original or primal problem as defined in Table 1.4, and repeated in Table 3.1, the dual problem for this example is *defined* in the theory as that shown in the lower part of Table 3.1. One non-negative variable is defined for each constraint in the primal. The numbers from the primal are all recycled: the values on the right-hand sides of the primal constraints become the coefficients in the dual's objective function; the coefficients in the primal objective function become the right-hand sides of the dual constraints; in the primal, the coefficients on the left-hand sides of the constraints form two columns each of three rows, and in the dual these columns are used as rows, with the numbers kept in the same order. Where the primal is in standard maximum form, the dual is in standard minimum form.

Before commenting on the interpretation of this dual problem, it is helpful to calculate its optimal solution. Because there are three variables, the graphical procedure cannot be used; instead, the solution may be found by extending the technique introduced in section 2.5, in order to find all the feasible extreme point solutions. First, convert the constraints into equalities by subtracting surplus variables y_4 and y_5. With only two constraints, each extreme point solution will have two non-zero variables (i.e. two basis variables). There are, of course, ten ways of choosing two variables from the extended list of five variables. For each of these ten cases, set the other three variables equal to zero, and solve. Only five of these cases have non-negative values for the basis variables. Hence there are only five feasible extreme point solutions; these are listed in Table 3.2, and it is obvious that the optimum is at $(y_1, y_2, y_3) = (2, 1, 0)$, where the objective function takes on the value of 1800.

These results have an air of familiarity. The minimal value of the objec-

Table 3.1 *The primal and dual problems for Example B*

The primal problem:
Find non-negative values for x_1 and x_2 so as to

maximise $\qquad\qquad 5x_1 + 3x_2$

subject to $\qquad\qquad 2x_1 + x_2 \leq 700$

$\qquad\qquad\qquad\quadx_1 + x_2 \leq 400$

$\qquad\qquad\qquad\quad 2x_1 + 3x_2 \leq 1{,}050$

The dual problem:
Find non-negative values for y_1, y_2 and y_3 so as to

minimise $\qquad\qquad 700y_1 + 400y_2 + 1{,}050y_3$

subject to $\qquad\qquad 2y_1 + y_2 + 2y_3 \geq 5$

$\qquad\qquad\qquad\quady_1 + y_2 + 3y_3 \geq 3$

Table 3.2   *Extreme points of the feasible region for the dual problem, Example B*

Values of the variables (including surplus variables)					Value of the objective function $700y_1 + 400y_2 + 1{,}050y_3$
y_1	y_2	y_3	y_4	y_5	
2	1	0	0	0	1,800
$2\frac{1}{4}$	0	$\frac{1}{4}$	0	0	$1{,}837\frac{1}{2}$
3	0	0	1	0	2,100
0	5	0	0	2	2,000
0	0	$2\frac{1}{2}$	0	$4\frac{1}{2}$	2,625

tive function is the same as the optimal solution to the primal problem, while the values of the variables are the same as the imputed values of the marginal units of the input supplies, already found in section 3.1. (In section 3.2, the discussion cheats a little: the result just found here is anticipated there by premature naming of the imputed values as y_1, y_2 and y_3.) These results are not merely an accident. It may be proved in the general case that the *optimal value for each of the variables of the dual problem measures the rate of change of the objective function of the primal problem,* as the quantity is varied on the right-hand side of the corresponding primal constraint. (Remember that only one such quantity is varied at once.)

Note also that the constraints of the dual problem have the kind of interpretation already discussed in section 3.2. For example, with y_1, y_2 and y_3 interpreted as the imputed values, the first constraint says that the imputed value (cost) of unit level of the first process (of the primal problem) is greater than or equal to the net revenue per unit level of this process. Further, the equality at the optimum –

$$5x_1 + 3x_2 = 1{,}800 = 700y_1 + 400y_2 + 1{,}050y_3$$

– signifies that the total net revenue is exactly assigned or imputed to the three input supplies.

3.5   THE PRIMAL AND DUAL PROBLEMS: SOME GENERAL RESULTS

The construction of the dual problem *is* simply a matter of definition. In the general case, alternative approaches are conceivable. Throughout, this book uses a single approach, in which both problems are in standard form; if the primal is a standard maximum problem, the dual is standard minimum, and vice versa. If the initial problem is not in standard form, it should be converted to that form before writing down the dual.

For the general standard maximum problem with p variables and m

constraints, as defined in section 1.9, the dual problem is:

find non-negative values for y_1, y_2, ...,y_p so as to

minimise $\quad\quad b_1 y_1 + b_2 y_2 + \ldots + b_i y_i + \ldots + b_m y_m$

subject to $\quad\quad a_{11} y_1 + a_{21} y_2 + \ldots + a_{i1} y_i + \ldots + a_{m1} y_m \geq c_1$

$$\vdots$$

$$a_{1j} y_1 + a_{2j} y_2 + \ldots + a_{ij} y_i + \ldots + a_{mj} y_m \geq c_j$$

$$\vdots$$

$$a_{1p} y_1 + a_{2p} y_2 + \ldots + a_{ip} y_i + \ldots + a_{mp} y_m \geq c_p$$

For those familiar with matrix notation, the pair of dual problems may be written very succinctly; if the primal is

maximise $\quad\quad c'x$

subject to $\quad\quad Ax \leq b$

$$x \geq 0$$

then the dual is

minimise $\quad\quad b'y$

subject to $\quad\quad A'y \geq c$

$$y \geq 0$$

(and vice versa).

For pairs of problems created by using this definition of the dual, there is a considerable body of mathematical theory. Some principal results are stated here without proof.

Theorem 1 In the optimal solutions to the pair of problems, the value of the objective function of the primal equals the value of the objective function of the dual.

This result has already been demonstrated for Example B. In the notation for the general problem, the theorem states that

$$c_1 x_1 + c_2 x_2 + \ldots + c_p x_p = b_1 y_1 + b_2 y_2 + \ldots + b_m y_m.$$

This equation supports another general proposition, again already seen for Example B, and now stated formally:

Theorem 2 The optimal value of any dual variable measures the rate of change of the optimal value of the primal objective function, as the value on the right-hand side of the corresponding primal constraint is increased. (Similarly, an optimal primal value measures the rate of change of the dual objective function, as a dual constraint is varied.)

This result may be illuminated (but not rigorously proved) by a simple examination of the above equation: as one of the b_i is increased by a small amount Δb_i, the right-hand side of the equation increases by an amount $y_i \Delta b_i$ and hence the left-hand side (which is the objective function of the primal) changes by the same amount in order to preserve the equality. (Remember that this applies only if the change Δb_i is such that the new value of b_i remains in the range for which the y_i value is valid – cf. the discussion of Example B.)

When applied to Example B, the above equation may also be examined in dimensional terms. The products $c_j x_j$ are in money units. Now the b_i are in various physical input units, and hence (to ensure the same dimensions on both sides of the equation) each y_i must be in money units per (appropriate) input unit.

Theorem 3 In the optimal solution to either problem, if a strict inequality sign holds in any constraint, then in the optimal solution to the other problem the corresponding variable is zero.

In the context of Example B, a strict inequality for the jth dual constraint means that the imputed cost of operating the jth (primal) process at unit level exceeds the net revenue, c_j. The theorem says that then the jth process is not used in the optimal solution; this result confirms part of the discussion given at the end of section 3.2. Equally, a strict inequality in a primal constraint implies that the input supply is not fully used; in that case, the theorem says that the imputed value of the input is zero.

Returning to the general linear programming problem, a related result is:

Theorem 4 In the optimal solution to either problem, if a variable takes on a strictly positive value, then in the optimal solution to the other problem the corresponding constraint is satisfied as an equality.

Again Example B may be used to illustrate: since $x_1 > 0$ in the optimal solution to the primal, then in the optimal solution to the dual

$$2y_1 + y_2 + 2y_3 = 5.$$

The economic interpretation has already been discussed in section 3.2: since the first process *is* used, the imputed cost of doing so equals the net revenue earned.

Clearly Theorems 3 and 4 are closely related to each other; they are often called 'complementary slackness' results (for reasons that need not detain us here). However: despite superficial resemblances, one theorem is *not* the converse of the other. Indeed, for neither theorem does the converse hold, because, as reported in Table 3.3, it is possible to have both a strict equality in the constraint *and* a zero value for the corresponding variable in the other

Table 3.3 *Types of relationship between variables and constraints in the optimal solutions of the pair of problems*

Case	Value of a variable in one problem	Causal link	Corresponding constraint in the other problem	Value of slack or surplus variable associated with that constraint
A	Strictly positive	→ (Theorem 4)	Equality (binding)	Zero
B	Zero	← (Theorem 3)	Strict inequality (non-binding)	Strictly positive
C	Zero	—	Equality (binding)	Zero

problem – see Case C in the table. (For the moment, ignore the table's final column.)

This Case C is associated with the condition of degeneracy; an example is to be found in Exercise 5 of section 3.6. It *is* something of an exception, in which the constraint is only just binding i.e. the optimal point lies *on* the constraint, but would not move if the constraint were eliminated.

In all the discussion so far in this section, reference to a 'variable' has been to one of the p variables in the standard maximum form or to one of the m variables in the standard minimum form (to use the notation for the general problem). Now introduce slack and surplus variables into the present discussion. If a constraint is binding, i.e. if in the optimal solution the constraint (in its original weak inequality form in the standard problem) is satisfied as an equality, then the slack or surplus variable that would convert the inequality form into an equality constraint takes a zero value in the optimum. If, on the other hand, the original constraint is non-binding, then the associated slack or surplus variable is strictly positive in the optimum. (These results are shown in the last column of Table 3.3.) This extension permits an alternative statement of the overall results: in the (exceptional) degenerate case, both the (original) variable and the corresponding slack or surplus variable in the other problem take zero values in the optimum; in the usual case, one of the variables is strictly positive and the other is zero.

The essence of these results on 'complementary slackness' applies also in the case of non-linear optimisation, and thus the complementary slackness properties appear again, in Chapter 7 below.

3.6   EXERCISES

(1) Solve the following problem by a graphical method:

find non-negative values for x_1 and x_2 so as to
maximise $\qquad\qquad\qquad x_1 + 2x_2$
subject to $\qquad\qquad\quad 2x_1 + x_2 \leq 40$
$$x_2 \leq 20$$

Then formulate the dual problem, and solve it graphically. Compare the two solutions and their properties with the aid of the theorems from section 3.5.

(2) Formulate the problem that is dual to the problem given in Exercise 1 of section 2.3. Solve this dual graphically, and compare the results with those obtained in Exercise 3 of section 3.3.

(3) Formulate the problem that is dual to the one given in Exercise 3 of section 2.3. Solve this dual graphically, and compare the solution with that of the primal problem.

(4) Formulate the dual for the primal problem given in Exercise 1 of section 3.3. Solve the dual by evaluation of the extreme points of the feasible region; and use the theorems from section 3.5 to help compare the results with those obtained in Exercises 1 and 2 of section 3.3.

(5) (a) Solve the primal problem

minimise $\qquad\qquad\qquad 2x_1 + x_2$
subject to $\qquad\qquad\qquad -x_2 \geq -4$
$$x_1 + x_2 \geq 4$$
$$x_1, \ x_2 \geq 0$$

by using a graphical analysis. (The optimum is degenerate: after adding surplus variables, the number of strictly positive variables is less than the number of constraints; cf. section 2.5.)

(b) Formulate the dual problem, and solve it graphically. Note that the optimum is not unique.

(c) Show that the primal optimum together with one of the dual optima illustrates Case C in Table 3.3.

3.7   ON THE USE OF THE DUALITY PROPERTIES

In empirical work with larger models, it may be necessary to find numerical solutions for both the primal and dual problems. When the simplex method (or any of its cousins) is used to solve the primal problem, the calculation automatically finds the solution to the dual. Indeed the simplex method uses the relationship between the problems to guide its iterations, and thus arrives simultaneously at both solutions. The computer package is invariably arranged to give output describing both solutions.

When linear models are used in economic theoretical analyses, it is sometimes possible to use the duality relationships to obtain important *qualitative* insights; for example, it may be possible to determine whether or not a variable will be zero in the optimal solution. Such theoretical models are formulated in general terms, without specification of precise numerical coefficients. In such contexts, the duality relationships may yield these important insights even though it is not possible to carry out numerical calculations to obtain explicit solutions.

To illustrate this approach with a very small example, consider the following model:

find non-negative values for x_1 and x_2 so as to

maximise $\qquad\qquad c_1x_1 + \quad c_2x_2$

subject to $\qquad\qquad a_1x_1 + \quad a_1x_2 \leqq b_1$

$\qquad\qquad\qquad a_2x_1 + 2a_2x_2 \leqq b_2$

Suppose that the theoretical context makes it clear that $c_1 > c_2$, and that a_1 and a_2 are strictly positive. Under these circumstances, will both processes be used, i.e. will both x_1 and x_2 be strictly positive?

To answer this question, formulate the dual:

find non-negative values for y_1 and y_2 so as to

minimise $\qquad\qquad b_1y_1 + \quad b_2y_2$

subject to $\qquad\qquad a_1y_1 + \quad a_2y_2 \geqq c_1$

$\qquad\qquad\qquad a_1y_1 + 2a_2y_2 \geqq c_2$

Now, whatever the optimal values of y_1 and y_2,

$$a_1y_1 + 2a_2y_2 \geqq a_1y_1 + a_2y_2 \geqq c_1 > c_2.$$

Thus the second dual constraint must be satisfied in the optimum as a strict inequality. Hence, from Theorem 3, $x_2 = 0$ in the optimal solution. (Of course, this example is so simple that this result can be obtained from direct inspection of the primal problem. However, the approach using duality relationships can work in more complex cases where direct examination fails to resolve the issue. Section 10.4 gives another application in the context of economic theory.)

3.8 EXERCISES

(1) Formulate the dual to the following problem. Solve the dual graphically, and hence solve the primal problem by making use of the duality theorems.

Find non-negative values for x_1, x_2, x_3 and x_4 so as to

maximise $\qquad\qquad 6x_1 + 4x_2 + 6x_3 + x_4$

subject to $\qquad\qquad x_1 + \quad x_2 + 2x_3 + x_4 \leqq 3$

$\qquad\qquad\qquad 3x_1 + \quad x_2 + \quad x_3 \qquad \leqq 1$

(2) (a) Formulate a model for the following situation, and then solve it graphically. (*Hint:* it is probably easiest to formulate a model in which each variable represents the number of widgets passing through the complete system in a certain way.) Widgets are manufactured by carrying out two *successive* processes. A firm has a plant with capacity for undertaking both processes, and in addition it can buy semi-processed widgets (i.e. widgets for which the first process has already been undertaken). The firm has three types of capacity whose supply is limited; the available amounts and the requirements per widget are shown in the table.

Type of capacity	No. of units available per day	No. of units of capacity required (per widget)	
		for first process	for second process
A	800	1	1
B	1350	1	3
C	400	0	1

The firm has effectively unlimited supplies of labour; however, the trade union involved is concerned about possible shortages of work for its members and has negotiated an agreement with the firm by which at least 75 per cent of the widgets produced must have been entirely processed in the plant. The firm's aim is to maximise the daily output of widgets.

(b) Formulate the dual problem and solve it by using the solution to the primal, in conjunction with the duality theorems. Interpret each of the dual variables.

(3) For the following primal problem, formulate the dual. *Without* calculating the solution to either problem, use the properties of the dual to show that $x_3 = 0$ in the primal solution.

Choose non-negative values for x_1, x_2 and x_3 so as to

maximise $\qquad\qquad 8x_1 - 4x_2 + x_3$

subject to $\qquad\qquad x_1 - 2x_2 \qquad \leq 10$

$\qquad\qquad\qquad\quad x_1 + \quad x_2 + x_3 \leq 12$

(4) Use the graphical method to solve the dual problem of the last exercise. Then use the duality theorems to find the primal solution from the dual solution.

3.9 FURTHER READING

Any textbook that treats linear programming in depth includes a discussion of duality. In their Chapters 3 and 7, Dorfman, Samuelson and Solow (1958) give a treatment that is particularly strong in economic interpretation. Beale (1968), Chapter 5 has a very brief discussion, with emphasis on the question of when both problems are feasible and have finite optima. (In the present book, that property has been assumed throughout.)

Chapter 4 of Vandermeulen (1971) gives a particularly interesting approach to duality theory, with emphasis on economic interpretations (and some comparisons with the Marshallian and Walrasian concepts of market equilibrium). Unfortunately (from the present point of view), his exposition supposes an intimate knowledge of the algebra of the simplex method.

4

More Linear Models

The *art* of model-building is learned from example and practice. This chapter first gives some further production examples, of greater complexity than the previous ones and designed to illuminate various points of model-building technique. Later sections present linear models from other areas of economic analysis and also bring out an equivalence between competitive equilibrium and constrained optimisation.

4.1 MULTI—STAGE MODELS

Where the process being modelled comprises a sequence of stages, the programming model must include representation of the links between the stages. To illustrate, consider a model of a tinplate plant that converts coiled steel strip into coated sheets (or sometimes coated strip), the traditional coating being tin. The product is used in making 'tin' cans, amongst other things.

The incoming annealed steel coil passes through temper mills. What happens next depends on the processes employed in the particular plant. Here suppose that four different alternative sequences are employed, leading to four classes of product. (Within each class, there are many varieties, e.g. in the width and thickness of sheet, in the thickness of the coating, and in the various physical and chemical properties. These variations are ignored in the present analysis, to permit the construction of a very simple, small-scale model. For many practical purposes, however, it would be necessary to take such variety into account, and the model would then be *very* much larger, generally with hundreds or even thousands of variables.)

The four alternatives are depicted in Figure 4.1. In two of these, the tempered coil passes through an electrolytic tinning line which deposits the coating. This tinplate coil may be sold as it is to customers, or it may be cut into sheets by tinplate shears and then sold in that form. In the other two processes, shears are used to cut the uncoated ('blackplate') coil. The resulting sheet is either sold directly to customers (who do the job of tin coating for themselves), or is dipped in pots of molten tin, to yield tinplate sheets that are then sold to customers.

Because variety within product classes is to be disregarded, we simply

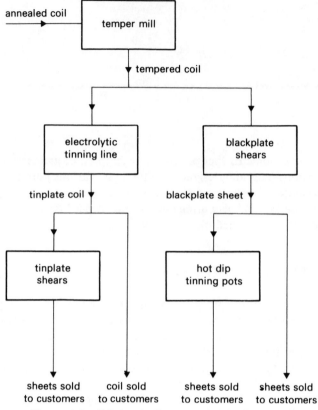

Figure 4.1   *Schematic diagram of a tinplate plant*

Table 4.1   *Data for the tinplate example*

Capacity of each piece of plant:	*tons per period*
temper mills	10,000
blackplate shears	2,000
hot dip tinning pots	1,200
electrolytic tinning lines	7,000
tinplate shears	5,000

No effective limit on availability of annealed coil.

Orders to be met from this period's production:	*tons*
electrolytic tinplate sheets	5,000
hot dipped tinplate sheets	1,000
blackplate sheets	400

Additional quantities of certain products may be sold:	*net profit (money units per ton)*
blackplate sheets	50
electrolytic tinplate coil	100

define total tonnages for each class, and then suppose that each piece of plant can have its capacity measured in terms of these aggregate tonnages, as at the top of Table 4.1. (In practice, the capacity of such plant depends to some extent on the mix of varieties being produced.) Also suppose that there is no loss or gain in weight as a batch of steel passes from one process to the next; this ignores (*inter alia*) the weight of the coating. (Clearly this is not always realistic; a later example shows how to incorporate change in weight or volume when modelling multi-stage processes.)

On the demand side, it is supposed that, in the period considered, certain orders are to be met and that there is a market for additional quantities of two of the products. Such additional sales earn the net profits shown in Table 4.1. The objective is maximisation of the total net profit for the period, subject to the capacity constraints, and subject to fulfilling the orders already accepted.

One way of building a model of this situation is to define as the variables the tonnages passing through each of the five pieces of plant; specific notation is introduced at the top of Table 4.2, which gives next the capacity constraints. Because there is a sequence of operations, the model needs 'interprocess balance' constraints; each of these says that the total tonnage leaving one piece of plant must equal the total tonnage received at the next

Table 4.2 *The model for the tinplate example*

Let the tonnages handled in each piece of plant be denoted:

temper mills	x_1
blackplate shears	x_2
hot dip pots	x_3
electrolytic tinning lines	x_4
tinplate shears	x_5

Capacity constraints:

$$x_1 \leq 10{,}000 \quad (1)$$
$$x_2 \leq 2{,}000 \quad (2)$$
$$x_3 \leq 1{,}200 \quad (3)$$
$$x_4 \leq 7{,}000 \quad (4)$$
$$x_5 \leq 5{,}000 \quad (5)$$

Inter-process balances:

$$x_1 - x_2 - x_4 = 0 \quad (6)$$
$$x_4 - x_5 \geq 0 \quad (7)$$
$$x_2 - x_3 \geq 0 \quad (8)$$

Orders to be met:

$$x_5 = 5{,}000 \quad (9)$$
$$x_3 = 1{,}000 \quad (10)$$
$$x_2 - x_3 \geq 400 \quad (11)$$

Non-negativity: $x_j \geq 0 \ (j = 1, 2, \ldots, 5)$

Objective function: maximise $50(x_2 - x_3) + 100(x_4 - x_5)$

stage. For example, for tempered coil leaving the temper mill, the balance is

$$x_1 = x_2 + x_4,$$

which becomes constraint (6) once all the variables have been transferred to the left-hand side. The electrolytic tinning line yields x_4 tons of tinplate coil and the next constraint could be written:

tons of tinplate coil produced = tons sold directly to customers
+ tons sent through tinplate shears.

But there is no variable that directly represents the weight of coil sold to customers. Since x_5 tons go to the shears, the weight of coil sold to customers must be $x_4 - x_5$; this is required to be non-negative, which is ensured by constraint (7). Similar analysis of the tonnage leaving the blackplate shears leads to constraint (8).

The remaining requirements relate to the markets. The plant is required to fulfil an order for 5,000 tons of electrolytic tinplate sheet; this requires $x_5 \geq 5,000$. Because there is no market for any extra quantity, it is legitimate to write the requirement as an equality, as in constraint (9). (However, if there were a joint product, it might be profitable to produce an excess quantity of the first product in order to benefit from the sale of an extra amount of the joint product; in that case, a constraint such as (9) should be left in inequality form.) Similarly constraint (10) represents the order for hot dipped tinplate sheets. Sales of blackplate sheets are $(x_2 - x_3)$ tons. Here there is a market over and above the initial order for 400 tons, so the requirement must be written as an inequality, as in constraint (11). (Incidentally, note that if constraint (11) is satisfied, constraint (8) is automatically satisfied. In that sense, (8) is redundant and may be omitted. This has the minor advantage of reducing the size of the model, which reduces computing costs. However, there is no obligation to hunt for redundancies, since the search is itself costly. Moreover, the omission of redundant constraints may reduce the richness of any duality analysis.)

In addition to the (fixed) profit from orders already contracted, there is a net profit of 50 money units per ton for the additional sales of blackplate sheets, and 100 money units per ton for the sales of electrolytic tinplate coil. Thus the net profit function to be maximised is

$$50(x_2 - x_3 - 400) + 100(x_4 - x_5).$$

The constant term, $50 \times (-400)$, may be omitted because (again) maximisation of the remaining variable part also maximises total net profit.

4.2   THE CHOICE BETWEEN ALTERNATIVE FORMULATIONS

In many circumstances, the model-builder can choose between alternative formulations. To illustrate this, consider another multi-stage example, one that deals with the distribution of a branded soft drink. To economise on transport costs, the firm manufactures a concentrated liquid in its factories and then dispatches this to local bottling plants, where the concentrate is diluted to produce twenty times the original volume of liquid, the diluted drink is bottled, and the bottles are distributed to local markets. In order to have a small model for the purpose of illustration, suppose (most unrealistically) that: there are only three bottling plants and four market locations; there are two factories, both of which can supply to each bottling plant; each market can be supplied by any of the bottling plants.

Most of the data for this problem are given in Table 4.3. Also suppose that per-unit manufacturing and bottling costs are the same in any location, and hence such costs are not varied by the decision on where these operations are carried out. Thus the problem reduces to that of meeting the specified demands at minimum transport cost.

For a first model, define a set of single-journey transport activities, in which (for example) x_{SA} denotes the number of thousand gallons of concentrate sent from factory S to bottling plant A, and (for example) x_{BG} denotes the number of thousands of gallons of diluted liquid sent from bottling plant B to market G. This gives a total of 18 activities and these are denoted in Table 4.4 by a reduced notation in which only the subscripts are shown (to save space); the first subscript represents the beginning, and the second subscript the end, of each journey. Table 4.4 is a tabular representation in

Table 4.3   *Data for the soft-drink example*

Manufacturing plants located at	S	T		
Capacities ('000 gallons of concentrate)	50	120		
Bottling plants located at	A	B	C	
Capacities ('000 gallons of diluted drink)	600	1800	800	
Demand centres located at	D	E	F	G
Quantities demanded ('000 gallons, diluted)	400	800	900	700

Transport costs (money units per thousand gallons of concentrate)

From/to	A	B	C
S	20	10	20
T	40	20	10

Transport costs (money units per thousand gallons of diluted drink)

From/to	D	E	F	G
A	3	5	6	7
B	3	6	8	4
C	4	5	2	5

Table 4.4 A first model for the soft-drink example

Variables:	SA	SB	SC	TA	TB	TC	AD	AE	AF	AG	BD	BE	BF	BG	CD	CE	CF	CG		
Manufacturing capacity:	1	1	1																≤	50
				1	1	1													≤	120
Bottling balances:	− 20			− 20			1	1	1	1									=	0
		− 20			− 20						1	1	1	1					=	0
			− 20			− 20									1	1	1	1	=	0
Bottling capacity:							1	1	1	1									≤	600
											1	1	1	1					≤	1,800
															1	1	1	1	≤	800
Demand requirements:							1				1				1				=	400
								1				1				1			=	800
									1				1				1		=	900
										1				1				1	=	700
Cost:	20	10	20	40	20	10	3	5	6	7	3	6	8	4	4	5	2	5		

which the coefficients of the constraints are shown in detached form (i.e. without the variable being explicitly included), each coefficient being associated with an activity variable according to the column in which it is located; again, this device saves space, and gives a clearer layout.

Constraints are required to reflect manufacturing capacity, bottling capacity, demand requirements and interprocess balances for the bottling plants. The details are given in Table 4.4. The bottling balances deserve one comment: because of dilution, the volume dispatched is twenty times the volume received. The last line of Table 4.4 shows the cost function to be minimised, based directly on the (constant) unit costs given in Table 4.3.

An alternative formulation for this soft-drink problem defines variables so that each relates to a complete sequence of processes, all the way through from manufacture to delivery to a local market. Thus, for example, x_{SAD} represents the number of thousands of gallons of diluted drink sent to market D, the bottling having been done at A with the concentrate coming from S. Since there are two manufacturing locations, three bottling plants and four markets, $2 \times 3 \times 4 = 24$ such variables are required, and these are listed, in a shorthand notation, in the column headings of Table 4.5 (the first subscript is placed above the other two simply to ease the problem of layout).

In building the model, care is required with the definitions of the variables and with the implications for the constraints. The above definition implies that unit level of the first activity (i.e. $x_{\text{SAD}} = 1$) corresponds to 1,000 gallons of diluted drink. However, for the first stage – manufacture of concentrate at S and transport to A – unit level corresponds to $1/20 \times 1,000$ gallons of concentrate. The capacity restrictions at the manufacturing plants are expressed in thousands of gallons of concentrate; thus for plant S, the capacity constraint is

$$\tfrac{1}{20}\left(x_{\text{SAD}} + x_{\text{SAE}} + \ldots + x_{\text{SCG}}\right) \leqq 50.$$

It is convenient to multiply both sides by 20, to give the first constraint in Table 4.5. *Interprocess balance constraints are no longer needed,* since the requirements (that what comes out of a bottling plant must match what goes in) are embedded implicitly in the new definitions of the variables. In calculating the cost of unit level of each activity, remember that 1,000 gallons of diluted drink require only 1/20 of 1,000 gallons of concentrate, and the unit transport cost for the concentrate stage must reflect this. The result of such calculations is the cost minimand shown in the last line of Table 4.5.

The alternative models may now be compared: the first has eighteen variables and twelve constraints, while the second has twenty-four variables and only nine constraints. For very large problems of this type, the difference could have computational significance; since computing time increases at a greater rate with extra constraints than it does with extra variables, the

Table 4.5 A second model for the soft-drink example

	S AD	S AE	S AF	S AG	S BD	S BE	S BF	S BG	S CD	S CE	S CF	S CG	T AD	T AE	T AF	T AG	T BD	T BE	T BF	T BG	T CD	T CE	T CF	T CG	
Manufacturing capacity:																									
	1	1	1	1	1	1	1	1	1	1	1	1													≤ 1,000
													1	1	1	1	1	1	1	1	1	1	1	1	≤ 2,400
Bottling capacity:																									
	1	1	1	1									1	1	1	1									≤ 600
					1	1	1	1									1	1	1	1					≤ 1,800
									1	1	1	1									1	1	1	1	≤ 800
Demand requirements:																									
	1				1				1				1				1				1				= 400
		1				1				1				1				1				1			= 800
			1				1				1				1				1				1		= 900
				1				1				1				1				1				1	= 700
Cost:	4	6	7	8	3.5	6.5	8.5	4.5	5	6	3	6	5	7	8	9	4	7	9	5	4.5	5.5	2.5	3.5	

second formulation may be preferable. But for problems of modest size, this aspect is likely to be unimportant, and considerations of convenience in building the model and in interpreting the results are likely to dominate. Yet other formulations are possible: for example, the first model could be expanded by introducing *explicit* variables to represent the volume of diluted drink bottled at each plant; this expansion may increase computing time, but may have advantages in terms of flexibility in use (e.g. if duality analysis is to be undertaken).

4.3 EXERCISES

(1) The blending problem of Example C (section 1.4) is adapted as follows:
- ingredients may still be purchased at the prices previously given, but are available only in limited amounts (measured in kg): oats 1,200; bran 1,000; flour middlings 500; linseed meal 1,700; soybean meal 800; gluten feed 8,000.
- the aim now is to blend (at minimum total cost) 6,000 kg of mixed feeding stuff of the initial specification, and 4,000 kg of another mixture meeting the following minimum requirements (expressed in proportions by weight): total digestible nutrients 0.74; digestible protein 0.15; calcium 0.0014; phosphorus 0.0055.
  (a) For this extended problem, formulate a linear model in which the output requirements are stated as inequalities (i.e. output $\geq$ 6,000, etc.). (Why is this approach valid?)
  (b) Consider the pattern of non-zero entries in the matrix of constraint coefficients. What links are there between the optimal decisions for the two blends? How are these links expressed by the pattern of non-zero entries?
(2) Use first principles (and nothing but first principles) to find the numerical solution for the tinplate model of section 4.1.
(3) In this tinplate problem, suppose that there becomes available an additional market opportunity: tempered coil may be sold at a net profit of 40 money units per ton. How should the model be adapted? How is the optimal solution affected?
(4) For the (extended) blending problem considered in exercise 1 above, convert the model to one of the standard forms and then formulate its dual. Interpret each of the dual variables.

4.4 A RICARDIAN ECONOMY

A linear model of a Ricardian economy is presented in this section. The model displays only a part of Ricardo's wide-sweeping economic system, however. A principal concern of Ricardo and other classical economists was to explain how population might grow, and how such growth might be checked by the fixity of the supply of land. In the linear model presented here, population size is regarded as being determined *exogenously* (i.e. determined outside the model, and taken as given for the purpose of the analysis). The model then concentrates on how the land is used. In this section, it is supposed that such use is planned by central direction, to maximise total output of the single crop – corn – that the land can produce. (The next section examines the workings of a competitive economic system for the same physical context.)

In this simple economy, society comprises three groups: landowners, capitalists and wage-earners. The economy is endowed with 50 acres of good land and 100 acres of poor land. On 1 acre of good land, 1 man-year of labour produces 40 bushels of corn, whereas 1 acre of poor land requires 2 man-years of labour to produce 30 bushels of corn. (These input-output ratios are supposed constant, no matter what the scale of production.)

In order to employ a labourer for one year, the capitalists have to pay in advance a wage of 10 bushels of corn. The capitalists have a wage fund of 2,100 bushels of corn, which is sufficient to pay 210 labourers. The population is large enough to be able to supply this amount of labour, and more.

Defining x_1 and x_2 as the acres of good and poor land put into production, the problem of finding the optimal production plan may be represented by the following model:

maximise $\qquad\qquad 40x_1 + 30x_2$

subject to $\qquad\qquad\quad x_1 \qquad\quad \leq \;\; 50$

$$x_2 \leq 100$$

$$x_1 + \;\; 2x_2 \leq 210$$

where the first two constraints reflect land supplies, and the third constraint the limit imposed by the wage fund.

From a simple graphical analysis, it is immediately clear that the optimal solution is $x_1 = 50$, $x_2 = 80$, with total output of 4,400 bushels. Thus all the wage fund is spent and all the good land is used; but some of the poor land is left unused.

Defining y_1, y_2 and y_3 as the dual variables corresponding to the three constraints, the dual is:

minimise $\qquad\qquad 50y_1 + 100y_2 + 210y_3$

subject to $\qquad\qquad\quad y_1 \qquad + \qquad y_3 \geq 40$

$$y_2 + \;\; 2y_3 \geq 30$$

In the optimal solution to this dual, $y_2 = 0$ (from Theorem 3, because some poor land is left unused); and the dual constraints are satisfied as equalities (from Theorem 4, because $x_1 > 0$ and $x_2 > 0$). Hence the solution is $y_1 = 25$, $y_2 = 0$ and $y_3 = 15$. These values are the marginal social products of the factors, i.e. the rates of change of gross output, if additional input supplies become available.

4.5 COMPETITIVE EQUILIBRIUM IN THE RICARDIAN ECONOMY

Suppose now that, instead of central direction of production, the decisions in the Ricardian economy are taken by the (large numbers of) individual capitalists and landowners who compete vigorously with each other in seeking to maximise their individual financial returns. As before, it is supposed that the wage rate of 10 bushels per man-year is given, and that the capitalists begin the year with an (aggregate) wage fund of 2,100 bushels. But rents for good and poor land (paid by the capitalists to the landowners) are to be determined by the competitive process.

It will now be argued that, in competitive equilibrium, these rents will take on the values of the dual variables, y_1 and y_2. This may be demonstrated informally by showing that *any* other values for the rents leave opportunities for capitalists to increase their financial rewards, and hence cannot be equilibrium values.

The wage fund is not large enough to permit the use of all the land, but is larger than that needed for the good land alone. In the absence of any rent payment, a capitalist would prefer to apply labour to good land, which is more productive. Owners of poor land will compete with each other to get small rents, and will drive the rent down to zero. At $y_2 = 0$, the return to the capitalist from the use of 1 man-year on poor land is $\frac{1}{2} \times 30 - 10 = 5$. If the rent of good land is less (greater) than 25, then the return to a capitalist from deployment of 1 man-year is greater (less) than $40 - 25 - 10 = 5$. Thus only at $y_1 = 25$ will the returns to capitalists be the same from both types of land. And since both will be used, these two returns must be the same for equilibrium.

Thus a competitive economy yields equilibrium rent levels that are just the same as the corresponding dual values for the problem of output maximisation. (Note that $y_3 = 15$ is not equal to the going wage rate; that rate is given exogenously in this model, and is not a price that is determined in the competitive solution.)

With land rents determined at the levels $y_1 = 25$, $y_2 = 0$, the distribution of the total output (income) would then be:

	(bushels)
landowners	1,250
labour	2,100
residual (to capitalists)	1,050
	4,400

The residual going to the capitalists reflects the scarcity of capital in the wage fund. If the capitalists spend 1,050 during the year, they begin the next crop-year with the same wage fund as before; in this case, the solution is a long-run equilibrium.

The results for this model illustrate the general proposition that a competitive equilibrium is the optimal solution for an appropriate constrained optimisation problem. In this instance, the constrained optimisation is a linear model. Another case that is equivalent to a linear constrained optimisation is considered in the next section.

4.6   AN ADAPTATION OF EXAMPLE A

Example A (cf. section 1.2) concerned the spatial allocation of supplies (available at two locations) to the firm's customers at three further locations, so as to minimise transport costs while meeting customer demands. In that model, total quantity available exactly matched the (predetermined) total quantity demanded. Suppose now that the quantity available at depot B is increased to 310 tons.

The new primal model is shown in Table 4.6. Although the customer demands have to be met exactly, it is convenient to write these constraints as: quantity sent to a customer is to be greater than or equal to the quantity demanded. This permits ready formulation of a standard minimum problem, and since it will never be worthwhile to send more than is needed (because to do so would needlessly increase transport costs), these constraints will always be satisfied as equalities in the optimum. The dual is then a standard maximum problem, also shown in Table 4.6.

The primal is so simple that it can be solved directly by using the principle of comparative advantage. In serving customers at D, E and C, location B

Table 4.6   *The adapted version of Example A*

Primal problem:
Find non-negative values for x_1, x_2, x_3, x_4, x_5 and x_6 so as to
minimise $\quad 5x_1 + 10x_2 + 12x_3 + 3x_4 + 4x_5 + 9x_6$
subject to

$$-x_1 - x_2 - x_3 \qquad\qquad\qquad \geq -100$$
$$\qquad\qquad -x_4 - x_5 - x_6 \geq -310$$
$$x_1 \qquad\qquad + x_4 \qquad\qquad \geq 50$$
$$x_2 \qquad\qquad + x_5 \qquad \geq 120$$
$$x_3 \qquad\qquad + x_6 \geq 180$$

Dual problem:
Find non-negative values for y_1, y_2, y_3, y_4 and y_5 so as to
maximise $\quad -100y_1 - 310y_2 + 50y_3 + 120y_4 + 180y_5$
subject to

$$-y_1 \qquad + y_3 \qquad\qquad\qquad \leq 5$$
$$-y_1 \qquad\qquad + y_4 \qquad\qquad \leq 10$$
$$-y_1 \qquad\qquad\qquad + y_5 \leq 12$$
$$-y_2 + y_3 \qquad\qquad\qquad \leq 3$$
$$-y_2 \qquad + y_4 \qquad\qquad \leq 4$$
$$-y_2 \qquad\qquad + y_5 \leq 9$$

has a cost advantage (per ton) of $6, $3 and $2 respectively. Thus it is optimal to apply B's capacity first to serving customers at D (where B's cost advantage is greatest); this gives $x_5 = 120$. Capacity is then applied to serving customers at E, giving $x_6 = 180$. The remaining capacity is then used for customers at C, giving $x_4 = 10$. The remaining customers at C are served from A, giving $x_1 = 40$. Hence $x_2 = x_3 = 0$, and some supplies at A are not used.

The dual may now be solved, with the help of the duality theorems. In the primal optimum, the first constraint is satisfied as a strict inequality, and hence (from Theorem 3), $y_1 = 0$ in the optimum. Also, since x_1, x_4, x_5 and x_6 are all strictly positive, then (from Theorem 4) the corresponding dual constraints are satisfied as equalities. This system of four equations may be solved readily, to give $y_2 = 2$, $y_3 = 5$, $y_4 = 6$ and $y_5 = 11$. Figure 4.2 summarises these dual results, and also the primal solution (with *solid* arrows indicating positive flows of the commodity, and unit transport costs shown alongside all the arrows).

The interpretation of the dual variables is orthodox. An additional ton at A would go unused; there would be no change in total transport cost, and hence $y_1 = 0$. But an additional ton available at B would go to C, and hence reduce total transport cost by $2; thus $y_2 = 2$. An additional ton demanded at C would come from A, and hence the cost increase would be $5. At D or E, an extra ton demanded would come from B, and hence would require an extra ton sent from A to C; the total cost increments would be $6 and $11 respectively.

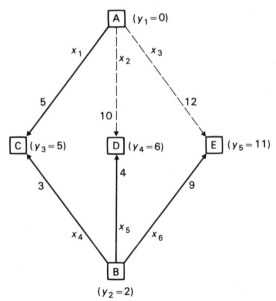

Figure 4.2 *Summary of the solution for the adaptation of Example A*

The problem may now be reinterpreted in a competitive setting: ownership of the supplies at A and B is now shared among a large number of competitive enterprises that seek to sell their supplies to customers in such a way as to maximise their financial returns; at each of C, D and E there are large numbers of customers seeking to acquire their predetermined demand quantities at the lowest possible prices. Competition between suppliers (in the face of aggregate excess supply) will drive down prices, but no supplier will be willing to sell at less than the variable cost (the transport cost).

Suppliers at B can deliver at lower cost into all three customer locations. But this advantage is smallest at C, and, since B cannot serve all the demand, customers at C will buy some supplies from A. To compensate those suppliers at A for the transport cost, the price must be at least $5; it will go no higher than $5 because of the competition among suppliers at A. Supplies from B will also sell for $5 at C (because of the competitive market there), which gives suppliers at B a profit of $2 per ton. The prices at D and E must give the same profit level (for, if they did not, it would be profitable for owners at B to switch supplies); hence the prices at D and E will be $6 and $11 respectively.

Thus the dual solution describes the prices that are determined in competitive markets, and the primal describes the competitively determined allocation quantities. Again, the competitive equilibrium is described by the optimal solution to an appropriate constrained optimisation problem. Of course, in this situation, minimisation of transport costs is a necessary condition for competitive equilibrium; if such costs were not minimised, an extra profit could be earned by appropriate reallocation of supplies.

4.7 EXERCISES

(1) In the version of Example A considered in section 4.6, suppose that there are now non-zero production costs, specifically $5 per ton at location A and $9 per ton at location B. Reformulate the primal model and use the principle of comparative advantage (as deployed in section 4.6) to solve this primal. Also formulate and solve the new dual. Interpret the results in a competitive-equilibrium setting.

(2) Repeat the analysis of Exercise 1 for the *original* version of Example A, in which the total supplies exactly equal the total demands. Show that the dual solution is not unique. Nevertheless consider what prices would be established in the competitive setting of this model.

(3) The world comprises two very simple economies, Agraria and Urbia, which trade with each other. Each economy uses one input and produces only two outputs, food and clothing. Agraria has 50 input units; its production activities need 1 input unit per unit of food, and 1 input unit per unit of clothing. Urbia has 100 input units, and per unit of food or clothing needs (respectively) 1 input unit and $\frac{1}{2}$ input unit.

    (a) Define four output variables for food and clothing production in each country, and formulate a linear model for the task of maximising aggregate

clothing output for a prescribed level of aggregate food output (where the aggregation is for the two countries combined).
(b) Formulate the dual model. Suppose that the prescribed food output level is such that Urbia *is* producing food. Use the duality theorems to show that Agraria will not produce any clothing.
(c) Comment on the economic sense of this result.

4.8 FURTHER READING

Many works in more advanced economic theory provide rigorous discussion of the general proposition that a competitive equilibrium is also the optimal solution of an appropriate constrained optimisation problem. For general equilibrium analyses using a linear programming formulation, one of the most accessible discussions is in Chapters 13 and 14 of Dorfman, Samuelson and Solow (1958); see also Chapter 9 of Kogiku (1971), and Chapter 9 of Lancaster (1968).

An entire book that exploits that theme is Takayama and Judge (1971); these authors present a large collection of programming models designed to enable the characterisation and computation of equilibria in various contexts, with emphasis on models with spatial and temporal elements. Although many of these models have non-linear objective functions, Part II presents linear pricing and allocation models. The analysis of Example A, given in section 4.5 above, is a particular case of the general analyses that Takayama and Judge present in their Chapter 3.

For some interesting empirical applications of this kind of model, see: Henderson (1958), who uses a linear programming model to calculate competitive output levels for the US bituminous coal industry, and then compares these with actual outputs in order to study the industry's deviations from the competitive norms; and Sternberger (1959), who studies the competitive position of North Carolina eggs in the US egg market, making allowance for transport costs.

In consumer theory, Lancaster's 'characteristics approach' can be developed with the help of linear programming; see Lancaster (1968), section 7.5. A simple model in international trade theory has also been studied in a linear programming framework; see Whitin (1953).

The empirical application of linear models to production planning problems has become relatively common-place. Two good examples are Manne (1958) and Kendrick (1967); in the latter, Chapters 2, 4 and 5 deal with a single-period model. Many applications can be found in agricultural economics; see, for example, the volumes from about 1952 onwards of the *Journal of Farm Economics* (now called the *American Journal of Agricultural Economics)*.

Practice in formulating linear models may be obtained from Naylor and Byrne (1963), which presents twelve hypothetical (and, inevitably, simplified) business problems.

5

Production Theory: The Linear and Neoclassical Models

This chapter develops some further properties of the linear model and gives economic interpretations in the context of production analysis. The discussion of these matters affords an opportunity to draw some comparisons with the neoclassical model.

In neoclassical economics, the firm (or, for that matter, any other agent) is taken to be well informed and rational. Thus knowledge of all (technically) efficient production plans is supposed to be available to the firm, and the planning task is reduced to that of selecting the (efficient) plan that best suits the firm's goal. For a theory that aims to produce general qualitative results, this approach is sufficient.

However, problems arise in making the approach operational for empirical implementation: identification of the efficient production plans would require considerable prior optimisation; and often it is simply not feasible to identify *all* such plans. These problems of implementation have been addressed in 'engineering economy', where, in simple cases, identification of all efficient plans *is* seen to be feasible (section 5.2).

The linear model, in contrast, does not require such prior optimisation, and the calculations are directed to the identification of the optimal plan using only the basic information that defines the production opportunities. Because of the restrictions to linear processes, the economic properties of the linear model are distinct from, though similar to, those of the neoclassical model. These comparisons are pursued in later sections of this chapter.

5.1 A FIRST COMPARISON BETWEEN THE NEOCLASSICAL AND LINEAR MODELS

The neoclassical and linear models differ markedly in their approaches to the specification of alternative production possibilities. Neoclassical thinking rests heavily on the traditional concept of *efficiency*. Colloquially, an efficient production plan is one that cannot be improved in such a way as to secure something for nothing. (For a proper definition of efficiency, see the glossary in Appendix B.)

The neoclassical model *begins* with the assumption that all the firm's efficient production plans have been identified, and can be described by a production function. (For a recent textbook exposition, see Varian, 1978, especially p.4) The economic planning task that remains is that of selecting among these efficient plans to find the one that best meets the goal of the firm. This latter task is sometimes referred to as that of resolving the problem of *allocative efficiency;* the earlier task of identifying the set of 'efficient' production plans is then referred to as the problem of establishing *technical efficiency*.

In recent years, economists have become increasingly aware that the problem of technical efficiency is by no means trivial (see, for example, Layard and Walters, 1978, p.208).

To see what is involved, it is convenient to examine here the case of the firm that produces two outputs and uses several inputs. At least one of the inputs is available only in limited amount, and hence the firm is limited with regard to the amounts of product it can make. To represent this limitation, many elementary textbooks present a diagram that portrays the production-possibility boundary (the set of all alternative efficient production points where, for a given level of one output, the amount of the other output is made as large as possible); it is usually supposed that this boundary has the shape shown in Figure 5.1. The process of optimisation is then portrayed as a simple search among these efficient points. Where, for example, the output prices are constant (not affected by the firm's scale of production), maximisation of gross revenue may be depicted geometrically as the task of finding the point of tangency between the curve and the highest iso-revenue line that intersects the production curve, as indicated in Figure 5.1. (This presupposes that the optimum occurs at a point where both outputs are strictly positive; see also section 7.1 below.)

For a linear model of this two-output case, a corresponding diagram may

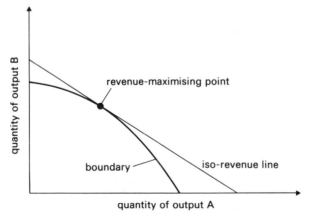

Figure 5.1   *The neoclassical production-possibility boundary*

be drawn, as in Figure 2.1 for the case of Example B. There is, of course, a very strong resemblance between the diagrams: the production-possibility boundary for the linear model approaches that for the neoclassical analysis as the number of (effective) factor limits increases. Furthermore, as seen in the earlier discussion of Figure 2.1, the process of optimisation in the linear model may be portrayed as that of finding the intersection of the production boundary and the highest relevant iso-revenue line.

Nevertheless, these similarities should not be allowed to obscure a fundamental difference: the neoclassical analysis supposes a prior knowledge of the complete locus of efficient production points. This assumption is in keeping with the general character of neoclassical theory, in which the firm is taken to have perfect information. While the assumption (that all efficient production points have been identified) may be acceptable for theoretical analysis, that approach is difficult to implement in empirical work. The linear model, in contrast, does not require such prior knowledge, and it is therefore easier to make it empirically operational.

In a simple linear model (such as Example B), it *is* possible to ascertain the complete locus, and indeed to use the graph as a way of finding the optimum point. But, as noted in earlier chapters, the general case of many inputs and many outputs requires the use of an algorithm to explore *some* of the extreme points of the feasible region in order to find quite directly the optimum extreme point. During this iterative process, the computation does *not* identify the complete set of efficient production plans; indeed generally that would not be feasible (at least at reasonable expense), and, even if it were, it would not be possible for the human mind to comprehend all the results. (For large dimensions, the data would be enormously complex; and, in any case, little of the information would be of value, since much of it would relate to commodity trade-offs that are not of policy interest.)

However, as a supplement to the normal optimising calculation for the linear model, it is possible to instruct the computer to explore a limited number of alternative (efficient) extreme points, in order to trace any particular trade-off that may be of interest. An interesting early example of this is to be found in a study of the production capabilities of the US petroleum refining industry, reported in Manne (1958): for the case where US production of JP4 jet fuel is to be increased from the level prevailing in the study's base period, Manne presents graphs showing how the output of all other products would have to be reduced (assuming the product mix, i.e. the output proportions, of these other products to be held constant). Part of the novelty of this interesting 1958 study lay in the demonstration of how, in practice, it *is* possible to compute such trade-offs in a complex case, a feat that had previously been taken for granted in neoclassical analysis. The next section presents an example showing the kind of prior optimisation required for just a simple application of the concepts of the neoclassical analysis.

5.2   ENGINEERING ECONOMY AND NEOCLASSICAL PRODUCTION THEORY

That the neoclassical production function *can* be made operational, at least in simple circumstances, is demonstrated by the development of engineering economy. Faced with choosing among many alternative policies, both in the long-run problems of design and in the short-run problems of operating decisions, engineers developed a systematic approach to the specification of these alternatives. In many circumstances, plant may be designed to combine factors of production (both current and capital inputs) in continuously variable proportions, and this led engineers to specify functional relationships in a manner broadly similar to that of the neoclassical production function, which also embodies this assumption of variable proportions. The engineers then applied simple financial criteria (e.g. cost minimisation for specified plant output capacity) to guide the choice among the alternatives thus described.

A common circumstance in engineering economy is the need to explore the trade-off between current and capital inputs. A classic example of this kind is now presented in detail, to illustrate the type and the amount of analysis required to obtain empirical results. The problem is to determine the optimal amount of heat-insulating material to wrap round a pipe used to transmit heat (perhaps embodied in the medium of steam) from a generator to a heat-consuming unit. The trade-off is obvious: increasing the thickness of the insulating material reduces the heat loss. To simplify the discussion, it is supposed that the other parameters have already been chosen. Let the heat output per hour be denoted y, and let x_1 denote the heat input per hour, which depends on the heat loss and therefore is to be determined; the pipe has already been chosen and S denotes its external surface area.

The first question relates to the class of *efficient* insulation configurations. Efficiency here requires that the insulating material be deployed in such a way as to minimise the rate of heat loss for a given amount of material (or to minimise the material required for a specified rate of heat loss). Thus policies such as leaving the insulating material unused in a heap on the factory floor, or of using it all on the second half of the length of the pipe, are ruled out as inefficient. Because the rate of heat loss from any given portion of the surface of the pipe is a decreasing function of insulation thickness, efficiency requires a *uniform* thickness of insulating material applied to the whole surface of the pipe, provided the drop in temperature, as the steam passes from one end of the pipe to the other, is relatively small. Thus thickness t of insulating material is the sole design parameter, assuming the choice of insulating material has already been made. The volume x_2 of the uniform cylinder of insulating material is then given approximately by

$$x_2 = tS. \tag{1}$$

There are two further physical relationships. First, from the principle of conservation of energy,

heat output = heat input − heat loss,

and, using H_L to denote the rate of heat loss, this may be written

$$y = x_1 - H_L. \tag{2}$$

The heat loss is influenced by the temperature difference between the steam and the external environment, and by the thermal properties of the pipe itself. Let T_1 denote the temperature inside the pipe, T_2 the external temperature, k the thermal conductivity of the (selected) insulating material, and C a constant depending on the dimensions of the pipe and on the thermal conductivity of its material. Empirical investigation shows that, to a good approximation, the heat loss is given by

$$H_L = \frac{T_1 - T_2}{C + t/kS}. \tag{3}$$

(Note the common-sense of this result: the heat loss increases with the temperature difference, the thermal conductivity k and the area S, and decreases with the thickness t.)

Equations (1), (2) and (3) may be combined to give the production function

$$y = x_1 - \frac{T_1 - T_2}{C + x_2/kS^2}, \tag{4}$$

where the values of T_1, T_2, C, k and S are taken as given.

For a given rate of heat output y, $x_1 \to y$ as $x_2 \to +\infty$; in other words, as the insulation is made ever thicker, heat loss tends to zero and heat input is reduced towards y. When no insulation is employed,

$$x_1 = y + \frac{T_1 - T_2}{C}. \tag{5}$$

Indeed, for a given y, the iso-product curve (i.e. the locus of points corresponding to alternative combinations of insulation and heat input for the required heat output rate) has the general shape shown in Figure 5.2.

Thus in this case, the iso-product curve asymptotically approaches the line $x_1 = y$, and at its other extreme it cuts the horizontal axis at the point given by equation (5). As x_1 increases, the curve falls monotonically, but at an ever-decreasing rate. Of course, these characteristics are determined by the particular physical relationships of this specific situation; and this

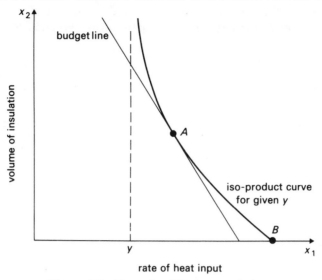

Figure 5.2   *Example of heat transmission*

iso-product curve, being a locus of *efficient* points, can be drawn only after identification of the class of efficient policies.

While this iso-product curve has some of the features traditionally supposed in elementary expositions of the neoclassical model, the present case does not reproduce all these features. Neoclassical analysis commonly supposes that it is necessary to employ at least a little of both inputs. In the present example, however, it is not physically necessary to use *any* insulation, and hence the iso-product curve cuts the horizontal axis at B.

The graph may also be used to illustrate the process of economic optimisation. Assuming constant unit prices for both inputs, a family of budget lines, each with slope determined by the price ratio, may be superimposed. (To avoid complications that are not germane, this supposes that a *per-period* cost – a rental concept – can be established for the capital input, the insulating material.) Each budget line corresponds to a specified outlay, and the lowest possible cost is determined by the line that just intersects with the iso-product curve. The graph shows a case where the budget line touches the iso-product curve, with the least-cost combination of inputs given by the coordinates of point A. However, another possibility is that insulating material is so expensive that the budget line is flatter than the slope at *any* point on the iso-product curve, in which case the optimum is at *B* (where the lowest possible budget line cuts rather than touches). In other words, if the insulating material is sufficiently expensive, none is used. In the general neoclassical analysis, it is commonly supposed that the optimal solution will occur at a point of tangency such as *A*; this example serves to remind us that the optimum may be at a boundary point such as *B* (at which one of the variables takes on a zero value). Where the optimum is at a tangency point, the per-period cost of an additional unit of insulation is equal to the cost of the heat saved (per period) by that additional unit of insulation.

5.3   EXERCISES

(1)   Electrical energy in the form of alternating current is to be transmitted from a single source via a copper cable (of return length $2L$) to a single consumer at distance L from the source. The thicker the cable, the lower is the energy lost in such transmission, the functional relationship being

$$\text{energy loss} = I^2 R,$$

where I denotes current flow, and the resistance of the (entire) cable is

$$R = \frac{2L\varrho}{A},$$

where A is the cross-sectional area of the cable, and ϱ is the coefficient of resistivity of copper. The energy output y required per period by the consumer determines the current flow, the relationship being

$$I = \frac{y}{E \cos \theta},$$

where E is the effective voltage at which the consumer requires the energy to be delivered, and $\cos \theta$ is the power factor of the consumer's load. Let g denote the density of copper. Using also the principle of the conservation of energy, find the production function relating energy output per period to energy input per period, x_1, and the weight of copper used in the cable, x_2. Explore the nature of the iso-product curve for a specified energy output rate, y.

(2)   If the price of energy input to this transmission line is p_1 per unit and the per-period 'rental' cost of the cable is p_2 per unit weight of copper, show that, for the cost-minimising cable design, the absolute value of the slope of the iso-product curve (where x_1 is placed on the horizontal axis of the graph) is equal to the price ratio p_1/p_2. Hence show that the optimal weight of copper to be used is

$$x_2 = y \frac{2L}{E \cos \theta} (g\varrho p_1/p_2)^{\frac{1}{2}}.$$

5.4   ACTIVITY ANALYSIS IN THE LINEAR MODEL

The iso-product curve of the neoclassical analysis has a close counterpart in the linear model. In order to explore this feature, consider the simple case of two inputs and one output (the same number of dimensions as in the example studied in section 5.2). For a specific example, suppose that labour and material are combined to make a single product, and that the available

Table 5.1   *A simple technology – an example*

Coefficients for each activity show the amounts for unit level of that activity:

Activity	A	B	C	D
Output of the product (kg)	1	1	1	1
Labour input (man-hours)	3	2	2.60	2.25
Material input (kg)	1	2	1.56	1.35

technology comprises four activities, whose input–output ratios or coefficients are as shown in Table 5.1.

First, consider activity A: operation of this at unit level is represented by point H in Figure 5.3; similarly if it is operated at level two (output and all inputs doubled), point J represents the outcome; at level three, point K. More generally, any (non-negative) level for activity A yields a point on the ray through the origin, and any point on that ray corresponds to a particular level of operation of the activity. If only activity A is available, the only input combinations that may be employed are those corresponding to points on this ray.

What input combinations may be used if only activities A and B are available? Obviously, combinations corresponding to points on rays A and B in Figure 5.4 are certainly feasible. For example, if 1 kg of product is to be made, this can be done by operating either at point H or at point L; in either case, one activity is used at unit level, and the other at zero level.

If both activities are used, each at level one-half, total output is 1 (kg), while the amount of material used is 1½ (kg) and the labour used is 2½ (man-hours). This corresponds to the point U, which is exactly half-way along the line from H to L. Similarly, any other point on that line corresponds to output of 1 kg, and hence the line HL forms (part of) the iso-

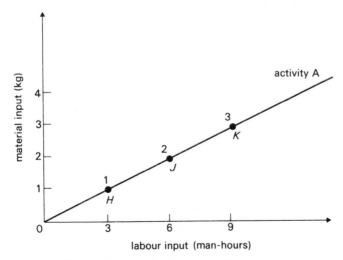

Figure 5.3   *An activity in the linear model*

product curve corresponding to 1 kg of output. This result shows that it is possible, when two activities are available, to employ inputs in *any* proportion that falls between the proportions specified in the two activities (here 1 : 3 and 2 : 2). More generally, although each activity involves commodities (inputs and outputs) in fixed proportions, variable proportions (intermediate between the extremes found in the available activities) may be achieved by using combinations of activities, with weights (levels) varied to give the desired overall proportions.

Before leaving Figure 5.4, note that the iso-product curve for 1 kg of output is completed by including the horizontal line to the right of H and the vertical line upwards from L. (If the factor endowment were more than 3 man-hours for each kg of material, then the excess labour can be left unused, in which case any point corresponding to 1 kg of material and more than 3 man-hours of labour lies on the iso-product curve for 1 kg of output. A similar argument applies when there is an excess supply of material.)

Now consider the addition of activity C (from Table 5.1) to the available technology. This uses the inputs in the ratio of 5 man-hours to 3 kg of material; as it happens, this is the same ratio as is used by an equal combination of activities A and B. For 1 kg of output, this equal combination (activity A at level one-half and activity B at level one-half) uses only 2.5 man-hours and 1.5 kg, whereas the same output from activity C requires 2.6 man-hours and 1.56 kg. Thus activity C is not an efficient activity, since it requires more of both inputs for given output. This result is illustrated in Figure 5.5 where V corresponds to the use of activity C at unit level. If V

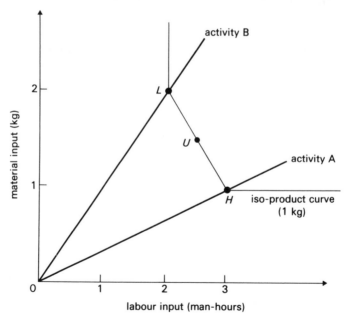

Figure 5.4 *Iso-product curve when there are only two activities*

were to be included, the iso-product curve would (so-to-speak) bend back upon itself, and thus this is the visual demonstration of inefficiency.

On the other hand, if activity D becomes available, this *is* efficient: although it uses inputs in the same 5 : 3 proportion, it uses at unit level only 2.25 man-hours and 1.35 kg of material (point W in Figure 5.5), both requirements being less than those of the relevant (equally weighted) combination of activities A and B (point U). Thus the iso-product curve now has four linear segments, and passes through L, W and H. Points on WH (for example) correspond to combinations of activities D and A. More generally, the iso-product curve (for two inputs) will have one more linear segment than the number of efficient activities. Also, in economists' jargon, the curve is convex 'towards the origin', i.e. it does not bend back as it would if it went through L, V and H. As the number of efficient activities increases, the curve becomes more like the smooth curve of the neoclassical analysis.

If the two inputs may be purchased at constant unit prices, then the usual budget (constant expenditure) lines may be added to Figure 5.5. The line closest to the origin and yet still intersecting the iso-product curve gives (at the point of intersection) the least-cost method of production. Generally this will be at a corner point (extreme point) such as L, W or H in Figure 5.5. Exceptionally, the budget line may have the same slope as one of the linear segments of the iso-product curve, in which case the least-cost plan is not unique – any point on that segment is equally attractive. There is a (conceptually straightforward) generalisation to the case with a total of m commodities.

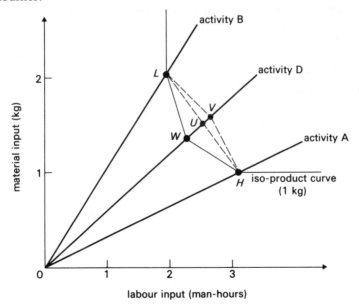

Figure 5.5 *Iso-product curve when there are three (efficient) activities*

Thus, in the case of two inputs and one output, the iso-product curve can be graphed from a knowledge of the technology. However, as indicated for the earlier linear-model context considered in section 5.1, in the general case of many commodities, computation of a least-cost production plan would go fairly directly to the optimum point, without attempting to trace the entire iso-production locus.

5.5 MARGINAL PRODUCT IN THE NEOCLASSICAL ANALYSIS

Where the production function permits variable factor proportions, it is often of interest to see how the optimal solution is altered if factor (input) utilisation or availability is altered. For the linear model of Example B, this question has already been considered in Chapter 3, for a limited degree of variation around the initial input supplies.

In this chapter, results are obtained for general cases in which a factor supply is varied over its entire feasible range. This section considers this question in the context of neoclassical analysis; the next section looks at the linear model. The analysis supposes that several inputs are used to make a single output. The question to be considered is: what happens when one input quantity is changed, while all other input quantities are held constant?

Let y denote the total amount produced of the single output, and let x denote the amount of the input whose supply is varied. The *marginal physical product* or *marginal product* is defined as the rate of change of total product as the quantity of the specific input is changed; in calculus notation, the marginal product is dy/dx. The *average product* is, of course, y/x.

Although the behaviour of average product and marginal product is an empirical matter, it is commonly found that marginal product declines as the input quantity increases. As a result, discussions of the neoclassical model in economics textbooks often take this as a premise, typically referring to it as the law of diminishing returns or the law of diminishing marginal productivity. Notwithstanding this terminology, it must be emphasised that the response is always an empirical question.

One case of diminishing marginal productivity is reported in Marani and Fuchs (1964): in an irrigation experiment conducted in Israel, extra increments of water applied to plots of cotton gave smaller and smaller increments of cottonseed and lint; indeed, the largest water application actually gave lower yields than the second largest (i.e. marginal product turned negative).

For a further example, consider the production function derived in section 5.2 for the instance of heat transfer. If the heat input x_1 is held constant while the volume x_2 of insulating material is increased, then the heat loss is reduced, and the heat output y is increased, as shown in equation (4).

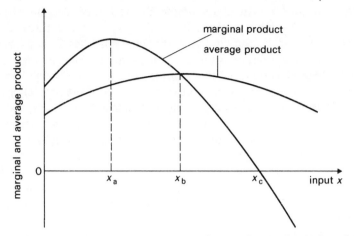

Figure 5.6 *Marginal and average product in the neoclassical model*

Furthermore, from (4),

$$\frac{dy}{dx_2} = \frac{T_1 - T_2}{kS^2} (C + x_2/kS)^{-2}.$$

Thus marginal product diminishes throughout the whole range of values of x_2, but never turns negative.

More generally, elementary economics textbooks commonly allow for the possibility that marginal product may not decline until the amount of the variable input is increased beyond a certain threshold level. The general case also permits the possibility that the marginal product eventually becomes negative. Thus the diagrammatic relationship between marginal and average product is commonly drawn as in Figure 5.6. In that case, of course, the marginal curve passes through the maximum of the average product curve (corresponding to input level x_b); at input level x_c, marginal product turns negative.

5.6 MARGINAL PRODUCT IN THE LINEAR MODEL

Although the neoclassical analysis accommodates a variety of specific forms for the production function, the linear model is more restrictive: although the number of efficient processes varies from case to case, and while the input–output coefficients for each of those processes remain to be determined empirically, the general style of the production function is fully specified, and universal diminishing marginal (physical) product is an automatic consequence of the assumption of linear processes (where the term 'diminishing' takes on a meaning to be explained below).

In order to have a particularly simple illustration of the general result, consider the technology specified in Table 5.1, with the three efficient activities A, D and B. Suppose that the enterprise has 2 man-hours of labour available and that, as available material input is increased from zero, marginal (physical) product of this input is to be measured on the assumption that the enterprise always maximises the output of the (single) product. For low levels of the material input, the firm uses activity A only (which is the most labour intensive): in terms of Figure 5.7 (which is an extension of Figure 5.5), the optimal point moves up the ray from the origin 0, reaching point R when available input is 0.67 kg. (This is the optimal point expressed in terms of quantities used: when available material is less than 0.67 kg, some of the 2 man-hours of labour is left unused; it is here assumed – as is often done in linear models – that an input may be left unused without cost, i.e. in this case, that unused labour does not 'get in the way' of labour being used, and hence that there is no reduction in output on account of the unemployed labour.)

As available material input increases beyond 0.67 kg, then the optimal point moves from R towards S (a mixture of activities A and D now being optimal, with all available labour being employed). Point S is reached when material input is 1.2 kg. A further increase in material input leads to a mixture of activities D and B being used, until material input increases to 2 kg, at which stage point L is reached. Further increases in material input do not add to output; in other words, beyond 2 kg of material, marginal product is zero. Inspection of the arithmetic shows that, between 0 and R,

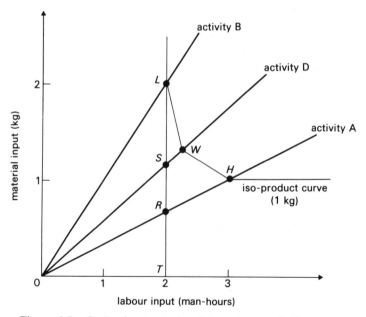

Figure 5.7   *Optimal output when labour input is held constant*

the marginal product is constant at 1 kg of output per kg of input. Between R and S, and between S and L, the marginal products are (respectively) 0.416 and 0.139 kg per kg of input. Thus the marginal (physical) product follows a declining step function, as shown in Figure 5.8: marginal product is constant on each step, but falls from one step to the next as input is increased.

More generally, for the case of one output and two inputs, marginal product always decribes a declining step function. This may be seen from consideration of Figure 5.7: if several equally spaced iso-product curves are added, it may be seen that these are crossed most rapidly, and at a constant rate, between T and R, less rapidly between R and S, and less rapidly again between S and L. While the size, position and number of the steps will vary from one technology to another (depending on the number of efficient processes and on the input–output coefficients), marginal product will never increase as the amount of the variable input increases. Moreover, marginal product never turns negative, provided that unwanted input can be left unused without cost, i.e. without interfering with production. In the neoclassical model, in contrast, there is no distinction between quantity used and quantity available: everything that is available is used (in the context considered here) because of the (usual) assumption that factor proportions may be varied over the whole range.

For this linear model (just as for the neoclassical analysis), the analysis extends immediately to the case of one output and more than two inputs: marginal product is defined for change in one input quantity, all other input quantities held constant. For the case of more than one output, rather than extend the analysis of marginal (physical) product, it is usually more useful to move to a concept of marginal revenue product, introduced in the next section.

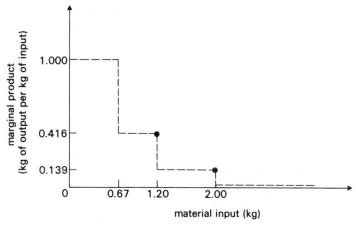

Figure 5.8 *Marginal product curve when labour supply is held at 2 man-hours*

5.7 MARGINAL REVENUE PRODUCT

The marginal revenue product of a factor is usually defined as the increase in revenue obtained by (optimal) employment of one extra unit of that factor, the supply of all other factors remaining unaltered. When only one product is made, the calculation is particulary simple: the marginal (physical) product is valued at the marginal revenue, i.e. the extra revenue obtained per unit of that output. When the firm sells at a constant price (e.g. in a perfectly competitive market), the calculation is even simpler:

marginal revenue product = marginal physical product × price.

This concept of marginal revenue product is the one that is customarily found in elementary textbooks, usually in the context of neoclassical production theory. It should be noted that the concept refers to the rate of change of *gross* revenue. The concept can also be applied in the linear model; and if the price of the output does not vary with the scale of production, then in that model the marginal revenue product is a step function, related through the product price to the underlying step function for marginal physical product.

When the enterprise makes two or more products, the situation is a little more complex, but the basic concept is the same: marginal revenue product of a factor is the rate of increase of (gross) revenue following from optimal deployment of a small increment in factor supply, other input quantities being held constant.

In the context of the neoclassical production model, this is the natural concept to use. There are no restrictions on the availability of factors and, at the optimum, the enterprise has completely adjusted its production arrangements to take account of factor and product prices. The marginal revenue product of a factor is then one piece of data that characterises that optimum. For this purpose, it is appropriate to measure marginal revenue product in terms of incremental *gross* revenue, and with all other input quantities held constant.

In the context of the linear model (and similar non-linear models), on the other hand, there is considerable emphasis on limits on the availability of inputs. In this situation, it may be desired to ascertain the optimal adjustment to the production plan when more of a limited factor supply becomes available, i.e. when the constraint relating to that supply is relaxed. Now such 'optimal adjustment' includes the possibility of *changes in the amounts used of other factors* but remaining within the constraints of the model, including the limits on the availability of these other factors.

In this context, then, marginal revenue product relates to the change in revenue that follows from re-optimisation, taking account not only of the change in the supply of the particular input but also of any consequent changes in the use of other factors, as required by re-optimisation and as permitted by the constraints. There is now no particular virtue in having a measure of the rate of change of *gross* revenue, since it is likely that costs will change as a result of changes in the amounts used of other inputs. Thus what is of interest is some measure of the rate of change of net (or, at least, semi-net) revenue. Exactly what costs are to be netted out will depend on the circumstances; examples are discussed below.

Furthermore, in the linear model, for any constraint that says 'amount of input used $\leq$ amount available', the associated dual variable will measure the rate of change of the objective function as the available amount of the input is changed. If the objective is to minimise the cost of achieving certain output targets, then increased availability of the particular input may reduce costs by permitting the substitution of more of this input in place of some amounts of other inputs. The dual variable then measures this rate of cost saving, which *is* a kind of marginal revenue product, though the sense of this concept is somewhat removed from that of the concept featured in the elementary textbooks.

More commonly, the objective may be to maximise profits; the dual then measures the rate of change of net revenue, and this is a marginal revenue product concept more closely related to the traditional one. Again, the precise nature of the net revenue concept depends on the details of the model, as examples will show.

Some of these general propositions are now illustrated by Example D, in which three factors are used to make two products, there being only two manufacturing activities in the technology. A description of the situation is given in the upper part of Table 5.2. The next part of the table gives the algebraic model; other formulations are possible, but the one given here is convenient for the present purpose.

In the model, the first three constraints say that the amount of an input used can not exceed the amount purchased. The fourth constraint represents the transport capacity limits, and the fifth the limit on the availability of factor B. Since the mechanics of finding the optimal solution are not of interest here, that solution is simply stated at the bottom of the table. Note that both the transport capacity constraint and the factor B supply constraint are binding. Indeed, the dual values for these two constraints are

$$y_4 = 0.4 \quad \text{and} \quad y_5 = 1.4.$$

This value of 1.4 for the supply constraint may be interpreted as a marginal *net* revenue product for factor B. From the usual definition of a dual variable, it measures the rate of change of the objective function as the right-hand side of the constraint is increased, i.e. as the factor supply is increased above 50 units. The objective function is net revenue, i.e. gross revenue from sales less outlays on factors, including the outlay of $1 per unit for the x_4 units of factor B. Now, as the right-hand side is increased above 50, x_4 *will* increase (because $y_5 > 0$) and hence the outlay on factor

Table 5.2 *Example D: production with several inputs and outputs*

The enterprise makes two products and uses three inputs. One unit of product 1 requires 1 unit of factor A and 2 units of factor B. For product 2, the corresponding requirements are 1 unit of factor B and 3 units of factor C. The supply of factor B is limited to 50 units; the total amount of all three factors that may be transported to the factory is limited to 120 units. A unit of product 1 sells for $8, a unit of product 2 for $7, and the three factors cost $2, $1 and $1 per unit, respectively. The enterprise seeks to maximise net revenue, there being no production costs other than the outlays on the factors.

Let x_1, x_2 denote the numbers of units made of products 1 and 2; let x_3, x_4 and x_5 denote numbers of units of factors purchased. The model may then be written:

Find non-negative values for x_1, x_2, x_3, x_4 and x_5 so as to

maximise $\qquad\qquad\qquad 8x_1 + 7x_2 - 2x_3 - x_4 - x_5$

subject to

$$
\begin{aligned}
x_1 \qquad\quad - x_3 \qquad\qquad &\leqq 0 \\
2x_1 + x_2 \qquad\quad - x_4 \qquad &\leqq 0 \\
3x_2 \qquad\qquad - x_5 &\leqq 0 \\
x_3 + x_4 + x_5 &\leqq 120 \\
x_4 &\leqq 50
\end{aligned}
$$

Optimal solution for this primal problem:

$$
\begin{aligned}
x_1 &= 16 & x_3 &= 16 & x_5 &= 54 \\
x_2 &= 18 & x_4 &= 50 & \text{Profit} &= \$118
\end{aligned}
$$

B will increase. Thus the dual measures the change in revenue after subtracting the increase in the outlay on this factor. Any changes in outlays on the other factors are also netted out, i.e. $y_5 = 1.4$ measures the change in gross revenue less the increase in outlays on all three factors. Thus, in this case, the concept of marginal revenue product that is measured by the dual value is one for which (1) the amounts used of the other factors are allowed to change, (2) all the changes in outlays are netted from gross revenue, and (3) all product quantities are allowed to change (because the problem is one of profit-maximisation rather than cost-minimisation).

These conclusions may be confirmed by a direct numerical check: let u and v denote the increases in the numbers of units manufactured of products 1 and 2, respectively, as one extra unit of factor B becomes available (and is used). From the input-output coefficients, it is clear that the extra units of factors used are:

$$
\begin{aligned}
\text{factor A:} \quad & u \\
\text{factor B:} \quad & 2u + v \\
\text{factor C:} \quad & 3v
\end{aligned}
$$

Since the transport constraint is (presumably) still binding, total units used must be unchanged:

$$3u + 4v = 0$$

For factor B

$$2u + v = 1$$

The solution of this pair of equations is: $u = 0.8$, $v = -0.6$. Thus, the changes in purchases of the three factors are 0.8, 1 and -1.8 units, respectively, and hence the change in net revenue is

$$8(0.8) + 7(-0.6) - 2(0.8) - (1) - (-1.8) = 1.4,$$

which confirms the above interpretation of the dual value.

One context in which this net, fully adjusted version of the marginal revenue product is useful concerns the price that the firm would be willing to pay for extra supplies. (This kind of situation was considered briefly at the end of section 3.1; it is now possible to explore the matter more formally and more thoroughly.) Suppose that the price of $1 per unit applies only to the initial 50 units of factor B, but that further supplies may become available at a higher price. Would it pay the firm to buy any extra? The dual value of $1.4 shows the increase in net revenue that may be earned per extra unit of factor B, over and above the *supposed* price of $1 per unit. Thus the marginal revenue product before netting the extra outlay on factor B (but after taking into account changes in outlays on other factors, as well as changes in gross revenue) is $2.4. Thus the firm should be willing to pay any price up to $2.4 per unit of factor B for extra supplies, or at least for the *first* extra units. Because the problem has been represented by a linear model, this marginal revenue product is, of course, a declining step function. For any sizeable increase in supplies, it will be necessary to ascertain the maximum amount of the increase in factor usage for which the (gross) dual value remains at $2.4. (The question of how to carry out computations on such step functions is taken up below, in section 5.9.)

Example D may be used also to illustrate a slightly different definition of marginal revenue product. Consider now the fourth constraint, which relates to the transport capacity limit. Suppose that this limit could be relaxed only if further investment is made. In order to make a comparison with the cost of such investment, the firm wishes to establish how much it could increase its net revenue by optimal deployment of such additional capacity. The dual value $y_4 = 0.4$ signals that net revenue would increase by $0.4 per unit of extra capacity. Again, care must be taken to establish the precise interpretation. This change in net revenue allows for extra gross revenue from extra product and for extra outlays on the factors. It does not, however, allow for the investment cost, which has not even been specified in the model. Thus, on this occasion, the dual value measures a marginal revenue product for which (1) the amounts used of the other factors are allowed to change (subject, of course, to the constraints of the model), (2) output quantities are allowed to change, and (3) from gross revenue, all outlays are netted except for the cost of the additional amount of the factor in question (here, transport capacity).

These examples illustrate a general lesson: in a linear model, the precise definition of a marginal revenue product varies from case to case, depending on how the model is constructed; thus careful exploration is needed to obtain the correct interpretation of the dual. (A further example, of greater subtlety, is discussed in section 9.1.)

5.8 THE COST FUNCTION AND THE CONCEPT OF MARGINAL COST

The objective of an enterprise may be to produce a list of *predetermined* output quantities (of distinct commodities) at minimum cost. Alternatively, the firm's aim may be to find the set of output quantities, and the set of input quantities to support those output levels, that together maximise profit. Even in the second case, production must be at minimum cost. If not, the output levels (found in the calculations) could be obtained at lower cost, which would yield higher profit, and hence the initial plan would not be optimal. Thus cost-minimisation plays an important role in the theory of the firm. (Beware, however, of certain other possible enterprise objectives – e.g. sales-maximisation, cf. Baumol, 1967 – in which the total cost of producing the selected output quantities is not minimised, in general.)

For the sake of simplicity, suppose now that there is only one output, and that this is produced using only two inputs. Employing y, x_1 and x_2 to denote the respective quantities, the neoclassical production function may be written

$$f(x_1, x_2) = y.$$

This function describes all the technically efficient production plans, for each of which, for given values of y and one of the input quantities, the other input quantity is made as small as possible. For some specified value of y, the iso-product curve is generally supposed to have the general character shown in Figure 5.9. (Note the contrast between this and the specific case shown in Figure 5.2.)

If the inputs are purchased in competitive markets (at prices that do not depend on the scale of purchases by the enterprise in question), then there is a family of budget lines (with slope determined by the price ratio). As in Figure 5.2, the least-cost plan corresponds to point A, where one of these budget lines touches the iso-product curve. This determines one point on the *cost function*, which describes the set of least-cost production plans for all alternative values of y. In this function, (minimised) total cost depends on the output level y and on the (given) input prices.

Turning next to the general case of several outputs and several inputs, the cost-function concept generalises in the obvious way. The rate of change of total cost, with respect to a change in one of the output quantities, is called

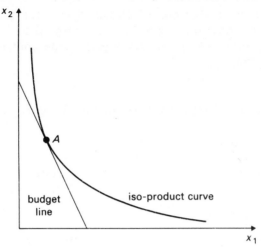

Figure 5.9   *Iso-product curve on neoclassical assumptions*

the *marginal cost* of that output. Implicit in this definition is the assumption that all other output quantities are unchanged. Thus this concept of marginal cost is appropriate when the firm is a cost-minimiser. This measure of marginal cost indicates the increase in cost if the firm is required to produce an extra unit of the commodity in question, while other output requirements are unaltered.

Of course, if the firm is instead a profit-maximiser, then this concept is inappropriate. (The argument is analogous to that given in section 5.7 for the concept of marginal revenue product of an input.) If such a firm is required to produce an extra unit of one output, it may be profitable to change the levels of some or all of the other outputs. In this case, the revenue consequences of these changes must be combined with the change in costs in order to arrive at a *net* marginal cost figure.

In particular, if the output in question is produced jointly with another product, then marginal cost under profit-maximisation may be less than that under cost-minimisation. For example, in electricity production, additional output at the peak may require investment in additional capacity. The new capacity will have lower *operating* costs than most if not all of the older plant, and thus the new plant will be operated off-peak as well. In producing the initial off-peak output level, this will give off-peak cost savings to be set against the capacity and operating costs incurred in meeting the extra peak demand. These savings should be recognised, of course, in a cost-minimising analysis. However, in a profit-maximising model there will be additional off-peak benefits: because of the lower off-peak operating cost, profit-maximisation will lead to a lower off-peak price and hence a higher off-peak output (provided there are no input restrictions that prevent, or make unprofitable, this expansion of output); the increase in off-peak output yields additional net revenue, which should be netted from the increase in (gross) cost in order to arrive at the (net) marginal cost.

These distinctions are further analysed, in the context of the linear model, in the next section.

5.9 MARGINAL COST IN THE LINEAR MODEL

The simplest case occurs when the aim of the firm is to minimise the total cost of meeting specified output targets. Each of these targets is represented in the linear model by a constraint that says 'quantity of the output must be greater than or equal to the target quantity'. In the optimal solution, the dual value (corresponding to this constraint) measures the rate of change of (minimised) total cost with respect to a change in the output target; hence this dual value measures marginal cost, i.e. a gross cost, measured on the assumption that no other output targets are altered.

For the linear model, it may be shown that marginal cost always follows a *rising* step function. And if the supply of one or more of the inputs is limited, then there is an upper limit on the amount that may be obtained of a particular output (assuming the scarce input is inevitably used in the production of that output).

These general propositions may be illustrated by a particularly simple case, Example E, whose situation is specified in the upper part of Table 5.3. Process B gives the cheaper method of production; its use is to be preferred to the extent feasible. When the required output θ is less than 50 kg, there is sufficient input available to permit all output to be obtained from process B. When θ increases from 50 to 51 kg, the output from process B has to be reduced to 49 kg. This releases 2 kg of the scarce input, which in turn permits 2 kg of output to be obtained by using process A. The cost of this level of use of process A is $10, while $3 is saved by reducing the level of process B. Thus the net incremental or marginal cost is $7. Similar switching from process B to process A continues as θ rises to 100 kg, beyond which no further increase is feasible. The optimal production arrangements are summarised in the lower part of Table 5.3.

When the objective is profit-maximisation, the dual value corresponding to a similar output target constraint measures the net marginal cost. In the case of several outputs, this measure reflects any opportunities there may be to earn additional profit by changing some other output levels. (Exercise 2 in section 5.11 illustrates this case.)

One other objective function that requires cost-minimisation is that of (Paretian) welfare-maximisation. In this case, the dual corresponding to an output target constraint measures the (net) marginal social cost, i.e. the rate of change of total welfare as the *required* output is increased. (Of course, there is a similar welfare-based concept for marginal revenue, i.e. welfare, product for an input available in limited supply.)

Table 5.3   *Example E and its marginal cost function*

An enterprise makes a single product, and has two alternative production processes. There is only one scarce input − the available quantity being 100 kg − and both processes need this input. Other inputs may be purchased in effectively unlimited quantities at fixed prices. The aim is to make θ kg of the product at minimum cost (where θ may be regarded as a parameter). The relevant data for the two processes are:

	Process A	Process B
Per unit level of process:		
output (kg)	1	1
cost of production ($)	5	3
no. of kg of scarce input required	1	2

The optimal production plan for output of θ kg is

		Total cost ($)	Marginal cost of last output unit ($)
$0 < \theta \leqq 50$	process B at level θ	3θ	3
$50 < \theta \leqq 100$	process B at level $(100 - \theta)$ and process A at level 2 $(\theta - 50)$	$7\theta - 200$	7
$100 < \theta$	infeasible	$+\infty$	$+\infty$

As in the discussion of marginal revenue product in section 5.7, the general moral is that, for any desired marginal cost concept, an appropriate model must be formulated; and, for any given model, care must be taken to interpret correctly any dual value that measures 'marginal cost'.

5.10   COMPUTATION OF THESE STEP FUNCTIONS FOR LINEAR MODELS

Although the entire step function is readily found for the simple case of Example E, such computation in realistic cases is by no means trivial. It is helpful to understand first the relationship between the step function and the geometry of the feasible region. In order to illustrate this, consider again Example B (described first in Table 1.3). The labour supply will now be varied over the entire range of values that may be of interest, and the marginal revenue product function (defined in terms of the rate of change of the objective function specified in Example B) will be established numerically.

If the labour supply is q man-hours, then, as q is varied, the labour constraint in Figure 2.1 shifts parallel to itself. It is easy to trace the travels of

Table 5.4 *Example B: the marginal revenue product for labour*

Let the labour constraint be denoted $2x_1 + x_2 \leq q$ where the labour supply, q man-hours, is regarded as a variable. Using Figure 2.1, the (primal) optimum solution point can be traced for all values of q. The following table lists the results, together with the optimal values for y_1, the dual variable corresponding to the labour constraint. (The calculation of these dual values is not detailed here.)

Range of values for q	Optimum point in Figure 2.1	Dual value (y_1)	Optimal basis
$0 < q < 350$	between 0 and B	3	$x_2\ x_4\ x_5$
$350 < q < 550$	between B and Y	2.25	$x_2\ x_4\ x_1$
$550 < q < 800$	between Y and R	2	$x_2\ x_5\ x_1$
$800 < q$	R	0	$x_3\ x_5\ x_1$

Note: at $q = 0$, 350, 550, and 800, the optimal basis is degenerate.

the optimum point, and these are summarised in Table 5.4, which also lists the sequence of dual values for the labour constraint. (Recall that the dual value measures the rate of change of net revenue, as defined in the objective function; this revenue function is measured after netting out a payment of 4 money units for each man-hour; cf. Table 1.3 and the discussion at the end of section 3.1.) The value for this dual variable moves from one step to the next (i.e. there is a discrete jump in the value) every time the optimum point moves through an extreme point of the feasible region in Figure 2.1. Thus, for example, as the supply increases through 550 man-hours, the optimum point passes through Y. (For those interested, Table 5.4 also shows the optimal basis for each step in the step function; recall that the concept of a basis is introduced in section 2.5.)

As this example shows, the dual value remains constant (i.e. remains on a single step) for a certain range of values of the input, and the end-points of the range correspond to a pair of adjacent extreme points in the feasible region. Thus when the optimising calculations are done by using the simplex method (or one of its cousins), which makes essential use of these extreme points, it is not at all difficult to obtain as a by-product of the main calculations those values of the input supply that correspond to the relevant sequence of extreme points. (Correspondingly, when it is a marginal cost function that is sought, interest focuses on those values of the output requirement that correspond to the sequence of extreme points.)

Most computer programs are arranged to output at least part of this information, upon request by the user. For a specified initial value on the right-hand side of the constraint of interest (e.g. in Example B, $q = 400$ for the labour constraint $2x_1 + x_2 \leq q$), the immediate interest is in the range of values on the right-hand side for which the quoted dual value applies (the range of values of q, viz. $350 < q < 550$, for which $y_1 = 2.25$ holds true). For obvious reasons, this is usually called right-hand-side ranging, and most program packages include this facility. Often, the program does not provide a direct method for providing similar information about the other steps in the step function. If necessary, however, this information may be obtained by repeated use of the right-hand-side ranging facility, starting each time with a different initial point. For Example B, the next application could begin with $q = 555$ to find the next step down the function. The user would then check to see whether the lower bound is $q = 550$; if it is, this ensures that no intermediate step has been missed. However, this ad hoc approach is cumbersome, and extravagant in computer time. This may discourage its use on large problems that are expensive to compute.

5.11   EXERCISES

(1)   In the optimal solution to the dual of Example D (introduced in section 5.7), the first three variables have values

$$y_1 = 2.4 \qquad y_2 = 2.8 \qquad y_3 = 1.4$$

(a)   Give a detailed interpretation of these dual variables.
(b)   The variables y_2 and y_5 both relate to extra supplies of factor B. Why is it that $y_2 \neq y_5$ in the optimum? (*Hint:* use a numerical exploration, broadly similar to that used in section 5.7, to find out what consequent changes there are in the optimal values of x_1, x_2, x_3, x_4 and x_5, when the second constraint is relaxed by one unit.)

(2)   In Example B (see Table 1.4), suppose that there is added to the model an output target constraint

$$x_2 \geq \theta$$

where θ is a parameter.
(a)   By inspection of the graph in Figure 2.1, find the value of the dual variable corresponding to this constraint, for all feasible values of θ. (*Hint:* first find the position and value of the optimum point, in terms of the parameter θ.)
(b)   Carefully interpret this dual variable.
(c)   In what economic context might knowledge of the dual value be useful?

(3)   A firm makes two products, named I and II, using any or all of three manufacturing processes, in each of which I and II are joint products. The data for the processes are:

	Process		
	1	2	3
Cost per unit level ($)	12	5	8
Output per unit level of process:			
units of product I	3	1	1
units of product II	1	1	2

The aim of the firm is to minimise the total cost of meeting contracts to supply 300 units of product I and ϕ units of product II, where ϕ is a parameter.
(a)   Find the marginal cost function for product II. (*Hint:* formulate the dual problem and solve it graphically for alternative values of ϕ.)

    (b)   For each range of values for ϕ, interpret the marginal cost results in terms of the manufacturing processes that are used.

(4)   For Example E (cf. section 5.9), formulate a linear model that is designed to calculate the amount of product that would be supplied by a profit-maximising firm, when the price of the product is a parameter, p. Calculate the supply function. How does it relate to the marginal cost function? What is the general moral?

(5)   For a linear model, with perfectly competitive markets, what is the relationship between the marginal revenue product function and the demand function for an input?

(6)   For the production circumstances of Example E, suppose that the (downward-sloping) demand curve for the product is $x = 105 - p$, where x is the number of kg demanded when the price is p. If the firm seeks to maximise its profit, what is the optimal price and output? The government now introduces a (flat-rate) tax of t per kg. What is the maximum value t can take without altering the optimal output level? For this value of t, who 'bears the tax'?

5.12   FURTHER READING

For an interesting but brief account of the development of engineering economy, see Chapter 8 of Smith (1961); this also gives some references to the engineering economy literature. Many empirical studies of production functions are to be found in Heady and Dillon (1961); see especially p. 535 for a case where marginal product declines and eventually becomes negative.

For linear programming analysis of the firm, see Dorfman, Samuelson and Solow (1958), who give a relatively elementary account in Chapters 6 and 7. (But beware of the erroneous implication – in the footnote on p. 166 – that marginal revenue product is *not* a step function!) Vandermeulen (1971) presents (in Chapters 5 and 7–11) a very detailed and fairly elementary discussion of the geometry of the programming model of the firm, and includes a thorough discussion of the step function, which (as he points out) may also be interpreted as supply and demand functions for products and factors. A brief formal analysis of the linear model of the firm appears in Chapter 7 of Kogiku (1971), while Intriligator (1971), Chapter 8, gives a formal, advanced treatment of the theory of the firm (some of which employs Lagrange multipliers, however; these are treated here only in Chapter 7 below).

6

Optimisation over Time

6.1 INTRODUCTION

In the previous chapters, time has not played a significant role in any of the models. Some of the situations studied are static, in the sense that all underlying conditions are unchanging over time. For such cases, the optimal policy is also unchanging; in empirical work, only one numerical solution has to be calculated, and this may be applied at all points of time. In the other situations, changes over time are not ruled out. However, it is supposed (implicitly) that the links between different points in time are so limited as to make it valid to model for a single time-period, considered by itself. Where plans are needed for a longer time-span, a sequence of single-period analyses may be used.

In practice, however, there are often significant links between periods, and these make the optimal policy for one period dependent on the policy adopted for other periods. For example, in the case of the animal feeding stuff, the cows may lose weight when their diet is changed, merely because a change has occurred; a sequence of separate optimisations would not capture this effect, and such analysis would not give a valid representation of the problem. In mining and manufacturing, the holding of stocks gives a strong interdependence between periods: production and sales at one time may affect the stocks carried over to a later time, in which case valid modelling requires recognition of the connection. Consumer behaviour is often time-dependent; in particular, consumption may be habit-forming, in which case consumer decisions (and producer's pricing policy) at one time influence consumption levels at later times.

Even with time-interdependence, the optimal policy *may* be unchanging over time, in which case a static analysis is sufficient. But such time-interdependence is generally coupled with changes in underlying factors. These changes may be endogenous, as (for example) when producer's price and advertising policies encourage consumer's habit-formation. Or the changes may be exogenous, when (for example) seasonal climatic changes lead to differences in crop availability.

In such cases, an optimal policy requires variation in the chosen values from one period to the next. Thus overall optimisation requires simultaneous calculation of policy variables for all relevant points of time, and it is this task that is studied in this chapter. (The problem of identifying 'all relevant points of time' is set aside initially, but is considered in section 6.6.)

6.2   MODEL FORMULATION: DISCRETE OR CONTINUOUS TIME

In building an optimising model for such problems, one of the first steps is to decide whether to formulate in discrete or in continuous time. This section considers that issue in the context of economic growth (an important area in economic analysis). In long-term theoretical models, it is often supposed that some economic magnitude (e.g. national income measured in real terms, or the general price level) will grow over time at a constant proportional rate.

Consider first the case where time is represented as a discrete magnitude. The time-measure t takes on only integer (or whole-number) values $t = 0$, 1, 2, 3, etc., and we speak of discrete time-periods. The economic magnitude M that is growing may be written $M(t)$ to indicate that its value depends upon time t. If the initial value (at time 0) is $M(0) = A$, and if M is growing at the rate of (say) 4 per cent per period, i.e. if its value is 1.04 times that of the previous period, then

$$M(t) = A(1 + 0.04)^t. \tag{1}$$

The magnitude M is defined only for these discrete time points, and its value jumps from one point to the next. The mathematician uses the term 'geometric growth' for such constant growth in discrete time.

An alternative representation treats time t as a continuous measure, which takes on all possible values *between* the integers, as well as the integer values themselves. Growth is now regarded as occurring at all moments in time, and so there is a steady increase in the size of the magnitude. It may be shown that the exponential function

$$M(t) = Ae^{rt} \tag{2}$$

has this property for a so-called *instantaneous* growth rate r, where r is strictly positive, and where the initial value $M = A$ at time $t = 0$. (Differentiation of this function gives

$$\frac{dM}{dt} = rAe^{rt} = rM$$

and hence the *proportionate* rate of change is indeed constant:

$$1/M \; dM/dt = r$$

Returning now to the particular case of growth of 4 per cent per period (for the formulation in discrete time), the question arises as to what is the equivalent instantaneous growth rate r for a continuous time formulation. By 'equivalent', we mean the value of r that gives the same result for $M(t)$

at time points 1, 2, 3, etc. From equations (1) and (2), this requires (for t any integer not less than 1)

$$Ae^{rt} = A(1 + 0.04)^t \qquad (3)$$

and, after taking logarithms of both sides, this yields

$$r \log e = \log(1.04)$$

which gives $\qquad r = 1.03922.$

Note that the numerical value of the instantaneous growth rate is a little smaller than the discrete rate of 1.04.

Thus for this example of constant proportional growth, if the empirical data are presented in discrete form, it is nevertheless possible to find a continuous-time formulation that is equivalent, in the sense discussed above. The converse also holds. Hence either formulation may be chosen, depending on which is the more convenient.

This conclusion holds more generally: whatever the context, it should be possible to formulate 'equivalent' models in discrete and continuous time, in which case the choice between the two models should rest upon mathematical or other convenience.

Those who are well trained in mathematics often prefer a continuous-time formulation, which may give elegance and which may result in a form that is particularly helpful for the qualitative investigations of economic theory. For empirical work, discrete-time formulations are often preferred. Also such formulations are more often amenable to low-brow mathematical analysis. The choice of formulation may determine which mathematical technique can be used. In particular, linear programming and associated techniques are essentially finite in character, and may be used only for discrete-time formulations; in multi-period linear models, separate activities or processes are defined for each time-period.

Most of the formulations used in this chapter are in discrete time. For such models, the choice of the length of time-period should be made on grounds of empirical convenience. In models of production planning, for instance, periods of a week or a month are commonly used. For investment-planning models, the basic time unit might be a year, although there it is common to have periods of different lengths within a single model. (The question of the *number* of periods to be included is considered below, in section 6.6.)

In formulating discrete multi-period models, it is essential to be very precise about the timing of activities. For example, the model must specify whether goods made in one period are first available for sale in that period, or in the next period (or even later). Sales or other withdrawals from stock may be regarded as occurring only at the beginning of the period, while goods might be put into stock only at the end of the period. The precise assumptions to be made must depend on the facts of the situation being modelled. But whatever they are, they must be precisely stated, since they can significantly influence the calculations. For example, if withdrawals in a period occur *before* additions to stock, there is less stock available for withdrawals, and more warehouse space available for additions, than if the timing were the other way round.

6.3   A MULTI-PERIOD EXAMPLE IN MANUFACTURING

For an example of a formulation using discrete time, consider a very simplified representation of a common problem arising in manufacturing industry, viz. how to schedule production so as to incur the least possible cost while meeting a fluctuating level of orders. Of course, stock-holding and changes in production levels both add to costs; thus the essential feature of the optimisation problem is the need to get an appropriate balance between holding stocks and varying the production rates.

The data for the example are set out in Table 6.1; note especially the timing assumptions.

The model needs stock-balance equations (which are comparable to the interprocess balances in multi-stage models):

stock at end of period t (i.e. after new production has been put into stock) = stock at end of period $(t-1)$ *less* sales in t *plus* amount manufactured in t.

Table 6.1   *Data for a multi-period example in manufacturing*

A firm makes a single product, the quantity manufactured in period t going into stock at the end of period t and being available for sale during period $t+1$. The firm is making plans for T periods, i.e. $t = 1, 2, ..., T$. It has already contracted to supply q_t tons, for $t = 1, 2, ..., T$. Opening stock (i.e. at end of period 0) is f tons ($\geq q_1$, by supposition). Manufacturing cost per ton is c_1 money units, and storage cost is c_2 money units per ton per period. The firm's aim is to meet the contract requirements at minimum cost, while reducing stock to zero at the end of period T.

Case   I   No further constraints on the firm's policy

Case   II   Capacity constraints:
              manufacturing capacity in period t is r_t tons $(t = 1, 2, ..., T)$
              storage capacity for storage from period t to period
                $t+1$ is s_t tons $(t = 1, 2, ..., T)$

Notation: Let u_t denote number of tons manufactured in
                period t $(t = 1, 2, ..., T)$
              and x_t denote number of tons carried in stock from
                period t to period $t+1$ $(t = 1, 2, ..., T)$

In the notation of this example, this becomes

$$x_t = x_{t-1} - q_t + u_t \qquad t = 2, \ldots, T-1 \qquad (5)$$

Also, since the opening stock is f tons,

$$x_1 = f - q_1 + u_1. \qquad (6)$$

It is always necessary to specify something about the closing stock; if this is not done in the present circumstances, the optimising calculations will ensure a zero stock since to do otherwise would cost money, without bringing in benefits recognised within the time-span up to period T. In the present case, there is an explicit requirement that the closing stock should be zero, and this gives:

$$X_T = 0 = X_{T-1} - q_T + u_T. \qquad (7)$$

To ensure that the sales contracts are met, the model must require

$$x_{t-1} \geqq q_t \qquad t = 1, \ldots, T \qquad (8)$$

Note that the first sales contract can be met only out of the opening stock, and this proves to be possible because it is given that $f \geqq q_1$. When (8) is applied to period T, it gives

$$x_{T-1} \geqq q_T.$$

Taken together with equation (7), this implies that

$$x_{T-1} = q_T \text{ and } u_T = 0.$$

These results have the obvious interpretation: in the penultimate period, the amount carried over into the final period is just sufficient to meet the sales contract of that final period, and there is no production in the final period. These properties hold for both of the cases specified in Table 6.1.

Case I

Where there are no further constraints, the model is as set out in Table 6.2. Note that the stock-balance equations have to be rearranged to put the variables on the left-hand side and the constants on the right-hand side.

As shown in the table, the objective function identifies both manufacturing and storage costs. However, the total quantity that is to be manufactured is fixed in advance, being the sum of the sales contract amounts less the opening stock. Since the unit manufacturing costs do not vary at all with

Table 6.2   *The model for Case I*

Find non-negative values for u_t $(t = 1, ..., T)$ and x_t $(t = 1, ..., T - 1)$ so as to

minimise $\qquad\qquad\qquad c_1 \sum_{t=1}^{T} u_t + c_2 \sum_{t=1}^{T-1} x_t$

subject to contract
requirements: $\qquad\qquad\qquad\qquad x_{t-1} \geqq q_t \qquad\qquad\qquad\qquad (t = 2, ..., T)$

stock balances: $\qquad\qquad\qquad\quad u_1 - x_1 = q_1 - f$

$$x_{t-1} + u_t - x_t = q_t \qquad\qquad (t = 2, ..., T - 1)$$
$$x_{T-1} + u_T \qquad = q_T$$

---

the timing of manufacture, the aggregate manufacturing cost is fixed, and
hence could have been omitted from the objective function.

Because this Case I is so simple, the optimal solution has a particularly
simple form:

> because there are no capacity constraints and because the unit manufac-
> turing costs are constant, there is no incentive to manufacture any earlier
> than is necessary to meet the delivery requirements, since earlier
> manufacture would incur storage costs; thus the optimal policy is to
> manufacture as late as possible, i.e. in each period immediately before the
> demand is to be met.

Thus, for most periods, the optimal policy is

$$x_{t-1} = q_t \text{ and } u_{t-1} = q_t.$$

However, at the beginning, opening stock f may exceed q_1, in which case
the remainder of that opening stock is used up in the next period (or
periods) before any manufacture takes place.

Case II

With the introduction of capacity constraints on manufacturing and
storage, the model must be extended in an obvious way. This is shown in
Table 6.3 for the specific example of $T = 4$. The obvious capacity constraints are added in the lower part of that table. Note particularly the
multi-period pattern of the coefficients on the left-hand side of the constraints; only in the first seven constraints is there any interdependence
between constraints (reflecting time-interdependence), and the interdependence is very limited.

The optimal policy is now likely to be more complex. With unit manufacturing costs still the same in all periods, there is again no cost incentive to
manufacture earlier than one period before selling the amount in question.

Table 6.3   *The model for Case II, assuming four time-periods*

minimise
$$c_1 \sum_{t=1}^{4} u_t + c_2 \sum_{t=1}^{3} x_t$$

subject to the constraints

$$
\begin{aligned}
u_1 - x_1 & = q_1 - f \\
x_1 & \geqq q_2 \\
x_1 + u_2 - x_2 & = q_2 \\
x_2 & \geqq q_3 \\
x_2 + u_3 - x_3 & = q_3 \\
x_3 & \geqq q_4 \\
x_3 + u_4 & = q_4 \\
u_1 & \leqq r_1 \\
x_1 & \leqq s_1 \\
u_2 & \leqq r_2 \\
x_2 & \leqq s_2 \\
u_3 & \leqq r_3 \\
x_3 & \leqq s_3 \\
u_4 & \leqq r_4
\end{aligned}
$$

and
$$u_t \geqq 0 \; (t = 1, ..., 4)$$

But now it may be infeasible to leave *all* manufacturing to the last moment. In other words, some of the manufacturing capacity constraints may become binding, in which case it becomes necessary to manufacture earlier and consequently incur storage costs.

In more realistic contexts, there may also be variation in unit manufacturing costs from one period to another. (In such cases, manufacturing costs *must* be included in the objective function.) The optimal policy may now be even more complex, since it may be desirable to manufacture ahead of time to take advantage of lower manufacturing costs. (See Exercise 1 in section 6.5.)

6.4   TIME DISCOUNTING, AND AN OPTIMISATION EXAMPLE IN CONTINUOUS TIME

If a money sum A is lent at an interest rate of $100i$ per cent per annum, with the interest paid at the end of each year and immediately reinvested (at the same interest rate), then after t years the sum grows to amount

$$V = A(1 + i)^t. \tag{9}$$

This is, of course, just another example of constant proportional growth and, being in discrete time, it may be described as geometric growth. As a result of the growth, the present value A at time $t = 0$ becomes a future value V at the end of year t.

Also of interest is the present value A corresponding to a sum V payable in t years' time, when the prevailing interest rate is $100i$ per cent. The expression (9) may be manipulated in the obvious way, to yield

$$A = \frac{V}{(1+i)^t} \tag{10}$$

For given V, A is of course a smaller amount, and for this reason (perhaps) it is customary to speak of 'discounting' the future sum to calculate its present value. Thus the present value or discounted value of a dollar to be received in the future depends on when it is to be received and on the applicable interest rate. If an individual can lend and borrow as he wishes at the interest rate $100i$ per cent, he will be indifferent between receiving $\$V$ in t years' time, or $\$A$ now, where A is determined by (10).

This process of time-discounting may also be considered in continuous time. Consider a sum invested to grow at an interest rate $100r$ per cent, where r is now an instantaneous growth rate. Of course, in practice interest can never be paid or credited in *exactly* this way, but the concept is valuable for two reasons: (a) daily calculation, now sometimes practised, comes very close to it; and (b) the conceptual equivalence of this case with the discrete-time formulation is often of value – as is illustrated by Exercise 2 in section 6.5. With an instantaneous growth rate of r, then, the future value is given by using an exponential growth function (as indicated already in section 6.2):

$$V = Ae^{rt}, \tag{11}$$

which is analogous to expression (9) for discrete time. Similarly, the discounted value A for a future sum V is

$$A = Ve^{-rt}. \tag{12}$$

In other words, the discounted value of a future sum is calculated by multiplying by the discount factor e^{-rt}.

With the help of this discussion of discounting in continuous time, it is possible to consider an example of an optimisation problem that goes a long way back in the writings of economists (at least as far back as Wicksell's *Lectures on Political Economy*, Volume 1, published in 1901).

A cask of wine may be sold now (where, on this occasion, $t = 1$ is used to denote the present), when its present value is $\$C$; or, if kept while its value increases with age and then sold at time t, the price it fetches will be

$$V = Ct \qquad \text{(for } t \geq 1) \tag{13}$$

(Note that, for $t = 1$, this expression reduces satisfactorily to $V = C$.)

With time discounting at an instantaneous rate of 100r per cent, the present value of the sum received from selling the wine at time t is

$$A(t) = Ve^{-rt}$$
$$= Cte^{-rt}. \tag{14}$$

The optimisation problem is to find the time t at which to sell the wine so as to maximise this discounted value $A(t)$. (This formulation implies that any storage costs are small enough to be ignored.)

The optimum may be found by deploying a simple ad hoc method. By differentiation of (13), $dV/dt = C$ and hence the *proportional* rate of growth of the value V is

$$\frac{dV/dt}{V} = \frac{1}{t}. \tag{15}$$

In other words, the value of funds invested in the wine grows at the instantaneous rate $1/t$. Now this rate decreases as t increases, and starts at unity when $t = 1$. Initially, then, the value grows at a greater rate than r, the interest rate (on the usual assumption that $r < 1$!). When $t = 1/r$, the two growth rates are equal, and, for $t > 1/r$, the rate of growth of the value of the wine is less than the interest rate. Thus the time to sell is when $t = 1/r$, since this maximises the value of invested funds at some distant future date, and hence maximises the discounted value $A(t)$. Note that the higher the interest rate r, the lower is the age t at which the wine should be sold.

This result may also be obtained by a routine application of the calculus conditions for an unconstrained maximum. (For those not familiar with that analysis, a brief account is given in Appendix A.) The first-order necessary condition for the maximisation of A is that $dA/dt = 0$. When applied to (14), this yields

$$\frac{dA}{dt} = C(-rte^{-rt} + e^{-rt})$$

$$= A\left(-r + \frac{1}{t}\right).$$

For all $t \geq 1$, $A \neq 0$, and hence the derivative can be zero only when

$$t = \frac{1}{r}. \tag{15}$$

The second-order condition makes use of

$$\frac{d^2A}{dt^2} = Cre^{-rt}(rt - 2).$$

When $t = 1/r$, this takes the value $-Cr/e$, which is negative. Thus the solution given by (15) is indeed a maximum.

6.5 EXERCISES

(1) For a variation of Case II of the manufacturing example considered in section 6.3, suppose that there is now a distinction in each period between straight-time and overtime working, with (constant) unit manufacturing costs of d_1 and d_2 respectively (the same for each period), and with (of course) $d_2 > d_1$. For period t, no more than a_t tons can be manufactured in straight-time working, with a limit of a further b_t tons in overtime. Also suppose now that product made in period t can be sold in the same period, and that the stock at the beginning of period 1 is zero. The other data are as previously specified.

For the case of three periods (i.e. $T = 3$), formulate a model in each of two alternative ways:
(a) with variables similar to those introduced in section 6.3;
(b) with variables x_{ij} to denote the number of tons made in period i in straight-time working, and assigned for sale in period j, for $j \geq i$; and variables y_{ij} for the corresponding magnitudes where manufacture is in overtime.

Hint: The second formulation does not require stock variables. Why not?

(2) A finance company offers interest of 16 per cent to investors who lend money to the company, and says it will credit the interest quarterly to the investor's account; in other words, 4 per cent of the current principal is added to the account each quarter, and the new principal earns interest in the next quarter. A second company offers 16.2 per cent, and operates in like manner except that it credits interest (8.1 per cent of the current principal) every six months. Both companies require the investor to deposit his money for a two-year term, and both companies lay down identical conditions. The two companies appear to be equally sound financially.

Which company offers the better deal? *Hint:* for each company, compute the equivalent instantaneous rate, using natural logarithms in your calculations. Why is it reasonable to use this rate to compare the investment opportunities?

(3) Like the owner of the cask of wine (section 6.4), the owner of a forest of trees (which are all the same age) has to decide the optimal time to cut the timber. Suppose that the value V of the timber in the forest grows over time t according to the function

$$V = ke^{\sqrt{t}}$$

Assuming an (instantaneous) discount rate r, and assuming also that there are no costs of upkeep for the forest, what is the best time to cut the timber if the aim is to maximise the discounted value of the receipts from sales?

Give an economic interpretation of your results.

6.6 THE PLANNING HORIZON

The choice of an optimal plan for the immediate future *may* depend on events in the much more distant future. For example, in considering investment in a very long-lived asset such as a highway, it may be wise to have regard to likely traffic levels over the next fifty years. And in the context of conservation of (depletable) natural resources, it may be appropriate to consider much longer time-spans; for example, in his 1973 paper 'The allocation of energy resources', Nordhaus builds a model that looks 150 years ahead.

Generally it may be expected that the influence on present plans of an event at a future date will be smaller, the further into the future that the event occurs. This property is reinforced by time-discounting, which reduces to very small amounts the present value of costs and benefits occurring in the very distant future. Nevertheless, *all* future time may have some impact, however slight, on the optimal policy for the immediate future. Thus, in building an optimisation model, it is desirable in principle to take into account all future time. This is usually described as 'choosing an infinite time horizon', where the *time horizon* is the date beyond which future events are ignored.

On the other hand, the further into the future we go, the harder it is to make accurate, or even sensible, forecasts. Also the amount of work required to perfom the optimising calculations increases as more of the future is included. Thus virtually all empirical work uses a *finite horizon;* that is to say, a specific date is chosen, and events beyond that date are largely ignored. To be more precise, there is no direct representation in the model of economic circumstances beyond that date, but it is often necessary to have some indirect representation of that future. An example has already been introduced in section 6.3, where it was observed (after equation (6)) that it is necessary to specify a closing stock at period T, the finite time horizon that is there employed. If nothing is specified, the optimising calculations for that case will ensure a zero stock. But, if the enterprise intends to continue in business after period T, then this is likely to be inappropriate, in which case it is necessary to specify some positive stock level, chosen with an eye to the likely business requirements of the ensuing period or periods. In this way, the required closing stock level is an indirect representation of the future beyond the time horizon. This illustrates a general point: the indirect representation is made by specifying one or more *terminal conditions* (as they are usually called).

The finite planning horizon may be used in either of two ways. If it is treated as a *fixed planning horizon,* the optimising calculations yield an optimal plan for all time up to that horizon. The whole of this plan is then executed. If the enterprise intends to act in the time beyond that horizon, a further plan must then be prepared as the horizon date draws near. (Everything said in this section about the planning horizon applies whether the model is formulated in discrete or continuous time; for the remainder of the section, however, the discussion is couched in terms of discrete periods, just to simplify the exposition.)

An example of the use of a fixed planning horizon is to be found in the practice of the Soviet economy (and in similar economies in Eastern Europe) of central planning using five-year plans. One feature of this approach (a feature that may be regarded as an advantage) is that high-level policy discussion is required only once every five years, when a (metaphorical) stock-taking is carried out. A disadvantage is that, in periods close to the horizon, the plan that is being executed is not very likely to be part of the long-term optimum, because so little of the future has been taken into account in its determination. Furthermore, an automatic execution of the whole plan necessarily requires the planner to ignore any unforeseen events that have occurred since the plan was compiled and before its later parts are executed. (See also the discussion of dynamic inconsistency in section 6.9 below.) For these reasons, it is commonplace to make revisions to the plan, perhaps on an ad hoc basis, in between the regular planning exercises that are conducted at five-year intervals.

This approach may be taken further, and systematised, by use of a *shifting planning horizon:* of the first plan, only that part relating to the first period is implemented; one period after the first plan is made, a second plan is determined, with the time horizon shifted forward by one period; again only the first part is implemented; and so on. For five-year plans (for example), the arrangement may be described symbolically:

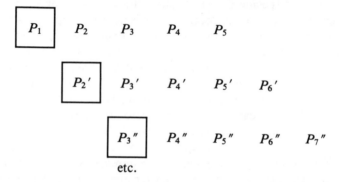

$$P_1 \quad P_2 \quad P_3 \quad P_4 \quad P_5$$

$$P_2' \quad P_3' \quad P_4' \quad P_5' \quad P_6'$$

$$P_3'' \quad P_4'' \quad P_5'' \quad P_6'' \quad P_7''$$

etc.

In the first plan, the components P_1, P_2, etc. each relate to one year of the five-year period. The components of the next plan are denoted by adding a prime; the horizon is now year 6. The boxed elements are implemented.

Whenever a finite planning horizon is to be used, the horizon should be sufficiently far off to ensure that events in the periods after the horizon have little impact on the determination of the first-period component of the plan. However, it is difficult to judge the size of this impact. Thus the trade-off between this concern for accuracy and the costs and difficulties of making forecasts is also difficult to judge. In practice, the choice may be based on guesses, with the hope that the chosen horizon does not lead to large errors as a result of ignored events after the horizon, while the forecasting demands are not made so difficult as to render worthless the predictions for the later periods.

In some contexts, there exists a *natural finite horizon,* such that it is certain that events beyond the horizon have no impact whatsoever on the choice of optimal plan for the first period. For example, in a given year, a firm that manufactures Christmas cards has a deadline for delivery to retailers. The printing and finishing of these cards may be spread over a considerable part of the year (in order to reduce costs by smoothing out production relative to the seasonal pattern of sales). However, it is most unlikely that it will ever be optimal to print cards for year $t + 1$ before the delivery deadline in year t. In that case, the deadline in year t may be regarded as a natural horizon. That is to say, forecasts for sales in year $t + 1$ and later years are not needed when scheduling production for year t. (However, for the planning, in year t, of investment in new printing equipment, forecast sales levels and other economic features after year t may have a major impact on the immediate optimal plan and, for this decision, the deadline of year t probably cannot serve as a natural horizon.) One study that makes use of the idea of a natural planning horizon is described in Modigliani and Hohn (1955).

While a finite horizon is generally used in empirical work, some studies in economic theory (and even some in applied analysis) use an infinite horizon, which may give a simpler formulation when the underlying conditions are unchanging or exhibit a steady rate of growth. Examples of such models are to be found in sections 9.3 and 10.2 below.

6.7   THE SHIFTING PLANNING HORIZON: AN EXAMPLE

In order to illustrate the use of a shifting planning horizon, and also to display some of the considerations that go into the choice of the length of horizon, consider now an example that is broadly similar to the case examined in Exercise 1 of section 6.5, and that has some similarity to the cases considered in section 6.3. The present emphasis, however, is on computation of the optimal solution rather than on the formulation of models.

As in those previous examples, the case concerns the scheduling of production so as to meet certain sales targets at minimum cost. The data for the example are set out in Table 6.4. As in the earlier cases, a linear programming model could be formulated. Indeed, that is how this case was

Table 6.4   *A shifting planning horizon example: the data*

Firm manufactures single product and seeks to meet demand requirements at minimum cost. Product made in a period is available for immediate sale. Stock at beginning of period 1 is zero.

Demand:	15 units per period up to and including period 9; 25 units per period indefinitely thereafter.
Manufacturing cost:	$6 per unit for first 20 units in a period; $11.50 per unit for next 10 units in a period.
Storage cost:	$1 per unit per period, with no capacity limitations.

first examined in the journal literature, by Modigliani and Hohn (1955). But then it was pointed out by Manne (1957) that the problem has a very simple structure, and that as a consequence the optimal policy may be computed directly. Specifically optimality is ensured if the computation is done in the following very simple way:

> review the sales requirements in 'due date' order; for each such requirement, assign production to the cheapest opportunity available at the stage at which the requirement is reviewed.

Of course, there is a trade-off between storage costs and the cost of overtime production (which is $11.50 per unit instead of the $6.00 per unit for production in straight-time working). As a result, it may prove desirable to manufacture in straight-time ahead of the demand date, in order to avoid the penalty of overtime working. A table of marginal costs (i.e. costs of production and storage) may be constructed from the data. Table 6.5 illustrates the trade-off possibilities and shows that it is cheaper to manufacture in straight-time working and to store for up to five periods than to embark on overtime production. The table of marginal costs thus helps to identify the cheapest opportunity available at each stage of the calculation.

The use of the computational approach may be illustrated with the help of a four-period shifting planning horizon. Although Table 6.4 provides an omniscient view of the future, it is now supposed that forecasts are made only four periods ahead (for the application of the four-period shifting horizon), and that the forecasts are completely accurate. Supposing that the planning starts in period 6 (with a zero initial stock), sales in period 6 are met by manufacture in that period. For sales in period 7, the cheapest opportunity available is to manufacture in period 7, all units being made in straight-time working. Similar policies apply in periods 8 and 9. This optimal plan is summarised in the first row of the upper part of Table 6.6. With the horizon shifted forward one period, the forecasts now identify the increase in sales in period 10, and the new optimal plan requires production ahead of demand (specifically 20 units rather that 15 units to be made in period 9, because the former arrangement avoids overtime working in period 10). This second plan is summarised in the second row. The remaining rows summarise the further plans made by repeated shifting forward of the horizon.

Table 6.5   *A shifting planning horizon example: marginal costs*

No. of periods, s:	0	1	2	3	4	5	6	7	8
Unit cost (in $) of production, and storage for s periods: production in									
— straight-time	6	7	8	9	10	11	12	13	14
— overtime	11.5	12.5	13.5	14.5	15.5	16.5	17.5	18.5	19.5

Table 6.6   *A shifting planning horizon example: some results*

To illustrate the use of the shifting planning horizon, consider the case where the horizon includes four periods. The method of calculation explained in the text leads to the following results:

	No. of units planned for production in period:									
Plan made in period:	*6*	*7*	*8*	*9*	*10*	*11*	*12*	*13*	*14*	*15*
6	15	15	15	15						
7		15	15	20	20					
8			20	20	20	20				
9				20	20	20	25			
10					20	20	25	25		
11						20	25	25	25	
12							25	25	25	25

The results of such calculations with differing planning horizons may be summarised thus:

No. of periods in planning horizon	*Actual no. of units produced in period:*								*Total cost, periods 6–13 ($)*		
	6	*7*	*8*	*9*	*10*	*11*	*12*	*13*	*Manufacture*	*Storage*	*Total*
3	15	15	15	20	20	25	25	25	1,042.50	5	1,047.50
4	15	15	20	20	20	20	25	25	1,015.00	20	1,035.00
5	15	15	20	20	20	20	25	25	1,015.00	20	1,035.00
6	15	20	20	20	20	20	20	25	987.50	45	1,032.50
7	15	20	20	20	20	20	20	25	987.50	45	1,032.50
8	15	20	20	20	20	20	20	25	987.50	45	1,032.50

Of course, only the first component of each plan is implemented. Thus the actual production schedule with a four-period horizon is as summarised in the *second* row of the lower part of Table 6.6. The other rows give similar summaries for alternative horizon lengths, from three periods to eight periods. This lower table sheds light on the desirable choice for the length of horizon. As the planning horizon is increased from three to six periods, the planning mechanism identifies at an ever earlier stage the rise in demand, and consequently advances the date at which the higher production level (of 20 units) commences. As a result total cost (for periods 6–13, inclusive) is reduced from $1,047.50 for the three-period horizon to $1,032.50 for the six-period horizon. Beyond a six-period horizon, there is no further improvement in planning, and the total cost is unchanged.

Thus, ignoring the costs of making forecasts and assuming that all forecasts are completely accurate, we see that the optimal choice of horizon is six periods. A shorter horizon leads to higher costs, and a longer horizon yields no further improvement and is therefore unnecessary. Of course, the analysis here is artificial: normally, forecasts cost money and are less than perfect, and then it is not possible to ascertain with certainty the optimal length of horizon. But this artificial example does serve to demonstrate the various factors at work that determine the optimal length of horizon.

6.8 EXERCISES

(1) A firm has contracted to supply the following amounts of its product in each of the next ten periods:

Period	1	2	3	4	5	6	7	8	9	10
Quantity (units)	8	11	15	20	9	11	14	20	8	12

Production costs are the same in each period: for the first 8 units made in the period, the cost is $4 per unit; for the next 4 units, $5 per unit; for the next 4 units, $7 per unit; and for the next 4 units (the last increment permitted by manufacturing capacity), $10 per unit. Product made in a period is available for sale in the same period. The product may be stored at a cost of $0.75 per unit per period; storage capacity is effectively unlimited. At the beginning of period 1, there is no stock on hand.

(a) Use the principle of 'review in due-date order' (cf. section 6.7) to find the production and storage plan that minimises the cost of meeting the sales requirements for these ten periods. (*Hint:* As your calculation of the production plan proceeds, make a summary record of it, by preparing a table of the following design, and showing in it how capacity in each period is earmarked for sales in the same or later periods.)

Period t	1	2	3	4	etc.
Capacity					
1st 8 units @ $4					
units @ $5					
9					
10					
11					
12					
units @ $7					
13					
14					
etc.					

(b) What happens to the level of stocks at the end of periods 4 and 8? Can we be certain that period 4 provides a natural horizon? And what about period 8?

(2) (a) For the problem described in the previous exercise, use the 'review in due-date order' principle in conjunction with a *shifting* planning horizon of two periods, to find the 'best' production and storage plan for the entire span of ten periods (i.e. the best plan available with a two-period shifting horizon).

(b) Compare the cost of this plan with that calculated in the previous exercise. In general qualitative terms, how does the new plan differ from the previous one, and why is its cost greater?

(c) What is the shortest shifting horizon that might be used for this problem (assuming sales contracts are determined sufficiently far in advance for the plan to be implementable)?

(3)   For the operation of its factory for the next five periods, a firm needs one machine of a specific type. It is about to instal such a machine, i.e. immediately before period 1 begins. This type of machine deteriorates with use, and hence the cost per period of operating the machine rises with age, as shown in the table below. The firm could find the money to pay for a replacement machine at the beginning of periods 3, 4 or 5, and it wonders whether it would be better to replace on one of these occasions, instead of using the original machine for the whole five periods. The firm pays $1,000 for a new machine, and it can sell a used machine at the price shown in the table.

Period t	1	2	3	4	5
Operating cost, machine aged t periods ($)	400	400	500	500	600
Value of used machine aged t periods ($)	750	400	300	200	100

Employing a fixed five-period horizon, find by a direct arithmetical procedure the least-cost plan on two alternative bases: (a) the remaining value of the machine in use at the end of period 5 is ignored, (b) the machine in use at the end of period 5 is valued at its resale price. Explain why the two bases give different results. What is the general moral for the specification of terminal conditions in models dealing with investment decisions?

6.9   CONSISTENCY IN INTERTEMPORAL OPTIMISATION

The previous discussion of the shifting planning horizon envisages revision of plans, so that those that are implemented in a period are not necessarily identical with those initially formulated for that period. Although the motive for such changes was not considered in that discussion, the most common reason for plan revision is the occurrence of changes in the environment, changes that have not been accurately foreseen by the planner.

In addition, however, whenever an economic agent makes a long-term plan that *can* be changed before all of it is implemented, the agent may simply change his mind, even though expectations have been verified. Such behaviour provokes the charge of inconsistent choice; it has become known as the problem of *changing tastes*. (There is no intention to limit this term to consumer behaviour; the problem can arise for all kinds of economic agent.)

The possibility of such inconsistency raises various fundamental conceptual problems, including that of defining what is meant by 'optimality' in such a context. These problems have led to the writing of a number of rather recondite papers. The pot was first stirred in a now-famous paper by Strotz (1955/6). Subsequent papers include Pollak (1968) and Hammond (1976). Although many of the issues go well beyond the level of this book, it seems best to give here a short introduction to some of the analysis.

In the context that he studied, Strotz found that inconsistency arises if and only if the individual discounts the utility of future consumption with a non-exponential discount function. In that case, Strotz proposed three alternative strategies that the agent might adopt, and these have been further studied by others, notably Hammond, who dramatizes the issue by using as an example the case of a potential drug addict. Before beginning to consume the habit-forming drug, the individual chooses between three options:

(1) take the drug for while, and then stop before health is impaired;
(2) take the drug indefinitely, and hence become an addict;
(3) decide not to take the drug at all.

One strategy (which Strotz calls 'myopic') is to choose at each stage the plan that *currently* seems best. Thus the individual initially may choose option 1, and then later switch to option 2 (because the problems of withdrawal now make option 2 look more attractive than persevering with option 1).

A second strategy is 'sophisticated': the agent rejects any plan that he will not (or cannot) follow throughout, and chooses whichever plan seems to be the best of those that can be executed in their entirety. Such *consistent* planning requires, of course, a very considerable knowledge and understanding of situations not yet experienced by the agent. Provided the potential addict is aware of the consequences of use of the drug, he chooses option 3, because that seems better than option 2.

A third strategy is one of *precommitment:* the agent will bind himself to follow the plan he chooses. For the potential drug addict, it is not obvious how it can be arranged (by the individual) for option 1 to be followed throughout. In other contexts, such precommitment may be institutionally feasible, for example when subscribing to savings plans such as Christmas clubs.

Although the conceptual importance (and, sometimes, the practical importance) of potential inconsistency is not to be denied, it seems likely, in most empirical contexts where optimal planning is formally pursued, that (i) the agent's discount function does not lead to inconsistency *and* (ii) there are major difficulties arising from unfulfilled expectations, and hence plan revisions are made for that very different reason.

Intertemporal consistency arising from a different cause has been studied in some later papers, beginning with Kydland and Prescott (1977). The argument here is that, if the planner seeks to optimise an economic system in which there are other economic agents whose decisions rest in part on their expectations of the planner's future policy actions, then this feedback invalidates the use of standard optimisation approaches. This argument goes well beyond the scope of this book, and soon reaches to the heart of the 'rational expectations' controversy. However, it may be noted here that this is a difficulty for the planner whose actions have a major impact on other important (influential) economic agents; in other words, it may bother government planners but is less likely to trouble individual agents such as firms and consumers.

6.10 FURTHER READING

For an interesting account of relatively straightforward multi-period modelling in manufacturing industry, see Chapters 3, 6 and 7 of Kendrick (1967) – although note that these models do make some use of integer variables (considered briefly in Chapter 8 below). Another empirical example of such modelling is given in Wein and Sreedharan (1968).

The conditions under which a finite horizon will serve as a perfect or adequate substitute for an infinite horizon can be explored rigorously in specific contexts. An interesting study of this kind, from the area of development economics, is to be found in Manne (1970). See also the transportation network study by Frey and Nemhauser (1972).

A close relative of the shifting planning horizon approach has become known as *recursive programming*, in which economic plans are determined by a sequence of optimising decisions. For example, the farmer may take his crop-acreage decisions a year at a time, each set of decisions being made in the light of current conditions and previous decisions. Day (1963) uses a sequence of linear programming models within this framework to yield predictions of agricultural production response in the Mississippi Delta; his account is very accessible (although a few parts of it make use of matrix algebra).

In Dorfman, Samuelson and Solow (1958), Chapters 11 and 12 present studies of optimisation over time in a very different context, namely the theory of growth and capital accumulation. The methods of analysis also differ to some extent from those considered in this book.

Optimisation over time can also be regarded as a particular kind of multi-stage decision process; such processes may be tackled by using the conceptual approach known as dynamic programming, which is the subject of Chapter 9 below.

In some respects, the use of a mathematical programming model (which requires a discrete-time formulation) is a relatively blunt instrument for the study of inter-temporal optimisation, although such models do have advantages in implementation for empirical work. For many studies in economic theory in recent years, optimal control theory (calculus of variations) has been applied to continuous-time formulations. The collection of techniques known as optimal control theory goes beyond the scope of the present book. However, interested readers will find a relatively simple introduction in Dorfman (1969), where the focus is on capital and growth theory. Among the many textbooks published in recent years, Kamien and Schwartz (1981) is one of the most accessible. There is a brief treatment in Chapter 5 of Benavie (1972). (Note, however, that it is better to study non-linear optimisation before turning to optimal control theory.)

7

Non-Linear Constrained Optimisation

Although linear models have been widely applied in economic analysis, and have led to important advances in both theoretical and empirical work, many economic contexts cannot be represented satisfactorily by such models, and thus it is important to have techniques for non-linear constrained optimisation. This chapter deals with the basic theory of such optimisation, and includes the non-linear equivalent of the duality theory that was developed in Chapter 3. The following chapter includes some discussion of computational aspects.

The theoretical analysis for non-linear optimisation is based on calculus. For those needing a refresher course, a brief review of basic unconstrained optimisation is given in Appendix A. In this chapter, the complications of *constrained* optimisation are first introduced one at a time: non-negativity requirements in section 1; and variables that are not restricted as to sign, but are subject to equality constraints, in section 3. These features are then brought together in section 5, which considers optimisation of non-negative variables subject to equality constraints. In section 7, this analysis is extended to the case of non-negative variables and inequality constraints.

7.1 UNCONSTRAINED OPTIMISATION OF NON-NEGATIVE VARIABLES

In the case of a function f of the n variables $x_1, \ldots, x_n$ that are unrestricted as to sign and are not subject to any other constraints, the first-order necessary conditions for a *maximum* are particularly simple:

$$\frac{\partial f}{\partial x_j} = 0 \qquad (j = 1, \ldots, n) \tag{1}$$

However, when the variables are required to be non-negative, the analysis becomes a little more complicated. For the case of just a single variable x, first consider the example shown in Figure 7.1. By assumption, $f(x)$ increases monotonically for all $x < x_A$ and then decreases monotonically for all $x > x_A$. Thus the maximum is at the point A, for which $df/dx = 0$. This

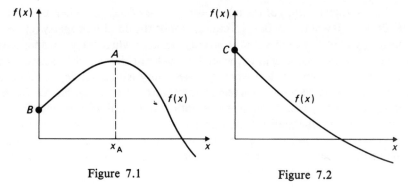

Figure 7.1   Figure 7.2

example shows that the presence of the non-negativity requirement does not necessarily alter the previous result. In the general case of n variables, provided the maximum is at an *interior point* of the feasible region (i.e. at a point where all $x_j > 0$), the first-order necessary conditions are just as before.

But there is also the possibility that a maximum may occur at a boundary or corner point. This is illustrated by a further single-variable example (shown in Figure 7.2), where $f(x)$ decreases monotonically as x increases. The point C (where $x = 0$) is a boundary point on the function $f(x)$, because any negative x is infeasible. The derivative $df/dx < 0$ at the corner point C, and to reduce x would increase f; but such reduction is not feasible, because of the non-negativity requirement. Hence the maximum is at the corner point C. This counter-example shows that $df/dx = 0$ is no longer a necessary condition when the variable x is required to be non-negative. Instead, the condition for a maximum is $df/dx \leq 0$, where the inequality holds if the maximum occurs at $x = 0$, and the equality when $x > 0$. Thus in all cases x, $df/dx = 0$.

For the general case of n non-negative variables, the first-order necessary conditions for a maximum may be stated thus:

$$\frac{\partial f}{\partial x_j} \leq 0 \qquad (j = 1, ..., n) \tag{2}$$

$$x_j \frac{\partial f}{\partial x_j} = 0 \qquad (j = 1, ..., n) \tag{3}$$

In each of the equations in (3), either $x_j = 0$ or $\partial f/\partial x_j = 0$. Exceptionally, both may be zero; this would occur in the case in Figure 7.2 if the curve $f(x)$ happened to be horizontal at $x = 0$ and declining for all $x > 0$. In the n-variable case, note that the maximum may occur at $x_j = 0$ for some j, and $x_j > 0$ for other j; in other words, the optimum may be on the boundaries specified by some of the non-negativity requirements, but inside the boundaries specified by the other requirements.

(This characterisation of the maximum — that $\partial f/\partial x_j < 0$ when $x_j = 0$ and that $\partial f/\partial x_j = 0$ when $x_j > 0$ — is reminiscent of the duality property (cf. section 3.5) where the dual value is strictly positive when the corresponding primal inequality is binding, i.e. when the slack/surplus variable is zero, and where the dual value is zero when the inequality is not binding, i.e. when the slack/surplus variable is greater than zero. The resemblance is, of course, not merely coincidental, since both results deal with essentially the same features of inequality constraints.)

Where the function is to be *minimised,* the first-order necessary conditions comprise equations (3) above, together with the following conditions (2'), in place of the earlier set (2):

$$\frac{\partial f}{\partial x_j} \geqq 0 \qquad (j = 1, ..., n) \tag{2'}$$

The sense of this may be confirmed by drawing a graph for a single-variable example in which $f(x)$ increases monotonically for all x.

7.2 LOCAL AND GLOBAL OPTIMA

The concepts of local and global optima were introduced in section 2.4, and it was remarked there that, in the linear model, a local optimum is always a global optimum. In non-linear optimisation, however, the situation is much more complex, as will now be demonstrated by the simple example shown in Figure 7.3.

This function of a single *non-negative* variable has a local maximum at D. That is to say, $f(x)$ has a larger value at D than it does for any other value of x in the immediate vicinity of D. (Mathematicians prefer a more precise definition: in the case of a single variable x, $f(x)$ is said to have a local maximum at $x = x^*$ if $f(x^*) \geqq f(x)$ for all x in an ϵ-neighbourhood of x^*, i.e. for all x such that $x^* - \epsilon \leqq x \leqq x^* + \epsilon$ for some positive number ϵ, however small.)

A further local maximum is found at E. By assumption, the function decreases monotonically for *all* $x > x_E$. Thus there are only two local maxima, viz. at D and E, and since $f(x_D) > f(x_E)$, $f(x)$ has a global maximum at D. (A global maximum occurs at a local maximum where $f(x)$ is larger than at any of the other local maxima. If two or more local maxima share this property vis-à-vis all other local maxima, then the global maximum is not unique.) In this example, both local maxima are at interior points. In contrast, there are local minima at G, on the boundary, and at H, an interior point; there is no finite global minimum.

Now the available optimisation techniques generally have the property that they search out a local optimum, and if the function is as complicated as that shown in Figure 7.3, then there is the additional problem of trying

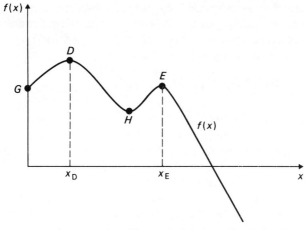

Figure 7.3

to discover whether any local optimum found is in fact also a global optimum. This task is not trivial; it is often difficult to be sure that all local optima have been discovered, and hence that the global optimum has been identified.

Fortunately many of the functions that arise in practice in economic (and other) applications have the property that there is only one local optimum, which must therefore also be a global optimum. Apart from the linear model (cf. section 2.4), there are some other cases where this property holds.

In order to facilitate discussion of these cases, we first turn to the concept of a convex set:

Definition   A set is *convex* if, for any two points in the set, all points on the line segment joining those points are also in the set.

In the single-variable case, if A and B are two points on the x-axis (corresponding to values x_A and x_B), then, for all λ such that $0 < \lambda < 1$, the point given by $x = \lambda x_A + (1 - \lambda)x_B$ is on the line segment joining A and B; as λ varies over its range, this expression describes *all* such intermediate points. (In the n-dimensional case, this algebra still applies provided that x, x_A and x_B are interpreted now as column vectors, each representing the coordinates of one point; those needing a review of basic vector properties may consult Appendix A.) An important example of a convex set is the non-negative space defined by $x_j \geqq 0$, for $j = 1, 2, \ldots n$. In the ensuing discussion, it is supposed that each function is defined over a convex set.

Definition   A single-variable function $f(x)$ is said to be *strictly concave* (over a convex set) if, for any two points on the function, the line segment joining these points lies everywhere below the function (except for the two end-points themselves).

This property may be expressed algebraically with the help of Figure 7.4, which pictures an example of a strictly concave function: for any two points A and B, corresponding to values x_A and x_B, and for any λ such that $0 < \lambda < 1$, strict concavity requires that

$$f[\lambda x_A + (1 - \lambda)x_B] > \lambda f(x_A) + (1 - \lambda)f(x_B),$$

where the left-hand side measures the value of the function at S corresponding to the intermediate value of x, and where the right-hand side is a convex linear combination of the values of the function at the end-points A and B, and hence measures the height of the intermediate point T on the line segment. In Figure 7.4, because of the shape of the function $f(x)$, it is clear that this property does hold for *any* pair of points A and B, and hence the function is indeed strictly concave. (For the case of n variables, the above algebraic inequality still applies provided x_A and x_B are interpreted as vectors.)

It may be proved that a strictly concave function has only a single local maximum, and hence that this local maximum is a global maximum. This may be illustrated by the example in Figure 7.4, where the point M yields a local maximum. The point H gives a local minimum, and, on the assumption that $f(x)$ decreases monotonically to the right of M, there are no other local optima, and M is therefore a global maximum.

The example of Figure 7.4 may be modified to show the significance of the requirement that the function $f(x)$ must be defined over a convex set. Suppose alternatively that $f(x)$ is defined over the values of x given by the *two* ranges $0 \leq x \leq x_A$ and $x \geq x_B$. The feasible set is no longer convex, since it has a gap between x_A and x_B, and a convex linear combination such as $\lambda x_A + (1 - \lambda)x_B$ is not in the set. In this second case, there is a local maximum at A and another local maximum at B; hence the theorem no longer holds.

Where the line segment lies *on* or below the function, the function is said

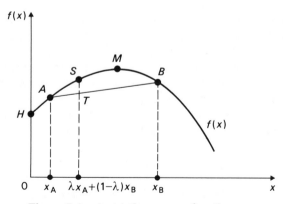

Figure 7.4   *A strictly concave function*

to be *weakly concave*. The algebraic condition then becomes a weak inequality:

$$f[\lambda x_A + (1 - \lambda)x_B] \geqq f(x_A) + (1 - \lambda)f(x_B).$$

This case embraces the possibility that the function may be linear over some or all of the feasible region. Again it may be proved that a local maximum is a global maximum. However, the global maximum *may* no longer be unique, i.e. there may be more than one point at which the function has a local maximum, all such points are equally good, and taken together they form a convex set. Thus (strict or weak) concavity is a valuable property since its presence greatly simplifies the task of finding a global maximum.

There is a corresponding definition for an opposite kind of case. Again consider a single-variable function:

Definition A function $f(x)$ is said to be *strictly convex* over a convex set if, for any two points on the function, the line segment joining these two points lies everywhere above the function (except for the two end-points themselves).

Note carefully that the word 'convex' is used in two distinct senses: the convex set refers to the set of feasible points x, while the convexity of the function refers to the 'shape' of the function f. Again, the algebraic property may be written as an inequality, this time as:

$$f[\lambda x_A + (1 - \lambda)x_B] < \lambda f(x_A) + (1 - \lambda)f(x_B).$$

As before, there is a category of functions that are weakly convex, where the inequality becomes a weak inequality. For a function that is strictly or weakly convex, it may be proved that any local *minimum* is a global

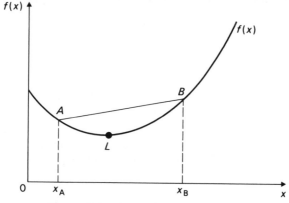

Figure 7.5 *A strictly convex function*

minimum; for strict convexity the global minimum is unique. Figure 7.5 shows an example for the case of a function of a single variable defined over the convex set $x \geq 0$.

Finally note that the global maximum of a concave function (and the global minimum of a convex function) may occur at boundary or corner points, rather than at interior points as illustrated in Figures 7.4 and 7.5. For the case of functions of a single non-negative variable, draw for yourself some illustrative diagrams.

7.3 OPTIMISATION SUBJECT TO EQUALITY CONSTRAINTS

The next step is to consider the case where the non-linear function is subject to *equality* constraints, but where the variables are *not* restricted as to sign. In order to have a simple introduction to the concepts, consider a *minimisation* example in only two variables:

choose values for x_1 and x_2 so as to

minimise $\qquad\qquad f = x_1^2 + x_2^2$ $\qquad\qquad\qquad$ (4)

subject to a single equality constraint $x_1 + x_2 = k$ $\qquad\qquad$ (5)

where k is a strictly positive constant.

For a fixed value of the function f, the alternative values for x_1 and x_2 describe a circle, with its centre at the origin. As f increases, the circle grows larger, as shown in Figure 7.6.

The following derivation of the solution for this example illustrates the rules for optimisation in this kind of context; the derivation is given here without proof, although subsequently some intuitive interpretation of the method is offered. The derivation begins with the definition of a new function L, which is obtained as follows. First rewrite the constraint as

$$k - x_1 - x_2 = 0. \qquad\qquad (6)$$

The rule employed here is to subtract the variables on the left-hand side of (5) from the constant term initially on the right-hand side. If this convention is adopted uniformly, it facilitates interpretation of some of the results, as will be seen below. Next, associate with the constraint a factor λ, which is called a Lagrange multiplier. In order to form the function L, the left-hand side of the constraint (6) is multiplied by λ, and then added to the original function f:

$$L = x_1^2 + x_2^2 + \lambda(k - x_1 - x_2). \qquad\qquad (7)$$

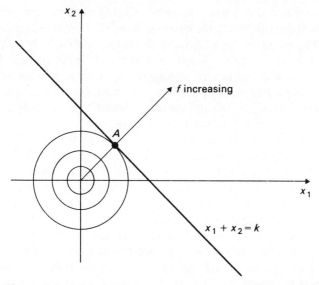

Figure 7.6   *Minimisation example with an equality constraint*

This may be regarded as a function (of three variables x_1, x_2 and λ), which is to be minimised without any constraints. Hence elementary calculus may be used: the first-order necessary conditions for a local minimum are

$$\frac{\partial L}{\partial x_1} = 2x_1 - \lambda = 0$$

$$\frac{\partial L}{\partial x_2} = 2x_2 - \lambda = 0$$

$$\frac{\partial L}{\partial \lambda} = k - x_1 - x_2 = 0$$

Solving these equations yields

$$x_1 = x_2 = k/2$$
$$\lambda = k$$
with $\qquad\qquad f = k^2/2 \qquad\qquad\qquad\qquad (8)$

In Figure 7.6, this solution describes the point A, which is the point on the constraint line that gives the smallest value of f; any other point on the line lies on a larger circle, and hence gives a larger value for f. From the figure, it is obvious that the solution is the unique local minimum, and is not a maximum; indeed, there is no finite maximum.

Also note what would happen if the constraint line were shifted away from the origin, i.e. if k were increased. Clearly the optimum point would move outwards, and hence the optimal value of f would increase. This is confirmed by equation (8), which also shows that $\partial f/\partial k = k$. Now $\lambda = k$, and hence $\lambda = \partial f/\partial k$; in other words, the optimal value of the Lagrange multiplier measures the rate of change of the minimum value of f as the right-hand-side value k of the constraint is increased. This result is similar to the interpretation of the dual value in a linear programming model; this comparison is discussed in more detail in section 7.7.

It is because of this interpretation of λ as $\partial f/\partial k$ that it is important to follow precisely the rules set out above for the formation of the Lagrangean function, L. The factor λ must be multiplied into the expression obtained by subtracting the variables from the right-hand-side constant (i.e. right-hand side in the original version (5) of the constraint). This derived expression is then to be *added* to the original function f, to give L. If these sign conventions are followed scrupulously, the resulting value for λ will always have the appropriate sign for λ to be interpreted as $\partial f/\partial k$, that is to say, as the rate of change of the optimal value of f as the right-hand side of the constraint is increased.

In considering the validity of this 'Lagrange multiplier method', it is intuitively helpful to notice that, in forming the function L, the expression that is added to the original function f must have zero value, provided the values for the variables x_1 and x_2 satisfy the constraint (5). This proviso is met because the method uses the condition $\partial L/\partial \lambda = 0$, which is the same as (5). Thus, minimising L is equivalent to minimising f.

The Lagrange multiplier method may now be stated for the general case,

Find values for the (unrestricted) variables $x_1, x_2, ..., x_n$ so as to

maximise (or minimise) $f(x_1, x_2, ..., x_n)$

subject to

$$
\begin{aligned}
g_1(x_1, x_2, ..., x_n) &= b_1 \\
g_2(x_1, x_2, ..., x_n) &= b_2 \\
&\vdots \\
g_m(x_1, x_2, ..., x_n) &= b_m
\end{aligned}
\tag{9}
$$

To begin the calculation, introduce a set of Lagrange multipliers $\lambda_1, \lambda_2 ... \lambda_m$, and form the Lagrangean function

$$
L = L(x, \lambda) = f(x) + \sum_{i=1}^{m} \lambda_i [b_i - g_i(x)]
\tag{10}
$$

where x denotes $x_1, x_2, ..., x_n$
and λ denotes $\lambda_1, \lambda_2, ..., \lambda_m$.

The first-order necessary conditions for a local optimum (maximum or minimum) are:

$$
\frac{\partial L}{\partial x_j} = \frac{\partial f}{\partial x_j} - \sum_i \lambda_i \frac{\partial g_i}{\partial x_j} = 0 \qquad (j = 1, ..., n)
\tag{11}
$$

$$\frac{\partial L}{\partial \lambda_i} = b_i - g_i(x) = 0 \qquad (i = 1, ..., m) \qquad (12)$$

Under favourable circumstances (depending on the precise nature of the functions f and g_i, as discussed in section 7.2), these $(m + n)$ equations (11) and (12) give a unique solution for the x_j and the λ_i. However, for all but the smallest cases, computation of these values is not a trivial task. Sufficient conditions for a maximum (or for a minimum) can also be established, but discussion of these is reserved for section 7.9 below. In economic applications, it is often simple to discriminate between a maximum and a minimum by using ad hoc methods.

In the optimal solution, $\lambda_i = \partial f / \partial b_i$. In other words, λ_i measures the rate of change of the optimal value of the function f as we increase b_i on the right-hand side of the corresponding constraint. In the previous illustrative example, the value of λ is positive. But, in general, these multipliers λ_i can be positive, zero or negative depending on the circumstances. To illustrate this proposition, consider an example that is an adaptation of the previous example:

choose values for x_i and x_2 so as to

maximise $\qquad\qquad f = -x_1^2 - x_2^2$

subject to $\qquad\qquad x_1 + x_2 = k$

where k is a strictly positive constant.

As an exercise, use the Lagrange multiplier method to show that in the optimal solution, $x_1 = x_2 = k/2$ with $f = -k^2/2$ and $\partial f / \partial k = -k = \lambda < 0$. Interpret the results with the help of a diagram similar to Figure 7.6.

7.4 EXERCISES

(1) Use the Lagrange multiplier technique to find the values for x_1 and x_2 that maximise $x_1 + x_2$ subject to $x_1^2 + x_2^2 = 1$, where x_1 and x_2 are *not* restricted as to sign. Interpret your results geometrically.

(2) Carry out a similar analysis to find the maximum of

$$e^{-x_1^2 - 2x_2^2}$$

subject to the linear constraint $2x_1 + x_2 = 1$, where x_1 and x_2 are not restricted as to sign.

   Consider the geometrical interpretation of your results; is there a finite minimum?

(3) Use calculus to find the values for x_1 and x_2 that minimise

$$f = x_1^2 + 6x_1 + x_2^2 + 9,$$

where the variables are not restricted as to sign. Illustrate graphically.

(4) For the same function f, use the calculus method to find the minimum when the variables x_1 and x_2 are required to be non-negative. Illustrate graphically.

(5) Noting that the iso-product curve of Exercise 1 in section 5.3 may be written

$$x_2(x_1 - y) = Cy^2,$$

where

$$C = 4L^2\varrho g/E^2 \cos^2\theta,$$

use the Lagrange multiplier technique to obtain the result for the optimal x_2, as quoted in Exercise 2 of that section.

(6) For the example discussed in section 5.2, and supposing that the price of insulating material is low enough to permit an interior optimum, use the Lagrange multiplier technique to show that, for a given heat output y, the optimal quantity of insulating material is

$$x_2 = S[k(T_1 - T_2)]^{1/2} (p_1/p_2)^{1/2} - CkS^2,$$

where p_1 and p_2 denote, respectively, the price of a unit of heat input and the per-period rental cost of one volume unit of insulating material. Note the way in which the optimal x_2 depends on the price ratio. What is the optimal value of the Lagrange multiplier, and what is the economic interpretation of this result for the multiplier?

7.5 EQUALITY CONSTRAINTS AND NON-NEGATIVE VARIABLES

The technique for handling non-negative variables may now be combined with the Lagrange multiplier method for dealing with equality constraints. First consider the general case where it is desired to find values of the non-negative variables $x_1, x_2, ..., x_n$ so as to maximise a general function f, subject to the m constraints given by (9) in the general problem stated in section 7.3. The Lagrangean function $L = L(x, \lambda)$ is formed as in expression (10) in that section, and this is now treated by using the technique introduced in section 7.1.

The first-order necessary conditions for a local maximum are

$$\frac{\partial L}{\partial x_j} \leqq 0 \qquad (j = 1, ..., n) \tag{13}$$

$$x_j \frac{\partial L}{\partial x_j} = 0 \qquad (j = 1, ..., n) \tag{14}$$

$$\frac{\partial L}{\partial \lambda_i} = 0 \qquad (i = 1, ..., m) \tag{15}$$

together with the implicit conditions

$$x_j \geqq 0 \qquad (j = 1, ..., n) \tag{16}$$

As before, it is often convenient to think of (13) as: either $\partial L/\partial x_j = 0$ *or* $x_j = 0$ (or both). Note also that (15) is an equality because the λ_i are unrestricted as to sign; in other words, conditions of the type (13) and (14) are required only for the non-negative variables.

If the function f is to be *minimised,* the first set of necessary conditions (13) becomes

$$\frac{\partial L}{\partial x_j} \geqq 0 \qquad\qquad (j = 1, ..., n) \qquad (13')$$

while the other conditions (14), (15) and (16) remain as before.

The use of this extension of the Lagrange multiplier method may now be illustrated by solving the following example:

choose non-negative values for the variables x_1 and x_2 so as to

maximise $\qquad\qquad f = -x_1 + x_2$ (17)

subject to $\qquad\qquad x_1^2 + x_2^2 = 1.$ (18)

An initial exploration may be made with the help of Figure 7.7. The equality constraint describes a circle of radius one unit and having its centre at the origin. The function f increases in the direction shown in the figure. If negative values were permitted for the variables x_j, the maximum would be at the point A where $x_1 = -1/\sqrt{2}$, $x_2 = +1/\sqrt{2}$ and $f = +\sqrt{2}$. (These results may be confirmed by treating an appropriate Lagrangean function by the method of section 7.3.)

When the non-negativity requirements are included, however, it is clear from the graph that the maximum will be at the point B, as will now be shown formally by using the Lagrangean technique of this section. The

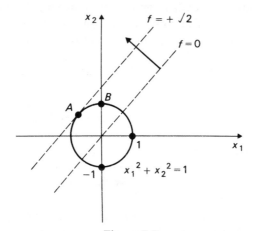

Figure 7.7

required Lagrangean function is

$$L = -x_1 + x_2 + \lambda(1 - x_1^2 - x_2^2), \tag{19}$$

(Again note how the expression in brackets is formed by subtracting the variable terms in the constraint from the right-hand-side constant term.) Application of the first-order conditions (13)–(15) yields

$$\frac{\partial L}{\partial x_1} = -1 - 2\lambda x_1 \quad \leqq 0 \tag{20}$$

$$\frac{\partial L}{\partial x_2} = +1 - 2\lambda x_2 \quad \leqq 0 \tag{21}$$

$$x_1 \frac{\partial L}{\partial x_1} = -x_1 - 2\lambda x_1^2 = 0 \tag{22}$$

$$x_2 \frac{\partial L}{\partial x_2} = x_2 - 2\lambda x_2^2 = 0 \tag{23}$$

$$\frac{\partial L}{\partial \lambda} = 1 - x_1^2 - x_2^2 = 0. \tag{24}$$

The derivation of the solution from these five results is not entirely straightforward. The working is now presented in detail in order to illustrate a computational strategy that may be used in small-scale examples.

The basic idea is to consider in turn the various cases that may be defined in terms of variables being either zero or non-zero in the optimum, and to reject cases that lead to infeasibility.

Case A: suppose that both x_1 and x_2 are non-zero. From (22) and (23), $x_1 = -x_2$, which implies that one of the variables is strictly negative. The supposition has led to infeasibility, and the case must be discarded.

Case B: suppose that $x_2 = 0$. This is immediately contradicted by (21), and this case too is ruled out.

Case C: the only remaining possibility is $x_1 = 0$, with x_2 non-zero. Equation (24) yields $x_2 = \pm 1$, and only the positive solution is feasible. Equation (23) then gives $\lambda = \frac{1}{2}$. Conditions (20), (21) and (22) are satisfied. Thus the only solution is $x_1 = 0$ and $x_2 = 1$, with $f = 1$ and $\lambda = \frac{1}{2}$; from Figure 7.7, it is clear that this is indeed the local (and global) maximum.

Note that condition (21) is satisfied as a strict equality, as it should be since the optimal value for x_2 is strictly greater than zero; the derivative

$\partial L/\partial x_2$ would be less than zero only if $x_2 = 0$ at the maximum. Also note that the interpretation of the multiplier λ may be made in the same manner as before. In order to see this more clearly, suppose that the constraint were of the more general form $x_1^2 + x_2^2 = k$, where $k > 0$. The optimal solution would then be $x_1 = 0$, $x_2 = \sqrt{k}$, $\lambda = 1/2\sqrt{k}$ and $f = \sqrt{k}$, with $\partial f/\partial k$ also equal to $1/2\sqrt{k}$. Hence λ again measures the rate of change of the maximum value of the function f, as the right-hand-side k of the constraint is increased.

7.6   EXERCISES

(1)   Use the Lagrange multiplier technique to find the values of the non-negative variables x_1 and x_2 that

maximise $\qquad\qquad\qquad f = x_1^2 + 2x_2^2$

subject to $\qquad\qquad\qquad x_1 + x_2 = 1.$

(2)   Similarly, find the values of the non-negative variables x_1 and x_2 that

minimise $\qquad\qquad f = x_1^2 + 2x_2^2$

subject to $\qquad\qquad x_1 - x_2 = k, \qquad\qquad$ where $k > 0$.

(3)   An individual consumes quantities x_1 and x_2 of two commodities and has a utility function $u = x_1 x_2 + 3x_2$. Unit prices of the two commodities are \$2 and \$1 respectively, and the consumer's budget permits expenditure of up to \$40 on these commodities. (Any unspent funds are *not* available for any other purpose.) Find the consumption quantities that maximise the consumer's utility. (*Hint*: by studying the marginal utility functions for each commodity, show that the consumer will wish to spend the whole \$40; then formulate and solve an appropriate constrained optimisation problem.)

7.7   INEQUALITY CONSTRAINTS: THE KUHN–TUCKER CONDITIONS

In economic applications, the constraints are commonly inequalities rather than equalities, and thus it is important to be able to extend the previous analysis. The general problem to be considered here is in the standard maximum form:

choose non-negative values for $x_1, x_2, ..., x_n$ so as to

maximise $\qquad\qquad f(x) = f(x_1, x_2, ..., x_n)$

subject to $\qquad\qquad g_i(x_1, x_2, ..., x_n) \leqq b_i$

for $\qquad\qquad\qquad\qquad\qquad i = 1, ..., m \qquad\qquad\qquad$ (25)

The Lagrange multiplier method of section 7.5 may be applied here, after the constraints have been converted to equalities by using the concept of the slack variable (introduced first in section 1.7). Specifically, to the left-hand side of the ith constraint, add a non-negative variable s_i:

$$g_i(x_1, x_2, ..., x_n) + s_i = b_i \quad (i = 1, ..., m) \tag{26}$$

The method of section 7.5 may now be applied directly. The Lagrangean function (now a function of the x_j, the λ_i *and* the s_i) is

$$L = f(x) + \sum_{i=1}^{m} \lambda_i [b_i - g_i(x) - s_i]. \tag{27}$$

The first-order conditions for a maximum are

$$\frac{\partial L}{\partial x_j} \leqq 0 \qquad\qquad (j = 1, ..., n) \tag{28}$$

$$x_j \frac{\partial L}{\partial x_j} = 0 \qquad\qquad (j = 1, ..., n) \tag{29}$$

$$\frac{\partial L}{\partial s_i} = -\lambda_i \leqq 0 \qquad\qquad (i = 1, ..., m) \tag{30}$$

$$s_i \frac{\partial L}{\partial s_i} = -s_i \lambda_i = 0 \qquad\qquad (i = 1, ..., m) \tag{31}$$

$$\frac{\partial L}{\partial \lambda_i} = b_i - g_i(x) - s_i = 0 \qquad\qquad (i = 1, ..., m) \tag{32}$$

Because the x_j and s_i are non-negative variables, these conditions include the usual properties, viz. either $x_j = 0$ or $\partial L/\partial x_j = 0$, as in (29), and either $s_i = 0$ or $\partial L/\partial s_i = 0$, as in (31). But the multipliers λ_i are unrestricted as to sign, and therefore the conditions (32) require simply that the corresponding derivatives should be equal to zero.

However, the conditions (30) show that, in the outcome, all the λ_i will be non-negative; this is an important general result of the analysis. As usual, each λ_i measures the rate of change of the optimal value of f as the corresponding right-hand-side value b_i is increased. This increase in b_i means a relaxation of the constraint: all the solutions that were feasible remain feasible, and some new solutions may become feasible. Accordingly, if the optimum changes at all, there will be an increase in the value of f. In other words, $\partial f/\partial b_i \geq 0$, and this explains why the λ_i turn out to be non-negative. (In any computation, the non-negativity of the λ_i depends on the Lagrangean function L being formulated in the manner previously specified, and this explains why it is important to follow the procedure and sign conventions recommended in that previous discussion.)

From the complementary slackness conditions (31), either $s_i = 0$ or $\lambda_i = 0$ (or, exceptionally, both are zero). In other words, if the constraint is binding in the optimal solution ($s_i = 0$), the Lagrange multiplier will (generally) be strictly positive. But if the constraint is not binding ($s_i > 0$), then the multiplier will be zero. These results are precisely similar to those obtained for dual values in the linear model (cf. the later part of section 3.5). Indeed, the Lagrange multipliers obtained in this section may be thought of as a generalisation of those dual values, since the multipliers apply in non-linear optimisation, where the non-linear problem (25) of this section includes as a special case the standard maximum form of the linear model.

The introduction of the slack variables has made it possible to show how to get the first-order conditions (28)–(32) for the standard maximum problem. However these slack variables may be eliminated from these conditions, by using the definitional equations (26). With some additional rearrangement, this yields the following alternative (and simpler) statement of the conditions:

$$\frac{\partial L}{\partial x_j} \leqq 0 \qquad (j = 1, ..., n) \tag{33}$$

$$x_j \frac{\partial L}{\partial x_j} = 0 \qquad (j = 1, ..., n) \tag{34}$$

$$b_i - g_i(x) \geqq 0 \qquad (i = 1, ..., m) \tag{35}$$

$$\lambda_i[b_i - g_i(x)] = 0 \qquad (i = 1, ..., m) \tag{36}$$

$$\lambda_i \geqq 0 \qquad (i = 1, ..., m) \tag{37}$$

In this form, these are known as the *Kuhn–Tucker conditions,* and they are first-order conditions for an optimum in the standard maximum problem. As before, note that (34) requires $x_j = 0$ or $\partial L/\partial x_j = 0$ (or, exceptionally, both equal to zero). Also (36) requires $\lambda_i = 0$ or $b_i - g_i(x) = 0$ (or both); these are again called *complementary slackness* conditions.

In order to apply the Kuhn–Tucker conditions, the Lagrangean function need *not* be in the form (27). Instead, it is sufficient to write L without explicit mention of the s_i:

$$L = f(x) + \sum_i \lambda_i[b_i - g_i(x)]. \tag{27'}$$

In order to facilitate understanding and recall of these Kuhn–Tucker conditions, it is helpful to describe and summarise them thus: conditions (33) and (34) are simply the standard conditions arising when L is differentiated with respect to the non-negative variables x_j in order to find a maximum; conditions (35) are the original constraints; equations (36) are the complementary slackness conditions for the constraints and the associated Lagrange multipliers; and (37) expresses the result that all the multipliers must be non-negative.

If the problem is to *minimise* a non-linear function subject to inequality constraints, one possible approach is to convert the problem to standard maximum form. Alternatively, the corresponding version of the Kuhn–Tucker conditions may be employed. If the problem is to

minimise $\qquad f(x_1, x_2, ..., x_n)$

subject to $\qquad g_i(x_1, x_2, ..., x_n) \geq b_i \qquad (i = 1, ..., m)$

then the Kuhn–Tucker conditions are:

$$\frac{\partial L}{\partial x_j} \geq 0 \qquad (j = 1, ..., n) \tag{33'}$$

$$x_j \frac{\partial L}{\partial x_j} = 0 \qquad (j = 1, ..., n) \tag{34'}$$

$$b_i - g_i(x) \leq 0 \qquad (i = 1, ..., m) \tag{35'}$$

$$\lambda_i[b_i - g_i(x)] = 0 \qquad (i = 1, ..., m) \tag{36'}$$

$$\lambda_i \geq 0 \qquad (i = 1, ..., m) \tag{37'}$$

These differ from the previous set only in the obvious ways. Note that the Lagrange multipliers are still non-negative (just as the dual values for a minimisation linear model are non-negative).

To illustrate the use of the Kuhn–Tucker analysis, consider this example:

choose non-negative values x_1 and x_2 so as to

maximise $\qquad f = -x_1^2 - x_2^2 + 4x_1 + 6x_2$

subject to $\qquad x_1 + x_2 \leq 6$

$$x_2 \leq 2.$$

The Lagrangean function is

$$L = -x_1^2 - x_2^2 + 4x_1 + 6x_2 + \lambda_1(6 - x_1 - x_2) + \lambda_2(2 - x_2).$$

Application of the Kuhn–Tucker conditions (33)–(37) gives:

$$\frac{\partial L}{\partial x_1} = -2x_1 + 4 - \lambda_1 \qquad \leq 0 \tag{38}$$

$$x_1 \frac{\partial L}{\partial x_1} = -2x_1^2 + 4x_1 - \lambda_1 x_1 \qquad = 0 \tag{39}$$

$$\frac{\partial L}{\partial x_2} = -2x_2 + 6 - \lambda_1 - \lambda_2 \quad \leqq 0 \qquad (40)$$

$$x_2 \frac{\partial L}{\partial x_2} = -2x_2{}^2 + (6 - \lambda_1 - \lambda_1)x_2 = 0 \qquad (41)$$

$$6 - x_1 - x_2 \quad \geqq 0 \qquad (42)$$

$$\lambda_1(6 - x_1 - x_2) \quad = 0 \qquad (43)$$

$$2 - x_2 \quad \geqq 0 \qquad (44)$$

$$\lambda_2(2 - x_2) \quad = 0 \qquad (45)$$

$$\lambda_1 \geqq 0 \qquad \lambda_2 \geqq 0 \qquad (46)$$

Again, there is no simple computational procedure for the solution of these conditions. As for the example in section 7.5, it is necessary to explore

Table 7.1   *Steps in solving Kuhn–Tucker conditions for an example*

Case	Assumptions	Reasoning from condition no.	deductive steps
A	$x_1 = 0$	44	$x_2 \leqq 2$
			$x_1 + x_2 < 6$
		43	$\lambda_1 = 0$
		38	$x_1 \geqq 2$
			contradiction
B	$x_1 > 0$	45	$\lambda_2 = 0$
	$x_2 = 0$	38 as equality	$x_1 = 2 - \lambda_1/2$
			$x_1 \leqq 2$
			$x_1 + x_2 < 6$
		43	$\lambda_1 = 0$
		40	$x_2 \geqq 3$
			contradiction
C	$x_1 > 0$	44	$x_2 \leqq 2$
	$x_2 > 0$		
Sub-case			
(i)	$x_2 < 2$	45	$\lambda_2 = 0$
		38 as equality	$x_1 \leqq 2$
			42 is inequality
		43	$\lambda_1 = 0$
		40 as equality	$x_2 = 3$
			contradiction
(ii)	$x_2 = 2$	38 as equality	$x_1 = 2 - \lambda_1/2 \leqq 2$
			42 is inequality
		43	$\lambda_1 = 0$ and
			$x_1 = 2$

various cases, defined principally by reference to whether each x_j is zero or positive. The details of the analysis are summarised in Table 7.1. After examination of Cases A and B is completed, it is clear that there is no feasible solution in which either variable is zero. Case C then has both variables strictly positive. From condition (44), x_2 has an upper limit of 2, and this prompts the definition of two sub-cases, having $x_2 < 2$ and $x_2 = 2$. The first of these again leads to a contradiction, but the second gives

$$x_1 = 2 \qquad \lambda_1 = 0$$
$$\hspace{6em} f = 12$$
$$x_2 = 2 \qquad \lambda_2 = 2$$

These values satisfy all the Kuhn–Tucker conditions, and the solution is unique. Inspection of the graph of the feasible region confirms that the solution is a (global) maximum.

7.8   EXERCISES

(1)   Find the non-negative values for x_1 and x_2 that

maximise $\hspace{8em} x_1^2 + x_2^2$

subject to $x_1 + x_2 \le 1$.

(2)   A profit-maximising enterprise sells a product for which the demand varies according to the time of day; specifically, in each day there is a peak period and an off-peak period, during which the respective (inverse) demand curves are

$$p_1 = b_1 - a_1 x_1$$

and

$$p_2 = b_2 - a_2 x_2,$$

where x_1 and x_2 are peak and off-peak demand quantities, and p_1 and p_2 are peak and off-peak prices. The constant coefficients a_1, b_1, a_2 and b_2 are all positive.

   The firm can obtain the use of production capacity at a rent of $\$k$ per unit per day (where one unit of capacity permits the production of one unit of the product in the peak period, and one unit in the off-peak period). There is also an operating cost of $\$c$ per unit of product made.

   (a) Write down the expressions for gross revenue in each period, and obtain expressions for marginal (gross) revenue.

   (b) Formulate a model to help the firm find the optimal amount of capacity to rent, and the optimal production levels for the two periods. (*Hint:* formulate the model in terms of quantities, and not prices.)

   (c) Derive the Kuhn–Tucker conditions for the optimum.

   (d) Suppose now that the optimal values for x_1 and x_2 are both strictly positive, and that the optimal capacity is not fully used in the off-peak period. Find the optimal production level for each period. For these optima, show that marginal gross revenue is equal to $\$c$ in the off-peak period, and to $\$(c + k)$ in the peak period; give an economic interpretation of these results.

(3)   A profit-maximising monopoly makes a single output from two inputs, capital and labour, where the respective quantities are denoted q, x_1 and x_2; the

production function permits inputs to be employed in any proportion. The price of the firm's output is denoted p. Suppose it can buy as much as it wants of the two inputs at constant unit prices of c_1 and c_2, respectively. Use $R = pq$ to denote revenue, and $\pi = pq - c_1x_1 - c_2x_2$ to denote profit.

(a) Use a simple calculus formulation to show that, if the factor proportions are chosen so as to maximise profit, then the ratio of marginal revenue products will equal the ratio of the input prices.

(b) Now suppose that the firm is regulated by government, which imposes a profit constraint expressed as an upper limit on the rate of profit per unit of capital employed, viz. $\pi \leq kx_1$ where k is a positive constant that is larger than the profit rate that can be earned elsewhere. Supposing the profit constraint is binding, use the Kuhn–Tucker conditions to explore how it affects the ratio of marginal revenue products in the new optimal plan. In your analysis, let λ denote the Lagrange multiplier associated with the profit constraint (where λ is defined in a manner that ensures that it is non-negative) and *assume* that $\lambda < 1$.

(c) Suppose that, other things being equal, the marginal revenue product of a factor decreases as the quantity employed increases. What does your result for the profit-constrained case imply for the utilisation of capital and labour, compared with the case of ordinary profit-maximisation?

(d) What is the economic significance of the assumption that $\lambda < 1$? (For some further insights into this model, see Averch and Johnson, 1962.)

7.9   THE KUHN–TUCKER CONDITIONS: QUESTIONS OF NECESSITY AND SUFFICIENCY

Although the Kuhn–Tucker conditions were described in section 7.7 merely as 'first-order conditions', the manner of their use prompts the question whether they are necessary conditions for a local optimum (either maximum or minimum, depending on which version of the conditions is being employed). Now it may be proved that these conditions are indeed necessary, provided only that the boundary of the feasible region is not too irregular or 'ill-behaved'. This vague property may be defined very precisely in terms of a *constraint qualification*. The details are not given here because the matter is rather complex, and because in economic applications it is very likely that the constraint qualification will be satisfied.

In particular, many economic applications have linear constraints only, and the following theorem then applies:

Theorem A   If a standard maximum problem has a non-linear objective function, while all the constraints are linear, then the constraint qualification is satisfied and the (appropriate) Kuhn–Tucker conditions comprise a set of necessary conditions for a local maximum.

Of course, a corresponding result applies for the standard minimum problem.

Now these necessary conditions may not be sufficient. However, as suggested by the discussion in section 7.2 of local and global optima for concave and convex functions, there are important cases where the Kuhn–Tucker conditions are both necessary and sufficient. In their pioneering work, Kuhn and Tucker themselves proved a result equivalent to the following:

Theorèm B In the standard non-linear maximum problem, if
(a) the objective function $f(x)$ is differentiable and (weakly) *concave* for all $x_j \geq 0$, and
(b) if each constraint function $g_i(x)$ is differentiable and (weakly) *convex* for all $x_j \geq 0$
then the Kuhn–Tucker (maximum) conditions are sufficient for a *global* maximum.

Furthermore, if the constraint qualification is satisfied, and if conditions (a) and (b) in the theorem are met, then the Kuhn–Tucker conditions are both necessary and sufficient for a global maximum.

For the standard non-linear minimum problem, in which $f(x)$ is to be minimised subject to constraints $g_i(x) \geq b_i$, the corresponding result is that, if $f(x)$ is weakly convex and the $g_i(x)$ are weakly concave, then the Kuhn–Tucker (minimum) conditions are both necessary and sufficient, provided the constraint qualification is satisfied.

Of course, these results apply in the particular case where all constraints are linear. In this circumstance, the Kuhn–Tucker conditions are both necessary and sufficient for a global optimum, provided the function f is (weakly) concave if a maximum is sought, or (weakly) convex if a minimum is sought. Many economic applications may be handled readily with the help of this result.

Some of the general significance of these results may be illustrated by analysis of the following *example:*

find non-negative values for x_1 and x_2 to

minimise
$$f = x_1^2 + x_2^2$$

subject to
$$x_1 + 2x_2 \leq 8$$

$$x_1 + x_2 \geq 1$$

It is useful first to explore the graph for the problem, shown in Figure 7.8. The objective function f describes a family of circles with centre at the origin; f increases with movement outwards from the origin. From inspection of the graph, it is obvious that there are local maxima at B and C (the global maximum being at C), and the global minimum is at D.

In beginning the algebraic analysis, note that f is indeed convex, as is easily seen by inspection of the function. The minimisation version of

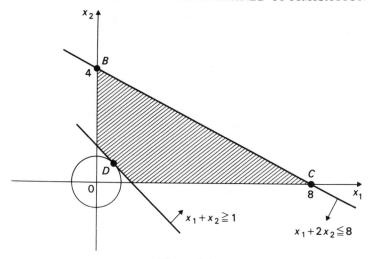

Figure 7.8

Theorem B applies, as does that for Theorem A. The Kuhn–Tucker conditions should be both necessary and sufficient. The first step in the Kuhn–Tucker analysis is to put the problem into standard minimum form, by converting the first inequality to

$$-x_1 - 2x_2 \geqq -8.$$

The Lagrangean function then is

$$L = x_1{}^2 + x_2{}^2 + \lambda_1(-8 + x_1 + 2x_2) + \lambda_2(1 - x_1 - x_2)$$

and, applying (33′)–(37′), the Kuhn–Tucker conditions for a minimum are

$$\frac{\partial L}{\partial x_1} = 2x_1 + \lambda_1 - \lambda_2 \qquad \geqq 0 \tag{47}$$

$$x_1 \frac{\partial L}{\partial x_1} = x_1(2x_1 + \lambda_1 - \lambda_2) = 0 \tag{48}$$

$$\frac{\partial L}{\partial x_2} = \qquad 2x_2 + 2\lambda_1 - \lambda_2 \geqq 0 \tag{49}$$

$$x_2 \frac{\partial L}{\partial x_1} = x_2(2x_2 + 2\lambda_1 - \lambda_2) = 0 \tag{50}$$

$$-8 + x_1 + 2x_2 \leqq 0 \tag{51}$$

$$\lambda_1(-8 + x_1 + 2x_2) = 0 \tag{52}$$

$$1 - x_1 - x_2 \qquad \leqq 0 \qquad\qquad (53)$$

$$\lambda_2(1 - x_1 - x_2) \qquad = 0 \qquad\qquad (54)$$

$$\lambda_1 \geqq 0 \quad \text{and} \quad \lambda_2 \geqq 0.$$

As usual, the various possible cases may be examined in turn:

Case A: $x_1 = 0$, $x_2 = 0$. This contradicts (53) and is ruled out.

Case B: $x_1 = 0$, $x_2 > 0$. Consider two sub-cases:
   (i)   If $\lambda_2 = 0$, (49) becomes $2x_2 + 2\lambda_1 = 0$, which requires $x_2 = 0$, giving a contradiction.
   (ii) If $\lambda_2 > 0$, (53) yields $x_2 = 1$ and substitution of this in (47) and (49) gives $\lambda_1 \leqq -2$, again a contradiction.

Case C: $x_1 > 0$, $x_2 = 0$. This may be ruled out by an analysis similar to that of Case B.

Case D: $x_1 > 0$, $x_2 > 0$. From (47) and (49), $2x_1 + \lambda_1 - \lambda_2 = 0$ and $2x_2 + 2\lambda_1 - \lambda_2 = 0$, giving $4x_1 - 2x_2 = \lambda_2$.

   Consider two sub-cases:
   (i)   If $\lambda_2 = 0$, $2x_1 + \lambda_1 = 0$, which implies $x_1 = 0$, a contradiction.
   (ii) If $\lambda_2 > 0$, $x_1 + x_2 = 1$. Now, if $\lambda_1 > 0$, from (51) $x_1 + 2x_2 = 8$, which gives a contradiction.
   If $\lambda_1 = 0$, (47) and (49) give $2x_1 - 2x_2 = 0$, leading to the results

$$x_1 = \tfrac{1}{2} \qquad \lambda_1 = 0 \qquad f = \tfrac{1}{2}$$
$$x_2 = \tfrac{1}{2} \qquad \lambda_2 = 1$$

These results satisfy all the conditions (47)–(54), and this solution gives point D in Figure 7.8.

Furthermore, it is the only solution for these Kuhn–Tucker conditions and it yields the (unique) global minimum. Thus the calculations demonstrate the sufficiency (as well as the necessity) of the Kuhn–Tucker conditions in this case: all points that do not give a global minimum are ruled out. In particular, the local *maxima* at points B and C are ruled out – indeed these points correspond to Cases B and C in the calculations.

Further insights may be obtained from study of the following variant of the example, in which the constraints remain unaltered but the function f is now to be *maximised*. Figure 7.8 still applies. Since f is still convex, Theorem B does not apply: the Kuhn–Tucker conditions may not be sufficient for a global maximum. Indeed, they prove not to be sufficient, as is now confirmed by direct calculation. Using (33)–(37) to obtain the new set of Kuhn–Tucker conditions, it is easily seen that each of the following sets of values is a solution:

point B:

$$x_1 = 0 \qquad \lambda_1 = 4 \qquad f = 16$$
$$x_2 = 4 \qquad \lambda_2 = 0$$

point C:

$$x_1 = 8 \qquad \lambda_1 = 16 \qquad f = 64$$
$$x_2 = 0 \qquad \lambda_2 = 0$$

Specifically note that point B is not a global maximum, although it does satisfy the conditions. But Theorem A does apply and thus the Kuhn–Tucker conditions are necessary. This is confirmed by the proposition that there are no local maxima except at B and C and the conditions are satisfied at both these points.

7.10   QUASI-CONCAVE AND QUASI-CONVEX FUNCTIONS

A class of function that is important in economic optimisation is exemplified by the symmetrical bell-shaped function, of a single variable x, shown in Figure 7.9. This function is defined over the set $0 < x < x_E$, and is an example of a *quasi-concave function*.

Definition: A single-variable function $f(x)$ is *quasi-concave* if and

only if $f[\lambda x_A + (1 - \lambda)x_B] \geq \min \{f(x_A), f(x_B)\}$

for all λ such that $0 < \lambda < 1$, where (as before) x_A and x_B are any two values of x in the permitted range.

The right-hand side of the algebraic relation is to be interpreted as the smaller of $f(x_A)$ and $f(x_B)$. As before, the left-hand side measures the value of the function for any intermediate value of x. For *strict quasi-concavity*, the weak inequality in the definition is replaced by a strict inequality.

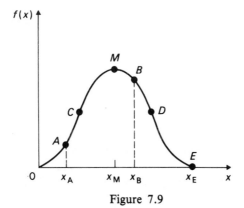

Figure 7.9

(And inspection of Figure 7.9 shows that this is in fact a case of strict quasi-concavity.)

If C and D are the points where the absolute value of the slope is greatest, then the function between C and D is strictly concave (cf. Figure 7.4). But $0C$ is not concave. This illustrates a general result: a (strictly) concave function is (strictly) quasi-concave, but the converse does not hold. In other words, concavity is more restrictive than quasi-concavity.

For a function of n variables, the above definition of quasi-concavity generalises in the usual way: x_A and x_B must now be interpreted as vectors that give the coordinates of the points A and B on the surface of the function. And for the definition of a *quasi-convex function,* the required algebraic relationship is

$$f[\lambda x_A + (1 - \lambda)x_B] \leqq \max \{f(x_A),\ f(x_B)\}$$

where the right-hand side signifies the larger of $f(x_A)$ and $f(x_B)$. The corresponding example of a (strictly) quasi-convex function is an *inverted* bell.

The term *quasi-concave programming* has been applied to the particular case of the (n-variable) standard maximisation problem (cf. equations (25) in section 7.7) in which the maximand $f(x)$ is quasi-concave and each of the constraint functions $g_i(x)$ is quasi-convex (in both cases, for all non-negative values of the x_j). For this case it may be shown that a local maximum is a global maximum; furthermore, if the maximand is strictly quasi-concave, then the maximum must be unique. These results are of value because they rest on weaker conditions than those of concavity, etc. as supposed in the original Kuhn–Tucker theory. The case was first studied in Arrow and Enthoven (1961), where sufficiency theorems and other important results are obtained.

The case is significant because of the role of quasi-concave functions in neoclassical economic theory. For example, the generalisation to n variables of the bell-shaped function of Figure 7.9 may be used in the study of the neoclassical utility function. Specifically, if attention is confined to the rising part of the curve ($0M$ in Figure 7.9), then a *horizontal* section through the function yields one of the usual consumer indifference curves (where such a curve is the locus of points yielding the same, constant level of utility). (It is easiest to visualise this for the case of two goods, consumed in amounts x_1 and x_2, with resulting utility $f(x_1, x_2)$; the functional surface is then literally a three-dimensional bell.)

Of course, a (strictly) concave function also yields the standard indifference curves. But, in the absence of a cardinal utility measure (which would determine the precise shape of the function), it is not possible to rule out the less restrictive case (i.e. a strictly quasi-concave function). Hence, for such neoclassical utility theory, it is helpful to have the analysis and results for the quasi-concave case.

7.11   FURTHER READING

A very accessible discussion of non-linear optimisation is given in Chapter 8 of Dorfman, Samuelson and Solow (1958). Formal and more advanced treatments are to be found in Chapter 2 of Benavie (1972), in Chapters 2, 3 and 4 of Intriligator (1971), and in Chapters 4 and 5 of Lancaster (1968). A brief review of much of the material is given in sections MR7, 8 and 9 of the Appendix in Kogiku (1971).

The 'constraint qualification' (mentioned at the beginning of section 7.9 above) is discussed by Intriligator (1971) in his section 4.3.

Chapters 1–5 of Dixit (1976) give a rather different approach to much of the material of this chapter and some earlier chapters.

In the duality theory of linear programming, we saw that, in the optimum, the largest value of the maximand equals the smallest value of the dual minimand. In non-linear optimisation there is a related result. The Lagrangean function, formed from (say) the standard maximum problem, may be thought of as a function L of the original variables $x_1, ..., x_n$, and the Lagrange multipliers $\lambda_1, ..., \lambda_m$. Using x^* and λ^* to denote the sets of optimal values, then it may be shown that

$$L(x, \lambda^*) \leqq L(x^*, \lambda^*) \leqq L(x^*, \lambda).$$

In other words, when the Lagrange multipliers take on their optimal values λ^*, the optimal values for x are those that make the Lagrangean function value as large as possible. Similarly, for $x = x^*$, the optimal values λ^* make L as small as possible. The task of finding the values x^* and λ^* that satisfy the above relations is called the 'saddle-point problem'. (This term derives from the fact that the function L is concave with respect to the x variables, and convex with respect to the λ variables; this is best visualised in three dimensions, when there is only one variable of each type, and the height of the saddle measures the value of the function L.) For brief discussions of this saddle-point property, see sections 5.4, 5.5 and 5.6 of Lancaster (1968) and section 4.3 of Intriligator (1971).

Some interesting applications of non-linear optimisation in microeconomic theory are given in Shone (1981).

8

Non-Linear and Integer Programming

While the Kuhn–Tucker conditions afford a valuable description of the optimal solution for the general problem in non-linear constrained optimisation, they do not provide an effective computational procedure for finding that solution. The first section of this chapter shows that the nature of the optimal solution makes the solution harder to find, and discusses briefly some general computational procedures. The next two sections consider two special cases of the general non-linear problem. These cases are important in economic analysis, and fortunately there are powerful special algorithms for them.

Although, traditionally, indivisibilities are largely ignored in economic analysis (especially in economic theory), their existence is an important fact of life. Later sections of the chapter introduce integer and zero–one variables, and show how these may be used in economic modelling, discuss the analysis of economies and diseconomies of scale, and show how the former may be modelled with the help of zero–one variables (thereby demonstrating an equivalence between indivisibilities and scale economies), and, finally, describe in general terms the computational procedures for integer programming.

8.1 NON-LINEAR PROGRAMMING: SOME GENERAL REMARKS

Some insight into the nature of the optimal solution to the general non-linear problem may be obtained by using an adaptation of Example B. Instead of the linear net revenue functions initially specified (cf. Table 1.3), suppose now that, for the two products, the respective net revenues per unit are

$$v_1 = 2(460 - x_1)$$

and

$$v_2 = 400 - x_2$$

(Such net revenue functions could arise when unit costs are constant and the two demand curves are linear but downward sloping – i.e. price diminishing with output x_j – while the two demands are independent – i.e. such that the quantity demanded of one product does not depend on the price of the other.)

The total net revenue is

$$\pi = 2x_1(460 - x_1) + x_2(400 - x_2)$$
$$= -2(x_1 - 230)^2 - (x_2 - 200)^2 + 145,800.$$

This last expression for π shows that the iso-net revenue curves are a nest of ellipses (as shown in Figure 8.1); each ellipse is centred on $(x_1, x_2) = (230, 200)$, the point marked W in the figure; and, if there were no constraints, the largest value for π would be 145, 800, which is obtained at W. (In the expression for π, each of the squared terms takes on the value zero, at this point W.) However, given the constraints of Example B, this solution is not feasible.

Instead of using the Kuhn–Tucker conditions, a low-brow solution procedure is now deployed. As shown in the figure, the constrained optimum is at the point where one of the ellipses touches the constraint line $x_1 + x_2 = 400$. At this point, the slope of the ellipse must be that of the line, viz. -1. This slope is also given (by differentiation of the iso-net revenue

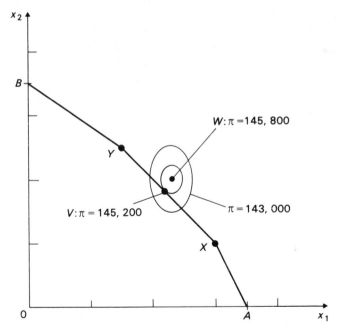

Figure 8.1 *Example B with a non-linear net revenue function*

function) as

$$\frac{dx_2}{dx_1} = -\frac{2(x_1 - 230)}{x_2 - 200}.$$

When this is set equal to -1, and the equation solved together with the equation of the constraint line, the constrained optimum is found to be at $(x_1, x_2) = (220, 180)$, shown as the point V in the figure.

In this case, although the optimum is still on the boundary of the feasible region, it is not at an extreme point. For optimisation of a non-linear function subject to linear (inequality) constraints, this is the general result when the unconstrained optimum lies outside the feasible region. However, the optimum *may* occur at an extreme point.

In other cases, the unconstrained optimum may lie *inside* the feasible region. In the non-linear version of Example B, suppose that the demand curves shift downwards to give the following new net revenue functions:

$$v_1 = 2(400 - x_1)$$

$$v_2 = 360 - x_2$$

These yield $\pi = -2(x_1 - 200)^2 - (x_2 - 180)^2 + 112,400.$

The unconstrained optimum is $(x_1, x_2) = (200, 180)$, which lies inside the feasible region; in other words, the solution is no longer even on the boundary! (The economic interpretation is immediate: because of the diminishing marginal revenues, the profit-maximising firm restricts output levels to such an extent that it does not utilise fully *any* of its available resources.)

If the constraints are non-linear too, the story becomes even more complicated; but it must be noted that in economic applications the constraints are usually linear. In addition, there can be problems in distinguishing between local and global optima, as already noted (for the case of unconstrained optimisation) in section 7.2.

Thus the linear programming computational device of searching among extreme points will not serve in (general) non-linear optimisation; rather, the general-purpose algorithms for non-linear problems must search more widely within the feasible region. For this reason, such algorithms are much less powerful than the linear programming procedures.

The principal computational approach to the general non-linear optimisation problem uses one or other of a family of *gradient methods*. Although the details vary from one method to another, most methods share the following basic characteristics. The (iterative) calculation begins with *any* feasible solution, although, as always, a 'good' feasible solution is preferable, since such will give a calculation with a 'small' number of iterations. Each iteration comprises a step from the previous solution point to a new point. The size of the step depends on the details of the algorithm, and may be limited by the presence of one or more constraints that act as barriers. The direction of the step is determined by the *gradient* of the objective function at the previous solution point. This may be visualised most readily in the case of two decision variables, measured on a horizontal plane; the vertical axis then measures the value of the function to be maximised. In moving from one point to another in the horizontal plane, the direction chosen is the one that gives the steepest ascent on the surface representing the objective function (where steepness is measured by the slope of the tangent plane at the starting point). Of course, in choosing a direction, allowance must be made also for the constraints and the non-negativity requirements, to ensure that the new point is also feasible. Provided the objective function is concave, a sequence of such iterations will move towards the (global) maximum. Although (in general) the process never converges exactly, it may be used to get sufficiently close to the optimum.

8.2   SEPARABLE PROGRAMMING

One of the special cases in which computation of the optimal solution can be relatively straightforward is that in which the objective function and the constraint functions are all separable. A function $f(x_1, x_2, ..., x_n)$ is said to be *separable* in the n variables if it may be written

$$f(x_1, x_2, ..., x_n) = f_1(x_2) + f_2(x_2) + ... + f_n(x_n).$$

In other words, the function may be separated out into a summation of functions, each of which is a function of a single variable. (Where the original function is not separable, it is sometimes possible to transform the variables in order to yield separability; this is discussed later.)

An economic example where separability occurs naturally is the gross revenue function for a firm selling two goods in imperfectly competitive markets, where the demands are independent. In particular, suppose that the demand quantity x_j is a linear function of own price p_j:

$$x_j = a_j - b_j p_j \qquad (j = 1, 2)$$

where a_j and b_j are strictly positive and the function is defined only for $p_j < a_j/b_j$ (which ensures that x_j is non-negative). The gross revenue received by the firm may then be written as a separable (quadratic) function *of the prices:*

$$R = p_1(a_1 - b_1 p_1) + p_2(a_2 - b_2 p_2)$$
$$= f_1(p_1) + f_2(p_2)$$

where the functions f_1 and f_2 are defined in the obvious way.

Returning to the general optimisation problem, if the constraints are all linear (as usually happens in economic contexts), then these constraint functions are, of course, all separable. All then hinges on whether the objective function is separable.

When it is, an approximate objective function may be substituted to permit a relatively simple form of calculation. Specifically, each separate function (of one of the decision variables) may be replaced by a *linear* approximation, as depicted in Figure 8.2 for the non-linear function $f(x)$, defined for the range $0 \leq x \leq a$ of the single variable x; this function is approximately represented by the sequence of linear segments $f^*(x)$, which is an example of what is known as a *piece-wise linear function*. Six linear segments have been used in the diagram; a closer approximation could be made by increasing the number of segments.

The simplex method for finding a linear programming optimum may then be used (in a slightly adapted form) in order to find a local optimum of the function $f^*(x)$; this solution approximates that for the original function $f(x)$. (For some details on how to reformulate the model in order to perform such calculations, see – for example – section 4.2 of Hadley, 1964.) Of course, the distinction between local and global optima (cf. section 7.2 above) still applies. For the range $0 \leq x \leq a$, the function $f(x)$ shown in Figure 8.2 is quasi-concave (cf. section 7.10), and there is only one local maximum, which (hence) is a global maximum; the method yields an approximation to that solution.

Incidentally, for empirical work, there should be no grounds for concern arising from the approximate nature of the solution. First, because of both

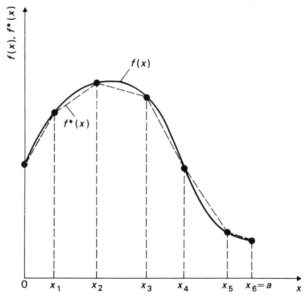

Figure 8.2 *A piece-wise linear approximating function*

conceptual and empirical difficulties, the model generally will be only an approximate representation of the intrinsic optimisation problem; in that context, an 'exact' solution may seem to give spurious accuracy. Secondly, as already remarked, the size of the error arising from the linear approximation may be reduced by increasing the number (and reducing the size) of the linear segments. In particular, for a problem known (or believed) to have only a single local optimum, once the location of that optimum has been identified rather roughly by an initial optimising calculation, a second optimising search may be executed in that locality, using a large number of small linear segments to represent the function there in order to obtain a more precise characterisation of the optimum.

As already noted, it may be possible to transform a problem to give separability when the original formulation has an objective function that is not separable. For an example, suppose that the firm selling two goods now finds that the demand functions are interdependent, with each demand quantity depending on both prices:

$$x_1 = a_1 - b_1 p_1 + c_1 p_2$$
$$x_2 = a_2 - b_2 p_2 + c_2 p_1$$

where c_1 and c_2 are both strictly positive (for the case where the goods are demand substitutes). The function for gross revenue becomes

$$R = p_1(a_1 - b_1 p_1) + p_2(a_2 - b_2 p_2) + (c_1 + c_2)p_1 p_2.$$

As it stands, the third term is not in separable form, being a product of the two decision variables, p_1 and p_2. But now define two new variables:

$$y_1 = \tfrac{1}{2}(p_1 + p_2) \qquad \text{and} \qquad y_2 = \tfrac{1}{2}(p_1 - p_2).$$

Then

$$p_1 p_2 = y_1^2 - y_2^2$$

and this may be used to substitute for the product term in the revenue function, which is thereby put into separable form. The (linear) equations that define y_1 and y_2 are added to the constraints of the model. (For some further discussion of this and other useful transformations, see section 4.5 of Hadley, 1964.)

8.3   QUADRATIC PROGRAMMING

The second special case for which there are powerful computational procedures is one in which the objective function is quadratic. The example in the preceding section, in which linear demand functions lead to a quadratic revenue function, illustrates the importance of this case in economic analysis.

The term *quadratic programming* is used to describe any computational algorithm that solves a problem in which a quadratic objective function is to be optimised subject to linear inequality constraints. If the decision variables are denoted $x_1, x_2, ..., x_n$, then the objective function, which may have both linear and quadratic terms in these variables, is denoted:

$$c_1 x_1 + c_2 x_2 + ... + c_n x_n + d_{11} x_1^2 + d_{22} x_2^2 + ... + d_{nn} x_n^2 \\ + d_{12} x_1 x_2 + d_{13} x_1 x_3 + ...$$

With the help of summation notation, this may be written more succinctly:

$$\sum_{i=1}^{n} c_i x_i + \sum_{i=1}^{n} \sum_{j=1}^{n} d_{ij} x_i x_j.$$

For those familiar with matrix algebra, the objective function may be written

$$c'x + x'Dx.$$

The importance of quadratic programming has led a number of people to devise algorithms; computer package programs for mathematical programming generally include one or more of these. All the algorithms are iterative in character, and some are close cousins to the simplex method for solving linear programming problems. The computing time and cost are somewhat greater than for a linear programming problem having the same number of variables and constraints; nevertheless the algorithms are powerful and 'well-behaved' and hence may be used with confidence on large problems. The computer program is usually designed to output the dual values (corresponding to the constraints), as well as the optimal values for the decision variables; these duals have the usual interpretation.

Now consider the *maximisation* problem. As indicated in section 7.2 above, provided the objective function is *concave,* any local maximum is a global maximum. This is the usual necessary condition for an algorithm to be able to find the optimal solution. Now the linear part of the objective function is necessarily concave. Thus, if the quadratic form

$$\sum_i \sum_j d_{ij} x_i x_j$$

is concave, then the entire fucntion, being the sum of two concave functions, is itself concave.

It may be shown that this concavity requirement is equivalent to the requirement that the quadratic form be *negative semi-definite,* (i.e. such that

$$\sum_i \sum_j d_{ij} x_i x_j \leqq 0$$

for all x_i. Furthermore, if the quadratic form is negative definite (i.e. such that

$$\sum_i \sum_j d_{ij} x_i x_j < 0$$

for any set of x_i other than all $x_i = 0$), then the global maximum is unique (because the objective function is now strictly concave) and the problem has a finite solution. In practice, there will be no difficulty even in the semi-definite case, and most computer packages can be relied upon to find the maximum if the quadratic form is either negative definite or negative semi-definite. (If the form is semi-definite, a so-called perturbation technique is used, if necessary.)

This leaves the practical question of how to ascertain whether the quadratic form is either negative definite or semi-definite. There is a systematic procedure for this evaluation, but the computation is not generally a trivial task for any but the smallest values for n. In practice, the nature of the quadratic form can usually be assured by the economic context: if the maximisation problem is soundly conceived, then the form will be concave. As an additional check, however, most computer packages contain a procedure for testing the quadratic form and delivering an appropriate message if all is not well.

The computer package generally requires that the quadratic form should be symmetric, i.e. such that $d_{ij} = d_{ji}$ (or, in matrix notation, that D should be symmetric). This requirement does not imply any loss of generality, since if any pair of coefficients d_{ij} and d_{ji} are not equal, a new set of coefficients f_{ij} and f_{ji} (and hence a new quadratic form) may be defined, having

$$f_{ij} = f_{ji} = \frac{d_{ij} + d_{ji}}{2} \qquad \text{for all } i, j.$$

In economic contexts, the symmetry often arises naturally (as is illustrated by the example in section 10.1). The symmetry may be exploited when preparing the data for input to the computer: instead of entering $d_{ij} x_i x_j$ and $d_{ji} x_j x_i$, it is easier to enter $2 d_{ij} x_i x_j$, making one such entry for each pair of subscripts having $i < j$ (the upper triangle in the D matrix); the example in section 10.1 illustrates.

Note that if the problem is one of minimisation, a well-behaved optimum (and hence a happy outcome for the computation) requires that the objective function be *convex,* which in turn requires that the quadratic form be *positive definite* or *semi-definite.* Again, the computer package tests for this.

8.4 INTEGER VARIABLES

In all the analysis so far, it has been supposed that all the decision quantities are continuously variable. In economic contexts, however, indivisibilities are common. In such cases, an implementable optimising solution must be in integers (whole numbers). Fortunately, in many instances it is sufficient merely to round any fractional results. For example, if an optimising calculation (supposing all variables to be continuous) suggests that an automobile manufacturer's profit will be maximised by the production of 847.23 vehicles per week, then, for all practical purposes, the rounded solution of 847 vehicles will be near enough to the integer optimum (if not actually that optimum); it is also likely to satisfy all the constraints (though this must be verified, of course).

On the other hand, if an optimising calculation (supposing all variables continuous) for aircraft scheduling were to recommend that the airline fly 1.42 Boeing 747 aircraft daily between points A and B, then it is by no means obvious whether the integer optimum requires the scheduling of one or two such aircraft (or, perhaps, the deployment of some other aircraft from the airline's fleet). For such contexts, where rounding requires a major departure from the fractional solution, it is essential to have an optimisation procedure that yields (non-negative) integer solutions.

It is interesting to note that a sub-class of linear programming problem has the property that *all* the extreme points of the feasible region have all-integer coordinates. In such cases, the optimum point necessarily has integer values for all variables, even though the model formulation is in terms of continuous variables. The defining characteristic of this sub-class is that the matrix of constraint coefficients should be *unimodular*. Without giving a formal definition, it may be noted here that a necessary condition for unimodularity is that all the constraint coefficients must be zero, or plus or minus one. An important case where unimodularity holds is the so-called transportation problem of linear programming; Example A (cf. section 1.2) is an instance of this case. (However the name is misleading: the case is defined by the classification of the matrix of constraint coefficients; applications occur also in contexts other than transportation.)

8.5 ZERO-ONE VARIABLES

While such integer variables arise naturally from indivisibilities in commodities, the related concept of the zero–one variable is a little more contrived, having been developed to give a helpful representation of discrete policy alternatives. It is convenient to begin with an example. In the so-called *fixed-charge problem,* some production process can be carried out (at any positive level up to a prescribed capacity limit) if and only if some fixed provision is made (e.g. investment in plant capacity); in the simplest model of this phenomenon, it is supposed that a fixed charge or cost c_1 is incurred if and only if capacity is provided, and that there is also a uniform cost c_2 per unit of output when the process is operated. If there were no fixed cost, the production process could be represented in an ordinary linear programming model. The presence of the fixed charge makes the modelling task more complicated.

A *zero–one variable* x_1 is one that takes the value 0 or the value 1; no other values are permitted. (Thus it is a special case of an integer variable.) Such a variable may be used to represent the discrete choice between providing or not providing the fixed capacity. The latter decision is represented by $x_1 = 0$, and the former by $x_1 = 1$. The fixed charge is then validly represented by the cost term c_1x_1. Now define x_2 as the number of units produced of the single output of the production process, with x_2 regarded as a continuous variable. The operating cost is then c_2x_2, and the total cost of providing capacity and operating the process is $c_1x_1 + c_2x_2$.

Suppose payment of the fixed charge c_1 provides capacity sufficient to enable the production of k units of output. If capacity *is* provided, then actual output is subject to the capacity limit: $x_2 \leq k$. If no capacity is provided, then x_2 must be zero, which may be written equivalently as $x_2 \leq 0$. These two requirements may be represented by a single constraint $x_2 \leq kx_1$ in which the alternative values for x_1 generate the capacity constraints for the two cases.

By using this device of the zero–one variable, it is thus possible to represent the link between the (discrete) capacity level and the (continuously variable) output level, and also to represent the costs of investment and operation. These expressions involving the zero–one variable x_1 can then be included in the entire optimising model, which typically will include further discrete and continuous variables representing other economic activities and processes.

Probably the single most important application of such modelling in economic analysis is in the area of long-term production planning, in which there are discrete investment alternatives, as well as continuous decision variables to represent operating levels. In this and other contexts, it is often necessary to find a representation for further logical requirements to be satisfied by the discrete variables. One common form of interdependence is that in which investment proposals are mutually exclusive. For example, prescribed investment schemes may comprise alternative uses for the same physical site or location. For n such investment proposals, a set of n zero–one variables x_j may be defined, each representing the level (zero or one) at which the investment is undertaken. Mutual exclusiveness may then be represented by the constraint:

$$x_1 + x_2 + \ldots + x_n \leq 1.$$

Bearing in mind that each x_j is a zero–one variable, it is clear that this permits no more than one project to be undertaken, while the inequality allows for the possibility that it may be optimal to undertake none of the projects.

Another example occurs in multi-stage processing, in which the output from plant A is needed as input to plant B. If x_A and x_B are defined as zero–one variables to denote the undertaking of investment in prescribed amounts of these types of plant, then the constraint $x_B \leq x_A$ prevents the creation of plant B without the creation of plant A. At the same time, it does not rule out any of the valid alternatives – construction of neither, of both, and of A alone. (Of course, this constraint is simply a variant of that used in the fixed-charge example.)

Situations in which there are both discrete and continuous variables are called *mixed-integer problems*. However, business/management contexts sometimes yield *all-integer* problems, in which all the variables are discrete. These usually require only zero–one variables, which are used to represent logical requirements. An example is the so-called *travelling salesperson problem*, in which the salesperson starts from a home city (to be denoted city 1), makes one visit to each of $(n-1)$ other cities, and then returns home. The distance between city i and city j is denoted d_{ij} (for all i, j), and the aim is to sequence the visits so as to minimise the total distance travelled. This is, in effect, a combinatorial problem, and it is this characteristic that makes it possible to model it solely in terms of zero–one variables. Each of these variables may be denoted x_{ijs}, which takes on the value 1 if the salesperson travels from i to j on leg s of the journey, and which otherwise takes zero value. The total journey length to be minimised is

$$D = \sum_{i=1}^{n} \sum_{j=1}^{n} d_{ij} \sum_{s=1}^{n} x_{ijs}.$$

The various logical requirements can be represented by simple constraints. For any given city i, only one leg begins there:

$$\sum_{j=1}^{n} \sum_{s=1}^{n} x_{ijs} = 1 \qquad (\text{for } i = 1, 2, ..., n)$$

Similarly, for any city j, only one leg terminates there:

$$\sum_{i=1}^{n} \sum_{s=1}^{n} x_{ijs} = 1 \qquad (\text{for } j = 1, 2, ..., n)$$

In any given leg s, only one pair of cities may be connected:

$$\sum_{i=1}^{n} \sum_{j=1}^{n} x_{ijs} = 1 \qquad (\text{for } s = 1, ..., n)$$

Also, if leg s ends in city j, then leg $s + 1$ must begin there:

$$\sum_{i=1}^{n} x_{ijs} = \sum_{m=1}^{n} x_{jms} \qquad (\text{for } j = 1, 2, ..., n \text{ and}$$
$$s = 1, 2, ..., n - 1)$$

(In this last constraint, note that m is used as a subscript to denote the destination city in leg $s + 1$, since j is there used as the subscript for the origin city for that leg.)

As is commonly the case, such logical requirements lead to linear constraints in which the non-zero coefficients are all $+ 1$, while the coefficients matrix has a low density. In this model, the objective function is also linear.

8.6   ECONOMIES AND DISECONOMIES OF SCALE

At this point, it is instructive to study economies and diseconomies of scale, in order to see how they may be modelled with the help of the formulations discussed in the earlier sections of this chapter.

For the sake of illustration, consider a production situation in which a single output is produced using several inputs, where all but one of the inputs is required in amounts strictly proportional to the output level. For a first case, the exceptional input is subject to *diseconomies of scale;* in other words, the marginal and average input quantities *increase* as the output level increase, according to a relationship depicted by the smooth curve $r = r(q)$ in Figure 8.3. Suppose also that all inputs are purchased at constant unit prices.

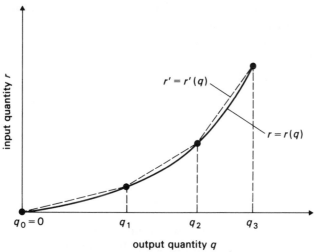

Figure 8.3   *Diseconomies of scale*

In principle, this situation could be handled by a non-linear programming formulation. However, it will now be shown how to construct a *linear* programming model that is an adequate approximation. First, the smooth curve $r(q)$ is approximated by a piece-wise linear function $r'(q)$; in the figure, a three-segment approximation is drawn. This is used in the algebraic formulation given next.

Define three activities, one corresponding to each of the three segments, with activity levels measured in terms of output, and denoted x_1, x_2 and x_3. In the first activity, the amount of the input per unit of output is measured by a_1, the slope of the first (linear) segment; the slopes a_2 and a_3 of the second and third segments play similar roles in the second and third activities. Since $a_1 < a_2 < a_3$, the first activity is cheaper to operate (per unit of output) than the second, and the second is cheaper than the third. If (for example) the aim is to produce specified output at minimum cost, the first activity will be preferred to the second, and the second to the third. If the desired output is greater than q_1, it would be invalid to use the first activity only in the optimal solution. Thus, to ensure a proper representation, it is necessary to place limits on the activity levels:

$$x_1 \leqq q_1; \ x_2 \leqq q_2 - q_1; \ x_3 \leqq q_3 - q_2.$$

This model now ensures that the activities are selected in the appropriate order and its optimal solution determines the appropriate levels for x_1, x_2 and x_3 to give the cheapest way of producing a total of q units of output, for any $q \leqq q_3$.

On the other hand, this modelling device fails if there are *economies of scale;* then $a_1 > a_2 > a_3$ (and the input function in the figure becomes flatter rather than steeper, as q increases). In this case, the third activity would be the cheapest, and the previous model would set $x_3 > 0$ even though x_1 may be zero. In other words, the cost-minimising calculation would (invalidly) count the scale-economy benefits, even when output was not large enough to qualify.

However, such economies of scale may be treated within a (linear) *integer* programming model with the help of zero–one variables y_1, y_2 and y_3, which are required to satisfy the following five constraints:

$$y_1 \geqq x_1/(q_1 - q_0)$$
$$y_2 \leqq x_1/(q_1 - q_0)$$
$$y_2 \geqq x_2/(q_2 - q_1)$$
$$y_3 \leqq x_2/(q_2 - q_1)$$
$$y_3 \geqq x_3/(q_3 - q_2)$$

These constraints serve to rule out invalid production plans. For example, if $x_1 < q_1 - q_0$ (the full amount that has to be produced at the high marginal cost a_1 before the advantage of the next lower marginal cost a_2 can be obtained), then the second constraint ensures that $y_2 = 0$, and, from the third constraint, $x_2 = 0$; the remaining constraints similarly ensure that $x_3 = 0$. (The zero–one variables do not appear in the objective function; they are used merely to secure a valid relationship between the x_j.)

8.7   INDIVISIBILITIES AND COMPETITIVE EQUILIBRIUM

For the Ricardian economy modelled in sections 4.4 and 4.5, it was shown that the (centrally planned) optimum can also be reached as an equilibrium outcome when competitive markets are used. Later (in section 4.8), it was noted that, in *linear* models generally, it is always possible to find (competitive) prices that will sustain an equilibrium at any given optimal solution found under central planning, and that the converse also holds. Furthermore, when the notion of *efficiency* was introduced in section 5.1, it was noted that all optimal solutions are efficient (cf. Figure 5.1 and the discussion comparing it with Figure 2.1). Thus the result for linear models may be rephrased: any efficient point can be sustained as an equilibrium by competitive market prices, and conversely any competitive equilibrium is efficient.

The question to be considered next is whether these results still apply in the cases of diseconomies of scale and economies of scale. The first case is easily resolved: as seen in the preceding section, diseconomies of scale may be represented by a linear model; hence the previous results still hold. This is hardly surprising since it is well known that competitive markets can (and do) coexist with such diseconomies.

Equally well known is the proposition that economies of scale cause difficulty for competitive markets: for example, if scale economies persist up to the level of total industry output, production of a commodity is eventually concentrated in a single enterprise, which then has market power that allows it to influence the price. In the preceding section, it was shown that centralised calculation of an optimum (when there are economies of scale) can be done with the help of integer variables, and this equivalence between scale economies and indivisibilies suggests that the price mechanism must have similar difficulty with indivisibilities.

This can be demonstrated explicitly for a simple example of two products, both indivisible in character, and made in amounts x_1 and x_2 subject to a (single) linear constraint, giving the set of integer feasible points (known, for obvious reasons, as lattice points) shown in Figure 8.4. The efficient point E is the optimal point for an appropriately defined optimisation problem (which necessarily has a non-linear objective function, if E is to be selected as the optimum).

As usual, uniform (competitive) prices give a straight price line; any such line that passes through E must pass below the feasible point S and/or the feasible point R. Thus, for *any* such prices, production plans corresponding

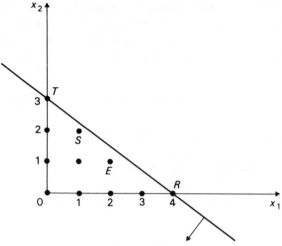

Figure 8.4

to R and/or S will yield greater value to the producer, and will therefore be preferred to E. Hence, although E is efficient, it is not possible to find (competitive) prices that will sustain an equilibrium at E. On the other hand, even in the integer case, all points that are competitive equilibria are efficient; in Figure 8.4 such points are R and T.

Thus, in the integer programming case, every competitive equilibrium is efficient, but not all efficient points can be sustained as competitive equilibria. The second of these results mirrors the inability of competitive markets to coexist with all cases of economies of scale.

8.8   INTEGER PROGRAMMING

In general, integer programming problems are much more difficult computationally than problems of comparable size but having continuous variables only. The reason for this is basically that typically there are many local optima; hence methods that depend on iterating from good to 'adjacent' better feasible solutions do not work. Thus the field of computational methods for integer problems is complex and untidy, since computational success is still to some degree an art, depending on practical experience of numerical work. Since our interest is not in computational algorithms *per se,* this section gives only a brief outline of some general ideas, to enable the model-formulator to have some appreciation of the methods that may be used and of their limitations. The term 'integer programming' is often confined to those cases in which the objective and constraint functions would all be linear if all the variables were continuous. This restriction is followed here, although some of the most general remarks do apply more broadly.

When there is only a very small number of integer variables, and when each can take only a small range of values (especially zero–one variables), it may be best to adopt a combinatorial approach: for each discrete alternative (i.e. for each feasible combination of values for the integer variables), first find the optimal solution for the problem couched in terms of the remaining (i.e. continuous) variables; then compare these 'local' optima in order to establish the global optimum. However, this soon becomes computationally inefficient as the number of discrete alternatives increases. (But methods of complete or partial enumeration have been used effectively on occasion for relatively large problems when *all* the variables are of the zero–one type.)

Failing such a combinatorial approach, most methods of (mixed) integer programming solve the problem initially as if all the variables were continuous, and then impose restrictions that rule out such invalid fractional values as are first obtained. The variety of programming approaches that have been advocated stem from differences in the design of the restrictions to be introduced. Some early theoretical word focused on so-called cutting plane methods, but computational experience with this approach seems to have been disappointing. Accordingly, most algorithms now use a *branch and bound* approach, whose general characteristics are described briefly.

Throughout the calculation, a record is kept of the best feasible solution so far found, and of the value m of the maximand for that solution. If all else fails, an initial solution and initial value of m is found by selecting a plausible set of feasible values for the integer variables and then solving for the continuous variables.

Suppose that one of the invalid fractional values obtained in the first calculation, when all variables are regarded as continuous, is $x_8 = 3.6$. Two new problems may be defined by 'branching' on this variable; one such problem adds the restriction $x_8 \geq 4$ and the other has $x_8 \leq 3$. Suppose that solving the first of the new problems gives a value for the objective function that is less than the current best feasible value, m. Irrespective of whether this new solution still contains illegitimate fractions, it is clear that the case with $x_8 \geq 4$ is no longer of interest – the value of m provides a bound that rules out this branch of problems (because when further restrictions are added to rule out invalid fractions, the value of the maximand cannot increase).

Calculation then continues for the branch where $x_8 \leq 3$. If this yields further fractional values, but a maximand greater than m, then it is necessary to create further branches, and examine further sub-cases. If one of these has no invalid fractions and a value greater than the initial m, it becomes the best feasible solution found so far.

This process of branching and bounding continues until there remain no sub-cases of promise, not yet examined. Here 'promise' means a solution with fractional values for integer variables and a maximand value greater than the current value for m. Clearly, there are only a finite number of sets of values for the integer variables (assuming a finite upper bound on each of these variables), and hence the branch and bound method will terminate in a finite number of steps although some finite numbers are very large).

Although such a pedestrian approach may look as if it will require a very large number of steps, computational experience has been relatively favourable. Where a solution yields more than one invalid fraction, there is a choice as to which variable should be selected for the next branching. Equally, at any stage, the list of promising but untested cases may be long, and it is necessary to choose which to examine first. Computational experience has led to refinements in the rules used to make these choices. In conjunction with improvements in computer hardware, these refinements have increased the size of problem that may be tackled at reasonable cost. In recent years, it has become practicable to solve problems with as many as 100 integer variables, along with a few thousand constraints and continuous variables; in the case of zero–one variables, solutions have been found at reasonable cost for problems with several hundred constraints and a few *thousand* zero–one variables. Unfortunately, branch and bound algorithms still are not very robust; while many problems run successfully, others of similar dimensions but differing numerical coefficients can absorb very large amounts of computer time without an optimum being established. Experience has shown that the calculation terminates more readily when the initial 'continuous' optimum gives a fair guide to the integer optimum. Since this cannot be assessed in advance, the novice must beware of possible dangers.

8.9 EXERCISES

(1) A consumer of two goods has preferences that are summarised in the (quadratic) utility function

$$U(x_1, x_2) = 20x_1 + 16x_2 - 2x_1^2 - x_2^2$$

where the (continuous) variables x_1 and x_2 denote the quantities purchased of the two goods. The unit prices of the goods are \$1 and \$2 respectively, and the consumer has a budget of \$15 available to spend on these goods. (The money cannot be used for any other purpose.)

(a) In the absence of any budget constraint, what quantities of the two goods would maximise the consumer's utility?

(b) Is it realistic to postulate a utility function that implies that there are consumption quantities at which the consumer is satiated?

(c) When the budget constraint applies, will the consumer wish to spend the entire \$15 on these goods? If so, what quantities will be purchased?

(2) Transform the following optimisation problem into one in which *all* the functions are separable:

choose values for x_1 and x_2 so as to

maximise $e^{ax_1 + bx_2^2}$

subject to
$$x_1 x_2 \leqq c$$
$$x_1 \geqq 0 \qquad x_2 \geqq 0$$

(3) Formulate a mixed-integer programming model for the following problem:

A manufacturer sells products A and B at unit profits of $1 and $2, respectively. Each unit of product A requires 2 kg of raw material; each unit of product B requires 3 kg. The available amount of the raw material is 100 kg. If any amount of product A is made, a set-up cost of $10 is incurred; similarly, for manufacture of product B, there is a set-up cost of $5. (The unit profits are net of all costs *except* these set-up costs.) The manufacturer wishes to find the profit-maximising production plan.

(4) Formulate an all-integer programming model for the following problem:

The director of the museum whose plan is shown in Figure 8.5 wishes to minimise the number of attendants needed to supervise the rooms labelled A–F. If stationed in a doorway connecting two rooms, an attendant can supervise both rooms.

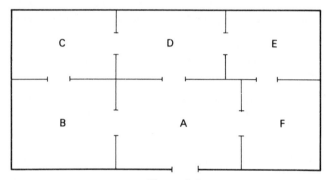

Figure 8.5

(5) Formulate a programming model for the following problem:

An art professor wishes to mail to another country eight books, whose weights (in kg) are: 5, 4, 4, 3, 3, 3, 2, 2. The professor wishes to put no more than four books in any one parcel, and seeks to minimise the number of parcels. The post office does not accept parcels weighing more than 13 kg.

(*Remark:* Although two parcels suffice, consider how you would formulate the model and execute the calculation of it, *without* this insight.)

8.10 FURTHER READING

Gradient methods for the general non-linear optimisation problem are discussed in some detail, and in a relatively advanced manner, in Chapter 9 of Hadley (1964). Chapter 4 of the same book gives a lengthy treatment of separable programming, while a short and fairly elementary discussion (focusing on computational practicalities – some of which are now a little dated) is to be found in Chapter 14 of Beale

(1968). The same two authors provide similar approaches to quadratic programming – see Hadley's Chapter 7 and Beale's Chapter 13. An interesting industrial application of separable programming is described by Beale, Coen and Flowerdew in Moore and Hodges (1970). (Incidentally, that volume also includes a general survey by Wolfe of non-linear programming methods – but some of the discussion is fairly advanced.)

Hadley (1964), Chapter 8, discusses the use of integer variables in various contexts; see in particular his section 8.9 for a slightly different formulation of the travelling salesperson problem, a formulation that has computational advantages. The later sections of Hadley's chapter deal with computational procedures for integer linear programming, but this has become dated in the light of more recent computational experience; for a useful (advanced) evaluation of that experience, see Beale's essay in Jacobs (1977), pp. 409–448.

Advanced discussions of various theoretical and computational aspects of non-linear programming (including duality theory for non-linear programming) are to be found in Abadie (1967). Many of the general methods of non-linear programming bring the user who is interested in empirical work into immediate contact with the numerical behaviour of computer codes. Although numerical questions such as accuracy and convergence go beyond the scope of this book, the reader who wishes to gain some appreciation of the problems of such numerical analysis may like to dip into Gill, Murray and Wright (1981), which is written in a relatively down-to-earth manner (though inevitably much of the discussion is rather technical).

An advanced examination of production theory for the case where goods are indivisible is given in Frank (1969). This extends the pioneering paper in *Econometrica* of Gomory and Baumol (1960), which attempts also to explore some duality theory for integer programming (although the results have proved to be disappointing). Those interested in the history of thought may like to know that the same issue of *Econometrica* contains the seminal paper by Land and Doig (1960) that was the first to propose a branch and bound approach to integer programming.

9

Dynamic Programming

The subject of this chapter is optimisation in multi-stage decision processes. This includes optimisation over time, although, as will be seen, such decision processes also occur in many other contexts. The optimisation approach that may be used in analysing such problems was developed about thirty years ago. It was named 'dynamic programming' and this name is now universally used. Nevertheless, the nomenclature is unfortunate, in that in other fields (notably linear and non-linear programming, and integer programming), the term 'programming' is used to denote computational algorithms (a convention that has been followed in this book). Dynamic programming, in contrast, is a mathematical theory of multi-stage decision processes. In other words, it offers a basic conceptual approach rather than a computational procedure; indeed, there is no general-purpose computational algorithm, and the design of the computational procedure for any individual application of the approach depends greatly on the circumstances of the case.

Many problems within the area of multi-stage decision processes can be tackled (in principle) by other methods. However, in many cases, these alternatives are computationally infeasible, or (at least) inferior to the dynamic programming approach. On the other hand, dynamic programming is not superior in all such cases. As always in optimisation, it is important not to prejudge how a problem should be formulated and a solution computed; each case must be examined on its merits.

Although the basic idea of dynamic programming is a simple one, its execution in any given context can require a lengthy chain of reasoning and (often) a great deal of formal (and, sometimes, frightening) mathematical notations. In an attempt to make the exposition as simple as possible, the approach used here is to present three simple, small-scale examples (which necessarily are very artificial) and then to use these to illustrate a discussion of the general properties of the approach.

9.1 A SIMPLE EXAMPLE

For a first example, suppose that a firm has a stock of Q units of a single commodity, which it sells in three distinct markets. These three markets are quite separate: any units sold in one market are consumed there; they cannot be transferred to either of the other markets. Using x_j to denote the (continuously divisible) amount sold in market j, the (inverse) demand functions for the three markets are

$$p_1 = a_1 - b_1 x_1$$
$$p_2 = a_1 - b_1 x_2$$
$$p_3 = a_3 - b_3 x_3$$

where all a_j and b_j are strictly positive. (As the functions indicate, the demand relationships are the same in the first two markets.) The revenues earned in the three markets are

$$R_1 = a_1 x_1 - b_1 x_1^2$$
$$R_2 = a_1 x_2 - b_1 x_2^2$$
$$R_3 = a_3 x_3 - b_3 x_3^2$$

The firm wishes to allocate its stock to the markets so as to maximise total revenue; it is assumed here that it *is* optimal to sell the entire stock.

In its application to this context, the fundamental dynamic programming principle yields the following proposition: *whatever* the commodity amount the firm decides to sell in any one market, the remaining amount must be divided optimally between the other two markets. This leads to a simple method of solution. Because the first two markets have the same demand function, symmetry requires that whatever is not assigned to the third market should be divided equally between these first two markets. Let the amount sold on each of the first two markets be denoted q; then $Q - 2q$ units are sold in the third market.

Using the revenue functions, the total revenue may now be expressed as a function of the unknown q:

$$R = a_3(Q - 2q) - b_3(Q - 2q)^2 + 2(a_1 q - b_1 q^2).$$

Suppose here that it is optimal to sell strictly positive amounts in all three markets. This implies an interior optimum (i.e. such that $Q > 2q > 0$), and hence a necessary condition for revenue-maximisation is that $dR/dq = 0$. This condition yields a single optimal solution:

$$q = [a_1 - a_3 + 2b_3 Q]/2(b_1 + 2b_3).$$

(The second derivative d^2R/dq^2 is negative, and hence this is indeed a maximum. In an empirical application, it would be necessary also to verify that it is optimal to sell in all three markets.)

This example serves to give an indication of the fundamental optimality principle that is the defining characteristic of the dynamic programming approach. For a general statement of this 'principle of optimality' we can do no better than turn to the words of Richard Bellman, the pioneer of dynamic programming, who wrote (Bellman, 1957, p. 83):

An optimal policy has the property that whatever the initial state and initial decision are, the remaining decisions must constitute an optimal policy with regard to the state resulting from the first decision.

In the present example, the initial state is the availability of Q units of the commodity, and the initial decision is the allocation of $(Q - 2q)$ units to the third market. The state resulting from this decision is that $2q$ units are left, and the remaining decisions (here just a single decision) concern the allocation of these units between the other two markets.

The proof of the principle is by contradiction: if the 'remaining decisions' are not optimal with respect to the state resulting from the first decision, then the entire set of decisions cannot be optimal, since the overall policy can be improved by appropriate change in the set of remaining decisions.

In the example, the calculation was made particularly easy because the first two markets are identical, and hence it could be seen immediately that the same quantities must be assigned to those two markets. However, this is not a necessary element in the use of the optimality principle, as may be seen by considering an adapted case in which the second market has the (inverse) demand function $p_2 = a_2 - b_2 x_2$ when $a_2 \neq a_1$ and $b_2 \neq b_1$. The procedure now requires a double application of the calculus technique.

Suppose that q_3 units are assigned to the third market. This leaves $(Q - q_3)$ units for the first two markets. Let q_1 denote the units sold in the first market. The revenue from these two markets is then

$$R_1 + R_2 = a_1 q_1 - b_1 q_1^2 + a_2(Q - q_3 - q_1) - b_2(Q - q_3 - q_1)^2$$

and this has to be made as large as possible by appropriate choice of a value for q_1, with q_3 regarded as given. As before, the first derivative $d(R_1 + R_2)/dq$ may be set equal to zero (the details are left for the reader to work through), and this gives a value of q_1 in terms of Q and q_3:

$$q_1 = f_1(Q, q_3)$$
$$q_2 = Q - q_3 - q_1 = f_2(Q, q_3).$$

The total revenue R may now be expressed as

$$R = r_1(q_1) + r_2(q_2) + r_3(q_3),$$

where the r_j are the appropriate functions. By substitution using the functions f_1 and f_2, this yields R as a function of Q and q_3, and the optimal q_3 may be found from $dR/dq_3 = 0$. The functions f_1 and f_2 are then used to calculate the optimal values for q_1 and q_2.

(Students of the theory of the firm will recognise that either of these versions of the problem can be solved in another way, using the necessary conditions for an optimum; namely, that the marginal revenues must be the same in all three markets, provided that it is optimal to sell all the stock and to sell in all markets. This alternative approach is slightly more convenient, computationally. However, the example still serves to illustrate the use of the optimality principle of Bellman; it also offers a reminder of the need to choose skilfully between computational procedures when alternatives are available.)

9.2 A SECOND EXAMPLE, HAVING DISCRETE ALTERNATIVES

A second example is given in this section. This has discrete alternatives, in contrast to the continuous nature of the decisions variable in the first example. This feature serves to give further insight into the use of the optimality principle.

The example concerns the road network depicted in Figure 9.1, where the lengths of the road links are shown in km. The link from point B to point E (for example) does *not* intersect with that from C to D; think of it as a case of one road passing over the top of the other without any connection at the bridge. Each link is a two-way road. The optimisation problem is to find the shortest route from point A to point H.

As already noted in section 8.8, in any optimisation problem for which the feasible policies comprise a finite set of discrete alternatives, the optimum may be found by a complete enumeration (i.e. by evaluating all the alternatives), provided this does not require too much computational effort. In the present case, the required computation is very slight; there are only eight possible routes, and these may be described by listing the intermediate points: BDF, BDG, BEF, BEG, CDF, CDG, CEF and CEG. The shortest of these is BDF, with a length of 16 km; and the shortest route is unique.

For large networks, however, complete enumeration is very expensive, if not infeasible, because of the very large number of alternatives that have to be considered. Then the dynamic programming approach is computa-

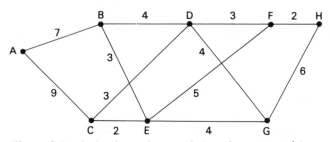

Figure 9.1 *A simple road network (not drawn to scale)*

tionally superior. The present small example is now used to illustrate its use.

The essential feature of the approach is to break up the task into a sequence of stages; in the present case, four stages are required. The first is to find the shortest routes to all points that are directly connected to A, i.e. to the points B and C. Clearly these are the direct routes, of lengths 7 and 9 km, respectively. These results are recorded in Table 9.1. The second stage is to find the shortest routes to such points in the network as may be reached from A after passing through only one intermediate point. For one such point, D, the alternatives are via B or via C. Now the shortest route passing through C and ending at D necessarily includes the shortest route from A to C, which is of length 9. Thus the shortest route via C to D is of length 12. Similarly the shortest route via B to D necessarily includes the shortest route from A to B, and hence is of length 11. Of these two routes, the one via B is shorter. Similarly, the shortest route to E proves to be via B, and is of length 10. These data are entered in the third and fourth rows of Table 9.1.

For the third stage, shortest routes are found to F and G. The shortest route to F via D necessarily includes the shortest route to D, and thus the best route to F via D is of length 14. Similarly, that to F via E is of length 15. The former is shorter, and is recorded in the table. The remaining calculations are left as an exercise.

Once the calculations are completed, the entries in Table 9.1 may be used to read off the overall result. The shortest route to H is of length 16, and passes through (in reverse order) F, D and B. This is confirmed by the earlier calculation.

In this example, the principle of optimality is used when considering (for example) a route from A via D to F. Here the implied given factor is the decision to approach F via D; the best such route must be optimal with respect to the remaining decisions, which concern the choice of intermediate point(s) between A and D. In other words, the shortest route via D to F must include (as part of the larger picture) the shortest route to D.

Once such routes have been calculated for all the points that are adjacent to F (here just the points D and E), the overall shortest route to F is established by direct comparison of all the alternatives.

Table 9.1 *Shortest routes for the simple road network*

Route to point	Length	Preceding point on shortest route
B	7	A
C	9	A
D	11	B
E	10	B
F	14	D
G	14	E
H	16	F

Clearly, as the size of the network is increased, even this dynamic programming approach requires an ever larger amount of computation. For all but the smallest networks, the use at each stage of the shortest routes to the previous stage reduces significantly the amount of computation compared with that needed in the direct approach of complete enumeration.

9.3   A MULTI-PERIOD EXAMPLE WITH AN INFINITE HORIZON

Optimisation over time is a field in which there is a particularly large number of successful applications of the optimality principle of dynamic programming. The example in this section uses a discrete time formulation (which arises naturally here from the economic context), and has an infinite horizon.

The optimising problem is that faced by a farmer who grows a single crop. Planting of the seed and harvesting of the crop take place within a single period, and cost a uniform \$$h$ per unit of crop *harvested*. Upon harvesting the total crop of q units, the farmer sells y units, in the same period, for an immediate revenue of \$$ky^{1/2}$. The remaining $(q - y)$ units are kept as seed, and are planted in the following period, when the harvest will be $a(q - y)$ units, where (of course) the growth factor $a > 1$. (Since marginal revenue in any period is $dR/dy = \frac{1}{2}ky^{-1/2}$, which is strictly positive for any y, it never pays to sell less than the entire amount left over after reservation of the seed portion.)

Because of the infinite horizon, the model has an infinite number of periods. It is supposed that cost, revenue and growth conditions are unchanging over time. Future costs and revenues are to be discounted using an interest rate r per period, and the farmer's aim is to maximise the discounted value of all future net cash receipts.

The farmer undertakes this optimising calculation in period 0, just after harvesting the crop of that period. The size of that crop will influence the optimal harvest and sales levels for ensuing periods. Suppose (for example) that the initial crop is very small; given his objective, the farmer may find it desirable to increase the crop size over succeeding periods, and at first this may lead the farmer to restrict sales to modest levels. Later crop sizes may be large. But, while marginal cost is constant at h, marginal revenue decreases as the sales level y increases. Thus, there is an upper limit to the profitable expansion of the crop size.

Furthermore, because all the underlying circumstances are unchanging over time, this upper limit is itself unchanging. In other words, there is an equilibrium harvest quantity q. If the initial harvest were at that level, then a policy of maintaining the same level in subsequent periods would maximise net revenue in each period, and also would maximise the discounted net revenue for the sequence of periods to the infinite horizon.

In practice, it is most unlikely that the initial harvest amount will be at the equilibrium level. Thus a time of transition may be expected, during which the farmer adjusts successive harvests to approach the equilibrium. This adjustment is *not* studied here. Instead the analysis of this section is confined to establishing the details of the equilibrium itself. This restriction means that the discussion avoids grappling with any difficulties there may be in relation to the nature (and indeed the feasibility) of the adjustment towards equilibrium.

With the harvest quantity at its equilibrium value, the future is unchanging: having harvested an amount q (in any of the periods), the farmer decides to sell an amount y in that period, and to reserve an amount $(q - y)$ as seed; when planted in the next period, this yields a harvest quantity $a(q - y) = q$ in that period. In period t, just after harvesting the amount q, the future prospect is precisely the same as that at the corresponding point of period $t + 1$: because of the assumption of an *infinite* time horizon, both futures contain an infinite sequence of identical periods, the same in both cases. These time points, just after harvesting, are examples of what are usually called 'points of regeneration': at each such point, the system is returned to the condition it was in at the corresponding point the previous period; in other words, the system has been regenerated. (This concept of regeneration points proves useful in a number of optimisation contexts; it is employed again in section 10.2 below, where there are also references to several other instances of its use.)

Given the equilibrium quantity q just harvested in period t, let $g_t(q)$ denote the net value (discounted to period t at interest rate r) of all the future revenues and costs that result from optimal deployment of this harvest; the stream of revenues and costs begins with sales revenue in period t, followed by harvesting costs and sales revenue in period $t + 1$, and so on. Then $g_{t+1}(q)$ denotes the net value (discounted to period $t + 1$) of the corresponding optimal stream of revenues and costs that begins in period $t + 1$.

The optimality principle may now be used: the optimal policy from period $t + 1$ onwards, whose value is $g_{t+1}(q)$ when discounted to $t + 1$, must be a component in the optimal policy from period t onwards. The value of this latter policy, $g_t(q)$ when discounted to t, also includes the sales revenue $ky^{1/2}$ earned in period t, and the planting and harvesting costs hq, incurred in period $t + 1$. When all values are discounted to period t, this relationship gives

$$g_t(q) = ky^{1/2} - (1 + r)^{-1}hq + (1 + r)^{-1}g_{t+1}(q). \tag{1}$$

On the previous argument about the stationary equilibrium, $g_t(q)$ and $g_{t+1}(q)$ relate to identical futures, and therefore must have the same value. (To see this, recall that each future time-span contains an infinite number of periods, and each of the two sequences of periods has the same pattern of revenues and costs. If there were a finite time horizon, one sequence would be shorter than the other. But the 'missing' terms at the later end of the shorter sequence would be heavily discounted, in calculating the net value, provided the time horizon is fairly distant and the discount rate is significantly larger than zero. On those conditions, the two values would be approximately equal. For a given discount rate, the difference would get smaller as the finite horizon is pushed further into the future. As the horizon goes to infinity, the difference tends to zero, and this gives the result that, for an infinite horizon, the two values are the same.) If the common value of $g_t(q)$ and $g_{t+1}(q)$ is denoted by $g(q)$, then the result may be expressed as

$$g_t(q) = g_{t+1}(q) = g(q) \qquad \text{for all } t \qquad (2)$$

The other property of the stationary equilibrium is that the quantity $a(q - y)$ harvested in any period is equal to the previous harvest, q. Thus

$$y = \frac{a-1}{a} q. \qquad (3)$$

After substituting from (2) and (3), the relationship (1) becomes

$$r\,g(q) = (1 + r)k\left(\frac{a-1}{a}\right)^{1/2} q^{1/2} - hq.$$

To find the q that maximises $g(q)$, set the derivative equal to zero:

$$r\frac{dg(q)}{dq} = \frac{k}{2}\left(\frac{a-1}{a}\right)^{1/2}(1 + r)q^{-1/2} - h = 0.$$

This yields

$$q = (1 + r)^2 \frac{k^2}{4h^2}\frac{a-1}{a}$$

and hence

$$y = \left\{(1 + r)\frac{k}{2h}\frac{a-1}{a}\right\}^2.$$

Also, for all $r > 0$, the optimal value of $g(q)$ is

$$g(q) = \frac{(1 + r)^2}{r}\frac{k^2}{4h}\frac{a-1}{a}.$$

(Since $d^2g(q)/dq^2 < 0$ for all $q > 0$, the solution also satisfies the sufficient condition for a maximum.)

Note the good sense of the solution: the optimal values for q, y and g increase with k and with a, and decrease with h, as is to be expected.

9.4 THE NATURE OF DYNAMIC PROGRAMMING

The examples of the preceding sections may be used here to throw light on the general nature of the dynamic programming approach. As noted at the beginning of the chapter, dynamic programming is a general strategy rather than a specific computation algorithm, and the precise form of the calculations depends on the nature of the optimisation problem in hand. Nevertheless, all applications of the approach share a common framework (besides the use of the optimality principle), and these common features are considered in this section.

The general approach may be used only if the optimising context requires *a multi-stage decision process,* or one that can be so regarded. In other words, the situation must require a sequence of decisions or a set of decisions that can be regarded as being sequential. In optimisation over time, there is very obviously a temporal sequence. For example, the farmer first takes this year's crop-allocation decisions, and then takes next year's, and so on. (Of course, all these decisions interact with each other; if they did not, the decisions could be taken separately, and the problem would be much less complex – and less interesting.) In the network example, the first decision is where to go after leaving A, the second decision is where to go next, and so on; in this case, the spatial framework provides a natural sequence. However, the sequence could begin from either the origin A or the destination H. Similarly, in multi-period problems, the sequence may work backwards in time – as is implicit in the infinite horizon case discussed in section 9.3, and is even more clearly the case in the finite horizon version that is the subject of Exercise 2 in the next section; alternatively, it is often equally convenient to work forward in time. In the first example (section 9.1), there is no natural sequence: the markets are independent of each other and hence the total revenue function is separable. Thus the markets may be considered one at a time and in any sequence, the only interconnection being the common stock of limited amount.

At each stage of a multi-stage process, there is a certain set of parameters that describe the state of the system at that stage, and these are usually called the *state parameters.* The farming example has only one state parameter at each stage, namely the size of the harvest. This harvest amount summarises the optimal strategy, so far, and is the only magnitude that influences the subsequent stages. For the first example, the one and only state parameter is the total amount of commodity allocated to the markets already considered. In the network example, each intermediate point just reached at the particular stage has a single parameter, namely the label of the immediately preceding point on the shortest route to the intermediate point in question.

Also at each stage, there is a set of *control* or *decision variables*. The farming example has just one, viz. the amount of crop to be retained for sowing in the following period. The network example has two decision variables, viz. the choice of previous point on the routes to each of the intermediate points about to be reached at that stage. A decision variable may be discrete (as in the network example), or continuous (as in the farming example). The applicable computational technique will depend crucially on which of these cases holds.

The optimal value of the objective function up to and including stage k is usually described as the *state function* for that stage. For the market example, the state function is the revenue earned in k markets that have been considered up to that stage. In the network example, the state function has one component for each intermediate point reached at that stage; each such component measures the length of the shortest route to that intermediate point.

For the dynamic programming approach to be feasible, it must be possible to use the optimality principle to develop a recurrence relation that permits the value of the state function for stage $k + 1$ to be determined from the value of the corresponding function for stage k. Using f_k to denote the value at stage k, then for the markets example the optimised value f_2 (revenue from the first two markets) is obtained from the argument that the two similar markets must be allocated equal amounts of the commodity. Hence

$$f_2(q) = 2(a_1 q - b_1 q^2).$$

Now f_3, the *optimal* revenue from all three markets, may be defined formally by using the recurrence relation

$$f_3(Q) = \max_{0 < q < Q/2} \ [a_3(Q - 2q) + b_3(Q - 2q)^2 + f_2(q)].$$

The notation on the right-hand side of this equation means that it is necessary to find the value of q (within the stated range) that maximises the function in the square brackets. This process yields the optimised revenue function, which is denoted $f_3(Q)$ because its size depends on the given total stock Q. (Compare this formal treatment with the informal approach used in section 9.1.)

In this example, the decision variable $(Q - 2q)$, being the amount allocated at this last stage, is a continuous variable, and a calculus method is used to undertake the optimisation (which is performed by varying q, since this is equivalent to varying $(Q - 2q)$. In the network example, the process of minimising the route length to a particular intermediate point is done by choice among discrete alternatives. This is effected by direct comparison of the alternatives, one for each of the intermediate points reached at the preceding stage. Although the mathematical approach used to achieve the optimisation varies from case to case, the basic idea is the same: the recurrence relation is used to find the value of the state function at stage $k + 1$ from a knowledge of that value at stage k.

From this variety in the form of the recurrence relation (and the consequent variety in the optimising procedure to be used), it follows that there cannot be a standard computer program, comparable to a computer package for (say) the simplex method for linear programming calculations. Instead, each distinct dynamic programming problem needs its own specially tailored algorithm. Fortunately, such algorithms are usually easy to code for a computer, whereas the simplex (and related algorithms) are not. Of course, the computational effort required in running such a dynamic programming code on a computer increases with the number of stages and with the number of state parameters and decision variables, other things being equal.

9.5 EXERCISES

(1) In the first multi-market example given in section 9.1 (for which the demand relations are the same in the first two markets), suppose that there is now a fourth market, for which the (inverse) demand function is

$$p_4 = a_4 - b_4 x_4.$$

Find the optimal allocations for all four markets.

(2) Consider an adaptation of the farming example (of section 9.3) in which there is a finite horizon, the cost of sowing and harvesting is ignored ($h = 0$), the discount rate $r = 0$, and in the last period the farmer wishes to sell the entire harvest immediately. For the four-period case in which the given harvest in the first period is 1,000 units, show that the optimal policy is as given in the table below.

Hints: Begin with the last period, in which (for given harvest amount q) the revenue is $f_1(q) = kq^{1/2}$. For the last two periods, use $f_2(q)$ to denote optimal revenue (starting with given harvest q in the penultimate period). Show that the recurrence relation that determines the optimal sales quantity y in that penultimate period is

$$f_2(q) = \max_{0 \leq y \leq q} \ [ky^{1/2} + f_1 \{a(q - y)\}]$$

Hence obtain the earlier recurrence relations, and then apply these results to the numerical data.

Period	1	2	3	4
Harvest quantity	1,000	2,925	8,100	18,225
Sales quantity	25	225	2.025	18,225
Revenue	5	15	45	135

(3) In the preceding exercise, the optimal harvest and sales quantities grow so rapidly over time as to make the results look unrealistic. What features of the model give such explosive growth, and how might the model be reformulated to give more moderate growth?

9.6 FURTHER READING

Although the pioneering book is Bellman (1957), a more accessible work is Bellman and Dreyfus (1962). In the latter, see especially: Chapter 1, for a not-too-advanced discussion, in the context of one-dimensional (deterministic) allocation processes, of the reasons why other computational procedures such as calculus may not work, and of the basic dynamic programming principle; Chapter 2, for an interesting discussion of multi-dimensional allocation processes – though here the analysis becomes rather more complicated.

A fairly thorough textbook treatment (occupying some 128 pages!) is to be found in Chapters 10 and 11 of Hadley (1964). Among other texts on dynamic programming are White (1969) and Jacobs (1967). There is a brief account in Chapter 13 of Intriligator (1971).

An interesting book that includes applications in diverse areas of economic theory is Beckmann (1968). Following the earlier work of Manne (1967), a recent book concerned with models for optimal investment in capacity expansion (of industrial systems such as telephone networks) is Friedenfelds (1981); this latter book makes much use of dynamic programming – see especially Chapters 4 and 5.

10

Some Further Economic Applications

Many books on optimisation focus exclusively on the mathemetical techniques. Some also consider fields of application. Rarely discussed, however, is the art of building the model, starting with a perception of the problem – a perception that may be incomplete or otherwise imperfect. The most effective way of conveying something of this art might be to present in detail some historical accounts of research projects, giving all the warts – including the false starts in modelling. Without going to those lengths, this chapter presents four applications, described in greater detail than is usual in published accounts, with some comment on various devices of model-building strategy and model use. It is hoped that these accounts will serve to bridge the gap between the simple world of the textbook and the more complicated world described (often, all too briefly) in research monographs and journal papers dealing with economic analyses that have used optimisation techniques.

The final section draws attention to publications containing such research reports, in economic theory and in empirical work in applied and policy analysis. It is particularly important for the student to read some of the empirical work, which shows how modern optimisation methods can handle large numbers of commodities (needed because commodities have to be defined very narrowly to secure sufficient commodity homogeneity), and serves to demonstrate a way in which much of modern economic analysis can be put to work in a complex world, notwithstanding the appearance of unreality in the elementary economics textbooks.

10.1 PEAK-LOAD PRICING AND CAPACITY DETERMINATION

This example, of profit-maximisation subject to capacity constraints, serves to illustrate an interesting and important issue in the interpretation of dual variables associated with capacity constraints, and also to demonstrate the use of quadratic programming. The problem to be modelled is one in which an enterprise invests in some capacity in order to provide a product or service to be sold in each of several time-periods, with storage of the product or service from one period to another being technically infeasible. Real-world instances include the use of generating capacity to provide electricity, and the use of transport infrastructure (such as rail or road tunnels, rail lines, toll highways or turnpikes, and airport runways) to permit the passage of transport vehicles. In all such cases, demand intensity varies over time, and the demand cycle (lasting a day, or a year where there is seasonal variation) may be divided into several shorter periods. In order to maximise profits, the enterprise seeks to determine simultaneously how much capacity to create and what price to charge in each period; it is supposed here that only one product or service is sold in each period.

Let price in period i be denoted p_i, and output q_i. Suppose that the operating cost of providing this output is c per unit, a constant that does not vary with the output level or with the period. Also let the demand cycle (say, one year) be divided into n periods, and suppose that the capital cost of providing capacity is equivalent to a rental figure of k per unit of capacity per year, where the constant k does not vary with the amount of capacity or with the degree of utilisation of capacity.

Net revenue per year is

$$\pi = \sum_{i=1}^{n} (p_i q_i - c q_i) - kq, \tag{1}$$

where q is the amount of capacity provided by the enterprise. The enterprise chooses values for q and the p_i so as to maximise this profit, subject to the obvious constraint that, in each period, output cannot exceed capacity:

$$q_i \leqq q \quad \text{for} \quad i = 1, 2, \ldots, n \tag{2}$$

For a first model, suppose that demand quantity is a linear function of own-price and does not depend on the prices in other periods:

$$q_i = a_i + b_{ii} p_i \quad \text{for} \quad i = 1, 2, \ldots, n \tag{3}$$

where the constants are $a_i > 0$ and $b_{ii} < 0$. Upon substituting this in (1), net revenue may be written

$$\pi = \sum_{i=1}^{n} (p_i - c)(a_i + b_{ii} p_i) - kq$$

$$= \sum_{i=1}^{n} \{b_{ii} p_i^2 + (a_i - c b_{ii}) p_i - c a_i\} - kq. \tag{4}$$

Note that this combines a quadratic function for gross revenue with a linear cost function, and hence the overall function is quadratic in the decision variables.

For specified p_i, (3) gives the quantity sold, and this may be substituted into the relevant constraint (2) to give

$$a_i + b_{ii} p_i \leqq q.$$

Since q is a policy variable, this is now transferred to the left-hand side, leaving a constant on the right:

$$a_i + b_{ii} p_i - q \leqq 0. \tag{5}$$

In this form, the constraint may now be interpreted: for period i, the excess of quantity sold over capacity must be non-positive.

This completes the general formulation of the model: the enterprise wants to choose q and the p_i (all required to be non-negative) so as to maximise (4) subject to the n constraints (5).

For a numerical illustration with five periods, suppose that demand forecasts have been made on the assumption that, in all periods, the same price $\bar{p}_i = \$15$ is to be charged; at this price, the demand quantities $\bar{q}_i$ are forecast to be those shown in Table 10.1; and at these demand points, the demand elasticity in each period is forecast to be $e_i = -1.5$. (With linear demand functions, the elasticities vary, of course, as we move to other points on the demand curves.) Such forecasts might be based on experience at another installation at which a uniform price is charged, and for which there is some evidence on demand elasticity. If our enterprise is contemplating price differentiation between peak and off-peak periods, the analysis has to be based as skilfully as possible on the scanty empirical knowledge of demand, gleaned from the simpler context. On the cost side, suppose that operating cost per unit is $c = \$2$ and that the per annum cost per unit of capacity is $k = \$10$.

From the demand function (3),

$$\frac{dq_i}{dp_i} = b_{ii}$$

and, since the demand curve passes through (p_i, q_i) and has elasticity

Table 10.1 *Numerical data for the case with independent demands*

i	Demand quantity $\bar{q}_i$ (when $\bar{p}_i = 15$)	Demand function parameters if $e_{ii} = -1.5$	
		a_i	b_{ii}
1	1,500	3,750	-150
2	1,200	3,000	-120
3	1,000	2,500	-100
4	800	2,000	-80
5	700	1,750	-70

$e_{ii} = -1.5$ at that point,

$$\frac{\bar{p}_i dq_i}{\bar{q}_i dp_i} = \frac{\bar{p}_i}{\bar{q}_i} b_{ii} = e_{ii} = -1.5.$$

With $\bar{p}_i = 15$, this gives

$$b_{ii} = -\frac{\bar{q}_i}{10}. \tag{6}$$

Similarly from (3)

$$a_i = \bar{q}_i - b_{ii}\bar{p}_i = \bar{q}_i - e_{ii}\bar{q}_i = 2.5\,\bar{q}_i. \tag{7}$$

These two results enable us to estimate the parameters a_i and b_{ii} for each of the demand functions, the results being as shown in Table 10.1. (Note how, in that table, the periods have been numbered in order of decreasing demand, with $i = 1$ representing the highest demand peak and $i = 5$ for the lowest demand level.)

When these data are substituted in (4), the profit function to be maximised is

$$3,450p_1 + 2,760p_2 + 2,300p_3 + 1,840p_4 + 1,610p_5$$
$$- 150p_1{}^2 - 120p_2{}^2 - 100p_3{}^2 - 80p_4{}^2 - 70p_5{}^2 - 26,000 - 10q. \tag{8}$$

The constraints (5) become

$$3,750 - 150p_1 - q \leqq 0 \tag{9}$$

$$3,000 - 120p_2 - q \leqq 0 \tag{10}$$

$$2,500 - 100p_3 - q \leqq 0 \tag{11}$$

$$2,000 - 80p_4 - q \leqq 0 \tag{12}$$

$$1,750 - 70p_5 - q \leqq 0 \tag{13}$$

When this is solved by using a quadratic programming algorithm (cf. section 8.3 above), the results are as shown in Table 10.2. In fact, the constant term $(-26,000)$ in (8) may be omitted from this quadratic programming calculation. However, if the calculation (with the constant omitted) gives an internal optimum, i.e. with $q > 0$, then the constant term must be taken into account to see whether the complete profit function is still positive; if it is not, then the true optimum is at the corner $q = 0$. As shown by the results in Table 10.2, in the present case the optimum profit

Table 10.2 *Optimal solution for the case with independent demands*

i	p_i ($)	q_i	dual ($)
1	17.0	1,200	7
2	15.0	1,200	3
3	13.5	1,150	0
4	13.5	920	0
5	13.5	805	0
		optimal $q = 1,200$	optimal $\pi = \$54,662$

(after netting out the constant term) is positive, and the optimal capacity is $q = 1,200$.

The dual values shown in the table are associated with the capacity constraints (9)–(13). Thus it is immediately obvious that these constraints are *not* binding in periods 3, 4 and 5; indeed the table also shows the extent to which optimal output in each of these periods falls short of capacity. For periods 1 and 2, however, the capacity constraints are binding. The economic interpretation of the dual values associated with the five capacity constraints raises some interesting questions that have to be analysed with great care.

In any multi-period problem in which the *same* level of capacity is available in two or more periods, any change in the amount of that capacity must apply in *all* the relevant periods. Yet the discussion of dual values (and, equally, that of Lagrange multipliers) has made it clear that each value refers to the rate of change of the objective function as the right-hand-side value is changed in one, and only one, of the constraints. How can these two considerations be reconciled?

As in all cases relating to the interpretation of dual values (Lagrange multipliers), the appropriate technique is to examine the single constraint in question, and to identify first the physical interpretation of a change in the right-hand-side value. Here, consider constraint (9): an increase in the right-hand-side from 0 to Δb_i (to use the notation of section 3.5) means that, in period 1 *only*, the quantity sold is now permitted to exceed capacity q by an amount of Δb_i (cf. the initial interpretation of (5)). Thus, strictly speaking, the change is not an increase in capacity as such; instead, it may be thought of as an increase in the amount of the supply of product, for period 1 only, available from an external source (e.g. from a plant other than the one being analysed). With this interpretation, change in one period only is now seen to be feasible; capacity, as such, changes simultaneously in all periods, but the change being considered here is not a capacity change.

The remaining issue is the interpretation of the rate of change of the objective function that is measured by the dual value. Before analysing this for the present model, consider a simpler situation in which the capacity q in constraints (9)–(13) is *not* a policy variable. Suppose instead that it is simply a constant, and the model then deals only with the short-run pricing problem of making optimal use of given capacity. The previous remarks on the interpretation of the change in the right-hand-side still apply: in period 1, the change refers not to an increase in capacity, but to an increase in external supply in that period. In that context, it is clear that the dual value measures the rate of change of net revenue ('profit') after allowing for the extra short-run cost c per unit of the extra supply (because of the term cq_1 in the objective function – see equation (1) above), but *without* netting out anything for the cost of extra capacity, since there is no term kq in the profit function in this short-run model.

Now, reverting to the original long-term model in which q *is* a policy variable (i.e. in which investment policy is considered as well as pricing policy), similar considerations apply. Although the profit function (4) now includes a term $-kq$, the change in the right-hand-side of (9) does not involve a change in q, and hence there is no change in capacity costs. As before, the extra external supply does change q_1 and hence there is an increase in the short-run costs cq_1. The dual variable for period 1 takes on the optimal value of $7 (as shown in Table 10.2), and this measures the rate of change of profit after allowing for the extra operating cost but without paying anything for extra capacity. Similarly, for period 2, the corresponding rate of change of profit is $3, and for each of the other periods it is zero.

Now, if the enterprise *were* to install one extra unit of capacity, this would permit one extra unit of output in each of the five sub-periods. These duality results show that, after allowing for the extra operating costs but without allowing for extra capacity cost, the net revenue of the enterprise would increase by $(7 + 3) = 10. This is the same as the per annum capacity cost of $k = 10, as it must be for an optimal level of capacity, for which a necessary condition is that marginal 'net' revenue (but before netting out the capacity cost) must equal the marginal cost of capacity. (Of course, in a short-run model in which capacity is fixed, this equality will not generally hold because the given capacity will not generally be optimal from a long-run point of view).

Some further analysis is instructive: in each period for which capacity is not fully used, profit-maximisation requires that marginal (gross) revenue should equal marginal (operating) cost. For any period, gross revenue $R = p_i q_i$ and marginal revenue is

$$\frac{dR}{dq_i} = p_i + q_i \frac{dp_i}{dq_i} = 2p_i + \frac{a_i}{b_{ii}}. \tag{14}$$

For the present numerical data, using (6) and (7) above, this becomes

$$\frac{dR}{dq_i} = 2p_i - 25. \tag{15}$$

Thus, for periods when capacity is not fully used, the profit-maximising marginal equality becomes

$$\frac{dR}{dq_i} = 2p_i - 25 = 2 = c$$

and hence

$$p_i = 13.5 \tag{16}$$

Thus in the present model, optimal price will be the same in all periods for which capacity is not binding, and this result provides a check on some of the quadratic programming calculations; in Table 10.2 the results for periods 3, 4 and 5 are now confirmed. (This kind of check can reveal errors in preparation and entry of data for the quadratic programming calculation.)

As an alternative to (15), marginal revenue may be expressed in terms of quantity q_i:

$$\frac{dR}{dq_i} = 25 - \frac{20}{\bar{q}_i} q_i. \tag{17}$$

When the capacity constraint is binding, $q_i = 1{,}200$ (as shown by the quadratic programming calculations) and then

$$\frac{dR}{dq_i} = 25 - 24{,}000/\bar{q}_i.$$

For periods 1 and 2, this yields marginal revenues equal to 9 and 5 respectively. Thus, for each of these two periods,

marginal revenue = dual value + marginal operating cost

where the dual value may now be interpreted as the contribution (in that period) to the marginal capacity cost.

This concludes the examination of the first model, which is based on the assumptions (3) that each demand is a linear function of own-price only.

For a second model, suppose that, in each period, demand is a linear function of all the prices:

$$q_i = a_i + \sum_{j=1}^{n} b_{ij} p_j. \tag{18}$$

The objective function becomes

$$\pi = \sum_{j=1}^{n} p_j \left(a_i - c \sum_{i=1}^{n} b_{ji} \right) + \sum_i \sum_j b_{ij} p_i p_j - c \sum_i a_i - kq \tag{19}$$

which is to be maximised subject to the constraints

$$a_i + \sum_j b_{ij}p_j - q \leqq 0 \quad \text{for } i = 1, 2, \ldots, n \tag{20}$$

For given cross-price elasticities e_{ij} (for $j \neq i$), measured (in a manner similar to that supposed in the first model) for initial values of $\bar{q}_i$ and $\bar{p}_i$, the coefficients b_{ij} are determined thus:

$$b_{ij} = \frac{\bar{q}_i}{\bar{p}_j} e_{ij} \quad \text{(for } j \neq i) \tag{21}$$

For a numerical illustration, again with five periods, suppose as before that $c = 2$ and $k = 10$, and that the cross-elasticities are as shown in Table 10.3. Also suppose that the *overall* price elasticity is $e_i = -1.5$; this is a generalisation of the assumption made in the first model and implies that if all prices are equal initially (i.e. all $\bar{p}_i = \bar{p}$) and if all are then varied by the same small amount (i.e. all $p_i = \bar{p} + \Delta\bar{p}$), then the response of the initial demand quantity $\bar{q}_i$ is such as to give an (overall) elasticity $e_i = -1.5$. In other words

$$e_i = \frac{\bar{p}}{\bar{q}_i}\frac{\partial q_i}{\partial \bar{p}} = \frac{\bar{p}}{\bar{q}_i}\sum_j b_{ij} = -1.5. \tag{22}$$

This may be rearranged to give

$$b_{ii} = -1.5\frac{\bar{q}_i}{\bar{p}} - \sum_{j \neq i} b_{ij} \tag{23}$$

and, upon substituting from (21), this may be used to give

$$e_{ii} = \frac{\bar{p}}{\bar{q}_i}b_{ii} = -1.5 - \frac{\bar{p}}{\bar{q}_i}\sum_{j \neq i} b_{ij}. \tag{24}$$

With $\bar{p} = \$15$ (as in the first model) and with the same $\bar{q}_i$ as in Table 10.1, equation (24) may be applied to calculate the new own-price elasticities,

Table 10.3 *Numerical values for the demand elasticities for the case with dependent demands*

i	$j = 1$	$j = 2$	$j = 3$	$j = 4$	$j = 5$
1	-2	0.4	0.1	0	0
2	0.5	-2.35	0.2	0.1	0.05
3	0.15	0.24	-1.99	0.1	0
4	0	0.15	0.125	-1.975	0.2
5	0	0.857	0	0.229	-1.643

Table 10.4   *Coefficients b_{ij} for the case with dependent demands*

i	$j = 1$	$j = 2$	$j = 3$	$j = 4$	$j = 5$
1	-200	40	10	0	0
2	40	-188	16	8	4
3	10	16	$-132.\dot{6}$	$6.\dot{6}$	0
4	0	8	6.6	$-105.\dot{3}$	$10.\dot{6}$
5	0	4	0	10.6	-84.6

shown in Table 10.3; equations (21) are then used to compute the b_{ij} shown in Table 10.4. (Note that the supposed values for the cross-price elasticities e_{ij} ($j \neq i$) yield $b_{ij} = b_{ji}$ in Table 10.4. This has been arranged to give symmetry in the substitution effects – cf., for example, section T.7 of the Technical Appendix in Green, 1971.)
From the initial data, (18) may be used to estimate the a_i:

$$a_i = \bar{q}_i - \bar{p} \sum_{j=1}^{n} b_{ij} \tag{25}$$

and from (23) this becomes

$$a_i = \bar{q}_i + 1.5\bar{q}_i = 2.5\bar{q}_i, \tag{26}$$

the same result as that obtained in (7) for the first model.
When the coefficients of (19) and (20) are estimated, the model becomes:

maximise
$$4{,}050p_1 + 3{,}240p_2 + 2{,}700p_3 + 2{,}160p_4 + 1{,}890p_5 - 10q - 26{,}000 +$$
$$80p_1p_2 + 20p_1p_3 + 32p_2p_3 + 16p_2p_4 + 8p_2p_5 + 13.\dot{3}p_3p_4 + 21.\dot{3}p_4p_5 -$$
$$200p_1{}^2 - 188p_2{}^2 - 132.\dot{6}p_3{}^2 - 105.\dot{3}p_4{}^2 - 84.\dot{6}p_5{}^2 \tag{27}$$

subject to
$$3{,}750 - 200p_1 + 40p_2 + 10p_3 \qquad\qquad -q \leqq 0$$
$$3{,}000 + 40p_1 - 188p_2 + 16p_3 + 8p_4 + 4p_5 -q \leqq 0$$
$$2{,}500 + 10p_1 + 16p_2 - 132.\dot{6}p_3 + 6.\dot{6}p_4 \qquad -q \leqq 0 \tag{28}$$
$$2{,}000 \qquad + 8p_2 + 6.\dot{6}p_3 - 105.\dot{3}p_4 + 10.\dot{6}p_5 - q \leqq 0$$
$$1{,}750 \qquad + 4p_2 \qquad + 10.\dot{6}p_4 - 84.\dot{6}p_5 - q \leqq 0$$

Use of a quadratic programming algorithm yields the optimal solution shown in Table 10.5. Compared with the previous case, the optimal capacity is slightly smaller, and the optimal profit slightly larger. With some non-zero cross-elasticities, some of the demand is now diverted from peak to off-peak periods. For example, in period 1 both price and output are

Table 10.5 *Optimal solution for the case with dependent demands*

i	p_i ($)	q_i	dual ($)
1	16.57	1,182	6.144
2	15.23	1,182	3.452
3	13.70	1,182	0.404
4	13.50	935	0
5	13.50	812	0
		$q = 1,182$	$\pi = \$54,946$

lower, because some of this period's demand is diverted to other periods; and, as a consequence, price is *higher* in periods 2 and 3. For the first three periods, the dual values shift in the same direction as the prices; the capacity constraint for period 3 is now binding. In periods 4 and 5, prices are unaltered but output increases slightly. This (limited) opportunity to divert some demand away from peak periods, and towards off-peak periods, is what makes it optimal to reduce capacity, and this leads to higher profit.

The above discussion brings out a general lesson: differences in results for related cases should be examined carefully, not only because of the intrinsic economic interest of the differences, but also because such scrutiny serves as a partial check on the general sense of the results, and hence as a check on their accuracy.

As in the case of independent demands, further analysis is of interest: it may be shown that in any period i, marginal revenue is

$$\frac{dR}{dq_i} = 2p_i + a_i / \sum_j b_{ij}. \tag{29}$$

(Note that (14) is, indeed, a special case of (29).) Since the new $\sum b_{ij}$ equals the b_{ii} of the first case, and a_i is the same as before, insertion of the numerical data in (29) yields the same result as (15), viz.

$$\frac{dR}{dq_i} = 2p_i - 25.$$

For each period when capacity is not fully used, the necessary condition for profit-maximisation (viz. marginal revenue = marginal cost) proves that the optimal price is $13.5, as before. This confirms the prices in Table 10.5 for periods 4 and 5. Again, the sum of the dual values is equal to the unit cost of capacity.

Many features of the example considered in this section have been suggested by the empirical case that is examined in Glaister (1976); study of that paper provides useful and interesting insights into some practical issues in empirical model-building in this area. For a reformulation of Glaister's model for interdependent demands, see Mills and Coleman (1982).

10.2 A SIMPLE MODEL FROM INVENTORY THEORY

While the batch-size model to be discussed in this section is of interest in its own right, it also serves to illustrate the use of an infinite planning horizon (cf. the remarks at the end of section 6.6 above). Although the model is so simple as to be rarely applicable just as it stands, it contains many of the basic ideas to be found in more complex and more realistic models for the optimisation of inventory levels in manufacturing industry and in wholesale and retail distribution. The model has also been used in monetary theory, especially in relation to the transactions demand for money.

The art of model-building plays a significant role in optimisation analysis. Often the most difficult task of the analysis is to identify all the aspects of the situation for which model assumptions have to be made, and to go on to make sensible judgements on the detailed bases of these assumptions. This simple batch-size model requires a considerable number of assumptions, and thus it provides a good illustration of this aspect of the model-building art.

For this simple model, it is supposed that a retailer sells a single (homogeneous) commodity, and obtains bulk supplies of this commodity from the manufacturer. The retailer's problem is to arrange these supplies at minimum cost. The model is formulated in continuous time.

The *demand* placed on the retailer is known with certainty, is not sensitive to changes in the price charged by the retailer, and occurs at a uniform rate of D units of the commodity per unit of time, over all future time (i.e. with an infinite time horizon). The retailer is obliged to meet all demands immediately they are placed on him, i.e. backlogging of orders is not permitted.

Supplies are dispatched from the manufacturer in batches. The size of any batch, to be denoted Q (a continuous variable), has no effective upper limit, and (of course) the context requires $Q > 0$. The retailer chooses when to place an order, and also chooses the size Q of the batch he orders. The batch is delivered after a time-lag, known with certainty, i.e. the batch always arrives at the time for which it is promised, and this time-lag is known to the retailer well in advance. The cost of a batch of size Q units is $\$(a + bQ)$, where $\$b$ is the unit cost of the commodity (with $b > 0$ and constant) and where $\$a$ (with $a > 0$ and also constant) is a batch cost, which is incurred every time a batch is ordered and which is independent of the size of the batch. This batch cost reflects the administrative costs of handling the order and billing the retailer, and possibly also the cost of setting up the manufacturer's equipment to make this particular batch (where the variety ordered by the retailer may differ from the other varieties produced by the manufacturer). On the other hand, the unit cost $\$b$ represents the cost of raw materials, energy and other inputs used during the manufacturing run.

Storage of the product by the retailer is feasible. There is no deterioration of the product in store; in other words, all the units put into the retailer's store are sold in due course. The storage cost is $k per unit of the commodity, per unit of time; this reflects the cost of operating the store, and the insurance and interest charges. There is no effective limit on the retailer's storage capacity. When delivered, the entire batch Q goes into the retailer's store instantaneously, and stock is available for sale as soon as it is delivered.

The retailer's *objective* is to meet all the demands placed on him for the commodity, while ordering supplies in such a way as to minimise his total costs. There is no time-discounting in the objective, and so the aim is to minimise cost per unit of time.

As is often the case in optimisation, it is both feasible and desirable to begin the analysis by making a preliminary examination to establish the nature of the opposing factors that must be balanced in the optimum. Here the trade-off is between batch costs, which are reduced by infrequent ordering of large batches, and storage costs, which are reduced by frequent ordering of small batches (since this gives a small average stock).

Some features of the optimal policy can now be established. Because of the (supposed) absence of uncertainty in both demand and supply arrangements, the retailer knows exactly when he will run out of stock. Ordering in sufficient time, he can ensure that the new batch arrives exactly at the moment the previous stock is exhausted. Hence 'safety stocks' are not needed, and cost is minimised by not having them.

Furthermore, because demand and supply conditions are unchanging over time, and the model has an infinite horizon each time the stock is exhausted (momentarily), the future looks the same as it did last time; in other words, such occasions are 'regeneration points', to use the concept introduced in section 9.3. Hence it will be optimal for the retailer to order the same size of batch each time.

Thus the optimal policy will require the stock level to behave over time in the manner shown in Figure 10.1. At time t_1, existing stock falls to zero, the new batch of Q units arrives as planned, and because it is taken into stock instantaneously the curve climbs vertically upwards. Because the demand rate D is uniform over time, the stock level follows a linear downward path, reaching zero at time t_2, when the next cycle starts. Each cycle is of the same duration, namely Q/D time units. (For another example of the use of this concept of regeneration points in inventory theory see Chapter 15, by Karlin, in Arrow, Karlin and Scarf, 1958. An investment example is to be found on p. 36 of Manne, 1967. The concept of regeneration points has also been used in consumer theory, in Flemming, 1969.)

This completes the main part of the analysis. It is now clear that there is only one decision variable, the batch size Q. The remaining task is to undertake a routine algebraic analysis to find the optimal value for Q, i.e. to find the optimal member of the family of uniform batch-size policies.

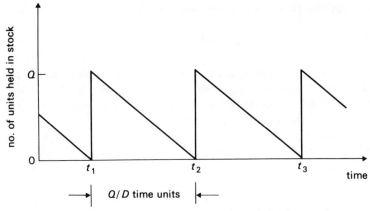

Figure 10.1 *Behaviour of the optimal stock level over time*

The first step is to obtain an expression for the total cost per unit of time. The ordering cost *per cycle* is $a + bQ$, and, since there are D/Q batches (i.e. cycles) per unit of time, then the supply cost per unit of time is

$$S = a\frac{D}{Q} + bD. \tag{30}$$

Since the stock level is reduced at a uniform rate over time, the storage cost per unit of time may be computed in terms of the average stock level $Q/2$, and hence is

$$H = k\frac{Q}{2}.$$

Thus the total cost per unit of time is

$$\phi = S + H = a\frac{D}{Q} + bD + k\frac{Q}{2} \tag{31}$$

and this is to be minimised by an appropriate choice of Q. Note that the second term bD is a constant, for the obvious reason that it represents the unit costs of supplying the given demand rate D.

The first-order necessary condition for a minimum of ϕ is $d\phi/dQ = 0$ and this yields

$$Q = + \sqrt{(2a\frac{D}{k})}. \tag{32}$$

Also note that this is indeed a minimum because the sufficient second-order condition is satisfied:

$$\frac{d^2\phi}{dQ^2} = \frac{2aD}{Q^3} > 0.$$

For the optimal Q, the minimised total cost is

$$\phi_m = bD + \sqrt{(2kaD)}. \tag{33}$$

The results of an optimisation analysis should always be scrutinised carefully, first to see what qualitative implications can be drawn out, and secondly to check the sense of the results — and such checks may save you from error. In the present case, note from (30) that the ordering cost decreases as Q increases, as it should, while the storage cost $kQ/2$ increases with Q. Equation (32) shows that the optimal batch size increases with the demand rate (which is intuitively obvious) but grows less then proportionately, which may be a little more surprising. This result is important because it contradicts a common rule-of-thumb that says 'keep in stock x days' supply'; this rule would require stock to double if the sales rate doubled, whereas the optimisation analysis shows that stock should increase by the smaller factor of $\sqrt{2}$. The result (32) also shows that the optimal Q increases with the ordering cost $\$a$, and decreases with the storage cost, $\$k$; both of these results seem sensible. From (33), note that the total cost increases less than proportionately as the demand rate increases; in other words, there are some economies of scale in this stock-holding/retailing function.

Finally, note the crucial role played by the infinite time horizon. When coupled with the assumption of a uniform demand rate, this ensures that the future does indeed look the same at each point of regeneration. If a finite time horizon were supposed, this property would be lost. For example, suppose that the above model yielded an optimal Q that corresponded to exactly three months' demand, while the retailer intended to close his shop (and have zero stock) in fourteen months' time. The model of this section could no longer be used. Instead it would be necessary to undertake a deeper analysis (which is not pursued here). Thus the infinite horizon gives a simpler analysis than a finite horizon, as is often the case.

10.3   A MULTI-PERIOD PROBLEM INVOLVING STOCKS

Although this problem requires the determination of the optimal level for an initial stock, the nature of the model proves to be very different from that of the preceding section. The problem requires little in the way of formal optimisation technique, and may be used to illustrate alternative ways of reaching the optimal solution.

The problem to be modelled may be described first in general terms: the board of a learned journal that is published at regular intervals (say, four times per year) wishes to decide how many copies of the next issue should be printed. The journal is well established and has a large list of subscribers to whom the next issue will be sent. From experience of previous issues, going back over many years, the board has found that there is usually a continuing demand for further copies of back numbers, a demand that may persist for many years after the issue is first made available. In the past, the board has printed more copies of an issue than were needed for immediate distribution to the then current subscribers; the extra copies are put into stock and are sold gradually as further orders come in. When the initial stock of an issue runs out, the board assigns rights in that issue to a reprint company, which immediately prints more copies. As still further demands come in, that company sells from its stock, and, for each copy thus sold, the company pays a royalty (at the time of sale) to the board of the journal. However, the royalty is quite small, and the board believes it is more remunerative to have its own large stock from the initial printing, and hence earn revenue from its own sales for quite some years after the issue is first published.

Thus a model is required to determine the optimal print number. For this purpose, it is convenient to work in discrete time, using periods each of one year in duration. Let the number of copies to be printed be denoted x, and let m denote the last year for which demand is met from the initial stock. (The present time is counted as the end of year 0). Of course, x and m are not independent variables; rather they are related to each other through the demand pattern. Suppose that the journal is sold at the price $\$p$ per copy, which is not changed over time. (In effect, the model abstracts from any price inflation. Alternatively, it may be regarded as being couched in constant prices; this approach is commonly used for multi-period modelling where the horizon is some years ahead.) In the present analysis, this price is to be taken as given. At this price, the number of copies sold in year t is predicted to be d_t for all $t \geq 0$, where d_0 denotes the number of current subscribers; thus

$$x = \sum_{t=0}^{m} d_t.$$

Suppose that such sales always occur at the end of the year in question.

Investigation of the printing costs shows that, to a good approximation, the costs that vary with the number of copies printed are effectively constant per copy; these are the costs of the paper and ink, of using the printing presses, and of binding each copy. There is also a fixed cost, not dependent on the number of copies printed, which is principally the cost of setting the type. Thus, let these printing costs be denoted $a + bx$, where this cost is incurred at the end of the year O, and where a and b are strictly positive constants. For the copies put into store, the board has to pay a storage cost of $\$s$ per copy for each year of storage, where s is a constant; the warehousing firm demands payment at this rate at the end of each year.

When a copy is sold from stock, the selling and distribution costs reduce the revenue received at that time to $\$fp$, where $0 < f < 1$. The royalty rate paid by the reprint company is g, where $0 < g < f$; thus, when the reprint company sells a copy at the end of year t (for $t > m$), the board immediately receives a fee of gp.

The board decides it wants to choose m (and hence x) so as to maximise the present value of the net receipts from the issue, where the present value is computed using a discount rate of $100r$ per cent. Since the model is in terms of constant prices, the value of r measures the discount rate expressed in real terms.

As is usual in optimisation analysis, it is useful to obtain first an intuitive understanding of the trade-offs between the opposing economic forces before going into the detailed analysis. For any given initial print number, x, consider the consequences of printing an extra copy. When this last copy is finally sold (i.e. when the stock becomes depleted) the board receives fp, rather than the smaller amount gp that would have come from the reprint company if this extra copy had not been printed. Against that benefit, however, the board incurs some extra printing cost, at time 0. If there were no storage costs, the picture would be particularly simple: as the print size increases, the benefit from the last copy comes later and later, and thus the present value of that benefit decreases. In period $t = 1$, the benefit may be supposed to be greater than the extra printing cost; but as t increases, the present value of the benefit will eventually decrease to such a degree that it becomes less than the extra cost. The last period before this happens determines the optimal value for m. When the per-period storage cost is taken into account, the present value of the sequence of storage costs (for this marginal copy) increases as its sale is postponed. Thus the presence of the storage costs alters the balance in the trade-off between costs and benefits, and the optimal value for m is smaller than before.

This general line of reasoning permits immediate construction of the optimising analysis. For a copy sold in period t, the present value of the revenue is

$$fp/(1+r)^t \qquad \text{for } t \leqq m$$

and

$$gp/(1+r)^t \qquad \text{for } t > m$$

For sale from the initial stock, the board incurs a printing cost of b (at time 0) and a sequence of storage costs, namely s at the end of period 1, s at the end of period 2, and so forth. This sequence has a discounted value of

$$S\{(1+r)^{-1} + (1+r)^{-2} + \ldots + (1+r)^{-t}\} = \frac{s}{r}[1 - (1+r)^{-t}]$$

and hence, for the sale of one copy from the initial stock in period t, the discounted net revenue is

$$\psi = fp(1+r)^{-t} - \frac{s}{r}[1 - (1+r)^{-t}] - b. \tag{34}$$

On the other hand, for a copy sold by the reprint company, the discounted net revenue is

$$\theta = gp(1+r)^{-t}. \tag{35}$$

Now, for a given t, the benefit of selling a copy from the initial stock rather than through the reprint company is

$$\psi - \theta = (1+r)^{-t}\left[(f-g)p + \frac{s}{r}\right] - \left(b + \frac{s}{r}\right). \tag{36}$$

On the right-hand side of (36), $(1+r)^{-t}$ is positive, and both expressions in the brackets [ ] and ( ) are also positive. As t increases, the first term decreases. On the supposition that $(\psi - \theta)$ is initially positive, the decrease in the first term means that $(\psi - \theta)$ eventually becomes negative as t increases. But $(\psi - \theta)$ remains positive for as long as

$$(1+r)^t < \frac{(f-g)p + \dfrac{s}{r}}{b + \dfrac{s}{r}}. \tag{37}$$

The process is now even more obvious: as t increases, the left-hand side of (37) increases, while the right-hand side is constant. The optimal value of m is given by the largest value of t for which the inequality still holds.

The numerical application of this result is now illustrated, using the following supposed values for the coefficients:

$$p = 4 \qquad f = 0.8$$
$$b = 1.1 \qquad g = 0.2$$
$$s = 0.035 \qquad r = 0.07.$$

The right-hand side of (37) then takes the value 1.812.

The relevant part of the table of compounding factors for $r = 0.07$ is:

t	:	7	8	9	10	11
$(1+r)^t$	:	1.6058	1.7182	1.8385	1.9672	2.1049

Thus the largest t that satisfies the inequality (37) is $t = 8$; but $t = 9$ has

$(1 + r)^t = 1.8385$, and this is much closer to 1.812. Thus it seems sensible to set $m = 9$ if an integer solution is desired. (Intrapolation is feasible – see below.)

It is interesting to see that the optimal value for m does not depend on the demand pattern d_t. This result occurs because the costs and benefits of printing an extra copy, and selling it in period t, are constant. Thus the corresponding function $(\psi - \theta)$ is constant, and does not depend on the scale x of the initial printing, or on the scale of the sales levels, the d_t. (However, if, for example, the initial printing cost were a non-linear function of x, the optimal value of m would necessarily involve the demand levels, d_t.) Note also that the result does not depend on the size of the lump-sum cost, a. An initial print run is to be executed in any event, and so this cost is not a variable in the optimisation.

Although it may not be too difficult to obtain fairly good estimates of p, b, s, f and g, the forecasting of the demand levels d_t will certainly be difficult, and there may also be some argument about the choice of an appropriate discount rate, r. Accordingly, alternative assumptions may be made about these two factors, sensitivity analyses conducted, and the results presented to the board. In order to illustrate this, consider alternative discount rates of 0.05, 0.07 and 0.09 and the three alternative demand patterns shown in Table 10.6. The results for the consequent combinations of assumptions may be presented as in Table 10.7. The board may then choose a print number in the light of all these considerations.

In obtaining the optimum condition (37), a direct comparison is made between costs and revenue for the marginal copy. This method is equivalent to deploying the usual first-order necessary condition for profit-maximisation, namely that marginal revenue must equal marginal cost. In the present case, however, the model is formulated in discrete time, and this yields the inequality form (37) rather than a precise equation. However, in

Table 10.6 *Alternative demand assumptions*

Demand case	Demand levels d_1	d_2	d_3	d_t for $4 \leq t \leq 8$	d_t for $t > 8$
A	80	50	40	30	30
B	80	50	40	30	20
C	80	50	40	20	10

Table 10.7 *Results of the sensitivity analysis*

r	Optimal m	Optimal print number, x A	B	C
0.05	11	410	380	300
0.07	9	350	340	280
0.09	7	260	260	230

applying the condition (37) to yield numerical results, as in Table 10.7, it is possible to treat time as a continuous variable. Thus (37) could be written as an equality; after taking logarithms, this becomes

$$t \log (1 + r) = \log \left[(f - g)p + \frac{s}{r} \right] - \log \left(b + \frac{s}{r} \right). \qquad (38)$$

On substituting the initial values, including $r = 0.07$, this yields $t = m = 8.8$, which readily compares with the integer results already presented for this case. In practice, the uncertainty relating to the demand forecasts is such that it is unnecessary (and unwise) to search for great precision in determining the value for m.

As an alternative to deployment of the first-order 'marginal revenue = marginal cost' condition, it is possible to write out the expression for the present value of total net revenue, and then search directly for the maximum. In order to do this, note that by using (34) and (35) for the case when the initial stock is exhausted at the end of year m, this present value is

$$\phi_m = \sum_{t=0}^{m} \left\{ fp(1 + r)^{-t} - \frac{s}{r} \left[1 - (1 + r)^{-t} \right] \right\} d_t$$

$$+ \sum_{t=m+1}^{\infty} gp(1 + r)^{-t} d_t - \left\{ a + b \sum_{t=0}^{m} d_t \right\}. \qquad (39)$$

As the initial stock is increased to a size that will make it last to the end of the year m instead of the year $(m - 1)$, the increase in net present value is

$$\Delta \phi_m = \phi_m - \phi_{m-1}$$

$$= \left\{ fp(1 + r)^{-t} - \frac{s}{r} \left[1 - (1 + r)^{-t} \right] \right\} d_m - gp(1 + r)^{-t} d_m - b d_m$$

$$= d_m \left\{ (1 + r)^{-t} \left[(f - g)p + \frac{s}{r} \right] - \left(b + \frac{s}{r} \right) \right\}. \qquad (40)$$

As m increases, ϕ_m increases as long as $\Delta \phi_m$ is positive. Thus the optimum occurs at the largest value of m for which (40) is positive. Since d_m is positive, this reduces to the previous condition (37). This second approach is more direct in concept but a little more cumbersome to implement.

(This problem of determining the optimal print number came to the author's attention in 1971, in connection with the affairs of the *Review of Economic Studies*. The analysis presented here was of some assistance to the board of that journal, notwithstanding some empirical and other difficulties in implementing the analysis.)

10.4 INVESTMENT APPRAISAL: SOME THEORETICAL RESULTS FROM THE DUALITY PROPERTIES

The following example shows how the properties of the dual model may give considerable insight into the qualitative characteristics of an economic problem, insight that may sometimes be obtained without any numerical calculation.

Consider a firm that wishes to evaluate some investment projects to ascertain which are worth undertaking. Let x_j denote the scale at which the jth project ($j = 1, 2, ..., n$) is undertaken, where the project scale is restricted to the range $0 \leqq x_j \leqq 1$. If the jth project is undertaken at full scale ($x_j = 1$), the project generates a sequence of cash flows a_{jt}, for $t = 1, 2$ and 3. Each project terminates in period 3, and has no residual value. The sign convention adopted is that $a_{jt} > 0$ denotes a cash outlay (investment in the project) in period t, while $a_{jt} < 0$ denotes a cash receipt from the project. If the project is undertaken at less than full scale, suppose that the firm experiences pro rata cash flows, $x_j a_{jt}$.

In each period $t = 1, 2$ and 3, the firm may also enter into lending and/or borrowing contracts, each for one period, and each at interest rate r. To help to finance all these activities, the firm has funds of amount B_t becoming available in each period t, and flowing from other assets owned by the firm. The firm pays no dividends, and does not dispose of these funds B_t in any way other than through the investment, lending and borrowing activities already described. The firm's aim is to maximise the value of assets held at the end of period 3.

To supplement the notation already introduced, let v_t denote the amount of money lent in period t; this earns interest, and the firm receives $(1 + r)v_t$ in period $t + 1$. Similarly, let w_t denote the sum borrowed in period t; the firm repays $(1 + r)w_t$ in period $t + 1$. Suppose that there are no limits on the scale of these borrowing and lending activities.

In the first period, the sum deployed in the investment projects is

$$\sum_j a_{j1} x_j$$

Note that some of the terms in this summation may be negative. The net amount lent in period 1 at interest r is $(v_1 - w_1)$. The total funds used must not exceed the sum available, B_1. Thus the budget constraint for the first period is

$$\sum_{j=1}^{n} a_{j1} x_j + v_1 - w_1 \leq B_1. \tag{41}$$

For the second period, the budget constraint is a little more complex, because the firm also receives $(1 + r)v_1$ and/or pays $(1 + r)w_1$ as a result of lending/borrowing contracts initiated in the previous period. Thus the constraint is

$$\sum_{j=1}^{n} a_{j2}x_j - (1+r)v_1 + (1+r)w_1 + v_2 - w_2 \leqq B_2. \tag{42}$$

Similarly, the constraint for the third period is

$$\sum_{j=1}^{n} a_{j3}x_j - (1+r)v_2 + (1+r)w_2 + v_3 - w_3 \leqq B_3. \tag{43}$$

The scale limits yield a set of n constraints

$$x_j \leqq 1 \qquad\qquad (j = 1, 2, \ldots, n) \tag{44}$$

Since the firm seeks to maximise assets held at the end of period 3, the objective is to

maximise $\qquad\qquad v_3 - w_3,$ (45)

and to do this the firm has to choose non-negative values for v_t and w_t (for $t = 1, 2, 3$) and for the x_j (for $j = 1, \ldots, n$).

To the primal problem represented by (41)–(45), a dual problem may now be formulated. Let y_t (for $t = 1, 2$ and 3) denote the dual variables corresponding to the budget constraints, and let u_j (for $j = 1, 2, \ldots, n$) denote the dual variables corresponding to the scale constraints (44). The dual problem is in the standard minimum form:

find non-negative values for the y_t and u_j so as to

minimise $\qquad\qquad \sum_{t=1}^{3} y_t B_t + \sum_{j=1}^{n} u_j$ (46)

subject to $\qquad \sum_{t=1}^{3} a_{jt}y_t + u_j \geqq 0 \qquad (j = 1, 2, \ldots, n)$ (47)

$$y_1 - (1+r)y_2 \geqq 0 \tag{48}$$

$$-y_1 + (1+r)y_2 \geqq 0 \tag{49}$$

$$y_2 - (1+r)y_3 \geqq 0 \tag{50}$$

$$-y_2 + (1+r)y_3 \geqq 0 \tag{51}$$

$$y_3 \geqq 1 \tag{52}$$

$$-y_3 \geqq -1 \tag{53}$$

Note that this has $(n + 6)$ constraints, corresponding to the $(n + 6)$ variables in the primal, the x_j and the v_t and w_t.

The structure of the dual problem permits the immediate deduction of some important results, without any need to obtain a numerical solution for the primal (which would not in any case be possible unless numerical values were specified for the a_{jt} and the B_t). From (48) and (49), it is immediately clear that $y_1 = (1 + r)y_2$, and from (50) and (51) that $y_2 = (1 + r)y_3$. Furthermore, from (52) and (53), $y_3 = 1$. Thus $y_2 = (1 + r)$ and $y_1 = (1 + r)^2$. Now, in the usual interpretation of a dual variable, y_t measures the rate of increase of the objective function as B_t is increased. The result for y_3 is immediately obvious: if B_3 is increased by a dollar, the assets held at the end of period 3 are automatically increased by a dollar too. For the result $y_2 = (1 + r)$, the interpretation needs a little more care: an extra dollar in period 2 will grow in value, and the result for y_2 shows that by period 3 it will grow to $\$(1 + r)$. This implies that (in general) the firm will be either lending or borrowing, at interest rate r, between periods 2 and 3. In either case, an extra dollar available in period 2 adds $\$(1 + r)$ in period 3 (by increasing v_2 or reducing w_2 by $\$1$). Similarly, if B_1 is increased by a dollar, the consequence for assets at the end of period 3 is an increase of $\$(1 + r)^2$. Between periods 1 and 2, the firm is (in general) either lending or borrowing at interest rate r; at the margin, the firm can transfer assets from one period to the next, at interest rate r.

Turning now to the investment activities, the dual constraints (47) imply

$$- \sum_{t=1}^{3} a_{jt}y_t \leq u_j \qquad (j = 1, \ldots, n) \tag{54}$$

Upon substituting the specific values for the y_t, the jth constraint becomes

$$- \sum_{t=1}^{3} a_{jt}/(1 + r)^t \leq u_j(1 + r)^{-3}. \tag{55}$$

Note that the left-hand-side value is the net present value (in period 0) of project j, with discounting done at the rate r.

Now consider various cases:

(i)   If the net present value $- \sum a_{jt}/(1 + r)^t < 0$, then (55) must hold as an inequality, since $u_j \geq 0$. From Theorem 3 (of Chapter 3) this inequality implies $x_j = 0$. In the optimal solution, the project is not undertaken.

(ii) If the net present value is strictly positive, two sub-cases must be examined:

(a) If (55) holds as an inequality, $x_j = 0$. Thus the scale constraint is not binding, and $u_j = 0$. Thus the right-hand side of (55) is zero, while the left-hand side is strictly positive. This contradiction means that this sub-case cannot occur.

    (b) Thus (55) must hold as an equality, and hence $u_j > 0$, which means that the scale limit is binding, i.e. $x_j = 1$.

Thus, if the net present value is strictly positive, it is optimal to undertake the project at full scale.

(iii)   If the net present value is zero, an inequality in (55) is ruled out (by an argument similar to that used in case (ii)). With (55) holding as an equality, $x_j \geq 0$. Also because the left-hand side of (55) is zero, $u_j = 0$, and hence $x_j \leq 1$. Thus, in the optimum, $0 \leq x_j \leq 1$; the project may be undertaken, but is not necessarily undertaken at full scale.

In the discussion of the optimal values for the y_t, it was remarked that *in general* the firm will be either lending or borrowing (at interest rate r) between any two adjacent periods. The exceptional case can now be explained. If there happens to be an investment project whose present value (at discount rate r) is exactly zero, then the firm *may* have no such lending or borrowing contracts for the particular pair of periods. Instead, as an alternative to lending or borrowing, the marginal investment project may be undertaken at strictly positive level, in order to transfer sufficient assets between periods at the interest rate r, which (in this case) can be earned *in* the project.

In conclusion, then, the exploration of the dual problem has given considerable insight into the nature of the optimal solution to the primal. Specifically, it has been shown that it is possible to work out the optimal plan by evaluating the projects one by one. To do this, the net present value is calculated for each project, using the interest rate r. If this value is strictly positive, the project should be undertaken at full scale; if it is negative, the project should not be undertaken; if it is zero, the project may be undertaken at some positive scale, as a (partial) alternative to entering into lending or borrowing contracts. Such contracts will be made to the extent necessary to finance investment projects having positive net present value, and/or to store value until the end of the final period.

Although these results are intuitively obvious, the duality analysis has provided a rigorous derivation of them. In more complex models, such duality analysis may give insights that are not intuitively obvious.

10.5 FURTHER READING

In economic theory, studies that seek to identify optimal policies, and that use formal optimisation methods, are to be found in a wide range of journals. In *Journal of Economic Theory*, *Journal of Mathematical Economics* and *Econometrica*, such studies are often written in a (mathematically) advanced style.

Papers in a more accessible style are to be found in, for example, *American Economic Review, Journal of Political Economy, Quarterly Journal of Economics* and *Southern Economic Journal*.

Most of the empirical studies using formal optimisation models are in the areas of pricing, output and investment decisions for individual enterprises, and for sectors of the economy such as the energy sector; there are also studies in fields such as transport, conservation and depletion of exhaustible resources, and urban planning. A particularly important source of such empirical studies is *Bell Journal of Economics*. Papers also appear in a range of journals for individual fields, such as *Journal of Transport Economics and Policy, Energy Economics*, and *Journal of Environmental Economics and Management*.

There follows a small personal selection of interesting empirical papers. The student who is considering whether to read these (or other) empirical studies, should note that linear (and, sometimes, non-linear) programming models are often relatively easy to follow, because there is little analytical development (other than that encompassed in the standard programming model). On the other hand, studies using the Kuhn–Tucker conditions or various special-purpose non-linear optimisations may deploy a considerable amount of mathematical argument before arriving at the optimisation itself, and such papers are often harder to master.

The selected papers are:

- Modiano and Shapiro (1980): a multi-period linear programming process model of the energy sector (focusing on depletable resource aspects) with an application to the USA.
- Manne (1976): in order to assess new technology in the energy sector, a non-linear programming model is solved to give an approximate result for a market equilibrium.
- Kennedy (1974): calculates a long-run equilibrium for a multi-commodity, multi-regional model of the world oil market, using a quadratic programming algorithm.
- Scherer (1976): a mixed-integer (linear) programming model is used to find the least-cost investment and operating plan for an electricity supply system (in upstate New York) for each of several given demand states and for alternative pollution constraints.
- Epple and Lave (1980): examines US federal government policy on helium conservation, using a non-linear programming formulation and the Kuhn–Tucker conditions.
- Dimopoulos (1981): evaluates multi-part pricing schemes for regulated enterprises, with an eye to distributional as well as efficiency aspects; uses a complicated non-linear formulation for which numerical optimisation is used (see below); application to a US electric utility.

This book has concentrated on analytical methods of optimisation (such as the Kuhn–Tucker conditions) and on well-defined numerical algorithms, which have guaranteed convergence to an optimum and which economise on computation by exploiting the mathematical properties of the solutions. For some complicated non-linear optimisation problems, such an approach may not be available; in that case, it is sometimes possible to find an optimum by simple numerical search of the objective function (response surface). (The last of the above papers uses this approach, although the details are not featured in the paper itself.) Such numerical search is little more than a sophisticated trial and error strategy, in which feasible points are sampled until the calculation reaches a point that appears to be at or near the optimum.

A related technique for empirical work is numerical *simulation*. This is used when it is not feasible to represent the behaviour of a system by an analytical model. This approach can be particularly helpful when the system has significant elements of uncertainty, as (for example) with rainfall needed to replenish water stocks (in a system of dams) used for electricity generation and/or irrigation. The effects of any proposed operating rule (for drawing water from storage) may be examined numerically by repeated trials with different numerical patterns of rainfall. An interesting water-resources study that uses this approach (as well as mathematical programming models) is Maass (1962).

Appendix A: Mathematical Prerequisites

In keeping with the aim of the book, the exposition requires as little prior mathematical training as possible. This appendix identifies these mathematical prerequisites; it is hoped that this review will be of assistance to those who wish to refresh their mathematical knowledge to facilitate study of this book. It must be emphasised that this appendix is only a *review:* although the account of basic concepts in section 1 is more or less self-contained, the calculus results of sections 2 and 3 are stated briefly, without proof. Section 4 gives references to a few elementary mathematical texts.

In the book, Chapters 1–4 deal exclusively with linear models; calculus is not used at all. Furthermore, the exposition of these chapters does not require any knowledge of vector and matrix algebra. Chapters 5 and 6 make limited use of some very elementary differential calculus. Chapter 7 is the most demanding mathematically: it requires further calculus techniques, including partial differentiation of functions of several variables; it uses the vector concept and the operation of vector addition; and it makes deeper use of the concept of a convex set or region. The remaining chapters require no additional mathematical knowledge.

The specific mathematical prerequisites may be grouped under appropriate headings and listed (broadly) in their order of appearance in the book.

1. MISCELLANEOUS BASIC CONCEPTS

Summation notation, $\sum$:

$$\textit{Example:} \quad \sum_{j=1}^{3} x_j = x_1 + x_2 + x_3$$

Inequality relationships:

$>$ greater than	e.g. $2 > 1$
$\geq$ greater than or equal to	e.g. $x \geq 0$

and, similarly, $<$ and $\leq$ (less than, less than or equal to)

Vector, which is defined as an ordered one-dimensional array

Example: on a graph, the point determined by $x_1 = 2$, $x_2 = 4$ may be denoted by the row vector [2 4]

or the column vector

$$\begin{bmatrix} 2 \\ 4 \end{bmatrix}$$

Vector addition: defined only when the vectors to be added are all row vectors, *or* all column vectors, and all have the same number of elements; to effect vector addition, add the corresponding elements.

Examples: [2 3] + [1 4] = [3 7]

and

$$\begin{bmatrix} 1 \\ 2 \\ 3 \end{bmatrix} + \begin{bmatrix} 4 \\ 5 \\ 6 \end{bmatrix} = \begin{bmatrix} 5 \\ 7 \\ 9 \end{bmatrix}$$

Convex set (region): a set is convex if, for *any* two points in the set, any point lying on the line segment that joins these two points is also in the set.

Extreme point of a convex set: a point in a convex set is an extreme point if it is *not* possible to find two other, distinct points such that the original point lies on the line segment joining these two points.

Exponential function, of a variable x, is of the form $y = b^x$, where the base b is positive. (The name of the function comes from the property that the variable x is used as an exponent in the function.)

Logarithm of a positive number: if the positive number y may be expressed as a power x of some base b (i.e. if $y = b^x$), then x is called the logarithm (to the base b) of the given number y (i.e. $x = \log_b y$).

The number e is a particularly important number because it serves as a very useful base in exponential and logarithmic functions. In order to define e, first consider the function $f = (1 + 1/n)^n$, where n is a positive integer. Some values of this function are: for $n = 1$, $f = 2$; for $n = 2$, $f = 2.25$; for $n = 3$, $f = 2.37$; and so forth. As n gets larger and larger, the value of f approaches 2.71828 (approximately!), and this case – with infinitely large n – is used to define the number e. Formally

$$e = \lim_{n \to \infty} (1 + 1/n)^n = 2.71828....$$

Logarithm to the base e: if $y = e^x$, then $\log_e y = x$. This is usually written more simply as $x = \log y$ or $x = \ln y$. Logarithms to the base e are called natural logarithms.

Discounting in continuous time: Given an interest rate r per period, the discount factor for period t is $1/(1+r)^t$. Suppose now that interest is compounded k times per period at rate r/k. The discount factor for period t is now $1/(1+r/k)^{kt}$. The denominator may be written alternatively as $[(1+r/k)^{k/r}]^{rt}$. Now, writing $n = k/r$, this becomes $[(1+1/n)^n]^{rt}$. Discounting in continuous time is equivalent to allowing k, and hence n, to become inifinitely large; then the discount factor becomes e^{-rt}.

2.   BASIC DIFFERENTIATION

The first set of results applies in the case of a (continuous) function y of a single continuous variable x, with the function denoted $y = f(x)$, in the general case.

The derivative of y with respect to x is defined as the rate of change of y, occasioned by an infinitesimally small increase in x; it is denoted dy/dx; and sometimes $f'(x)$ is used as an alternative notation.

Rules of differentiation for particular cases:

The derivative is given by the expression shown in each of these cases

$f(x)$ a constant: $dy/dx = 0$

$f(x) = x^n$: $dy/dx = nx^{n-1}$ where n is any integer or *fraction*

$f(x) = g(x) + h(x)$: $dy/dx = f'(x) = g'(x) + h'(x)$

$f(x) = uv$ (where u and v are functions of x): $dy/dx = v\,du/dx + u\,dv/dx = vu'(x) + uv'(x)$

$y = g(u)$, and $u = h(x)$: $\dfrac{dy}{dx} = \dfrac{dy}{du} \cdot \dfrac{du}{dx}$

Example: $y = (x^2 + 3x)^{1/2}$ Let $(x^2 + 3x)$ be denoted u.

Then $y = u^{1/2}$ with $u = x^2 + 3x$

$dy/du \quad = \tfrac{1}{2}u^{-1/2}$ and $du/dx = 2x + 3$

Hence $dy/dx = \tfrac{1}{2}(2x + 3)(x^2 + 3x)^{-1/2}$.

$y = \log x = \ln x$: $dy/dx = 1/x$

$y = e^u$ with $u = u(x)$: $dy/dx = e^u \cdot du/dx$.

Example: if $y = e^{2x^2+x}$, let $u = 2x^2 + x$; then $dy/dx = (4x + 1)e^{2x^2+x}$

The second derivative is obtained by differentiating, with respect to x, the first derivative dy/dx; the result is denoted d^2y/dx^2.

Example: if $y = 3x^4$, $dy/dx = 12x^3$ and $d^2y/dx^2 = 36x^2$.

The following gives some generalisations that apply when y is a function of several independent variables x_1, x_2, ..., x_n.

Partial derivative: suppose x_j, one of the independent variables, is allowed to change, while all the other independent variables are held constant. The partial derivative of y with respect to x_j is defined as the rate of change of y for an infinitesimally small increase in x_j, and is denoted $\partial y/\partial x_j$.

Example: $y = x_1^2 + 2x_2 + 3x_3^3 + 5x_1x_2$

Then $\partial y/\partial x_1 = 2x_1 + 5x_2$

$\partial y/\partial x_2 = 2 + 5x_1$

$\partial y/\partial x_3 = 9x_3^2$

Second-order partial derivative is defined, as before, as the appropriate derivative of a first-order derivative.

Example: $y = x_1^2 + (2 + 5x_1)x_2$

$\partial y/\partial x_1 = 2x_1 + 5x_2$, $\partial^2 y/\partial x_1 \partial x_2 = 5$

and $\partial^2 y/\partial x_1^2 = 2$.

3. UNCONSTRAINED OPTIMISATION

In unconstrained optimisation, the independent variable(s) – x or x_j for $j = 1, 2, ..., n$ – may take either sign; and there are no other constraints on the values that may be taken by the independent variable(s).

For a function $y = f(x)$ of a single variable, x:
A necessary condition for a minimum or a maximum at $x = a$ is that $dy/dx = f'(x) = 0$ at that point.

A set of sufficient conditions involves the second derivative. The function has a maximum at $x = a$ if at that point $dy/dx = 0$ and $d^2y/dx^2 < 0$. The sufficient conditions for a minimum are $dy/dx = 0$ and $d^2y/dx^2 > 0$.

For a function of several independent variables:

In general, the sufficient conditions are complex, but are not used in this book. However it is easy to note that in the case of two independent variables u, v a set of sufficient conditions for a maximum of the function $y = g(u, v)$ is

$$(1) \quad \frac{\partial y}{\partial u} = 0 \qquad \frac{\partial y}{\partial v} = 0$$

$$(2) \quad \frac{\partial y^2}{\partial u^2} < 0 \qquad \frac{\partial y^2}{\partial v^2} < 0$$

$$(3) \quad \frac{\partial y^2}{\partial u^2} \cdot \frac{\partial y^2}{\partial v^2} > \left(\frac{\partial^2 y}{\partial u \partial v}\right)^2$$

For a minimum, the inequalities are reversed in the conditions denoted (2). The conditions denoted (1) are necessary for a maximum or minimum.

4 FURTHER READING

There are, of course, many textbooks of basic mathematical techniques. The following is just a small sample.

For study of calculus, there is an old but trusty work:
R. G. D. Allen (1938) *Mathematical Analysis for Economists,* London: Macmillan.
A *very* elementary treatment of a little calculus is
S. G. B. Henry (1969) *Elementary Mathematical Economics,* London: Routledge & Kegan Paul.
For linear algebra, see
G. Mills (1969) *Introduction to Linear Algebra,* London: Allen & Unwin.
A more advanced work in that field is
G. Hadley (1961) *Linear Algebra,* Reading, Mass.: Addison-Wesley.
For a good selection of material in both calculus and linear algebra, the student of economics might try
D. S. Huang (1969) *Introduction to the Use of Mathematics in Economic Analysis,* New York: Wiley.
An alternative for students with more of a business orientation is
B. V. Dean, M. W. Sasieni and S. K. Gupta (1963) *Mathematics for Modern Management,* New York: Wiley.

Appendix B: Glossary of Economic Terms

To help the reader who may have only a limited background in economic theory, this glossary provides *very brief* definitions of some of the economic terms that are used, but not fully explained, in the text. For fuller (and more rigorous) definitions, the reader may wish to consult a dictionary of economic terms, such as

G. Bannock, R. E. Baxter and R. Rees (1978) *The Penguin Dictionary of Economics* (2nd edn), Harmondsworth, Middx: Penguin.

D. W. Pearce (ed.) (1981) *The Macmillan Dictionary of Economics,* London: Macmillan.

A. Seldon and F. G. Pennance (1975) *Everyman's Dictionary of Economics,* London:J. M. Dent.

The reader may also find it useful to study some longer articles given in an encyclopedia, such as

D. Greenwald (ed.) (1982) *Encyclopedia of Economics,* New York: McGraw-Hill.

In the entries in the following list, a term is italicized if it is the subject of another entry.

Comparative static analysis
An *equilibrium* that holds before some *exogenous* change occurs is compared with the new equilibrium that results from that change.

Competitive equilibrium
An *equilibrium* situation in a *perfectly competitive* market.

Cross-price elasticity of demand
The ratio of the proportionate change in quantity demanded of one good to the proportionate increase in the price of another good, in a situation in which the demands are dependent (sometimes called 'interdependent'), i.e. in which the quantity demanded depends on the price(s) of related good(s) as well as on its own price.

Demand elasticity (with respect to price)
The ratio of the proportionate change in quantity demanded to the proportionate increase in own price (which causes the change in demand quantity). ('Own price' means the price of the good in question.)

Diseconomies of scale
These exist when total production costs increase more than proportionately with output as the scale of production of the good is increased.

Economic dynamics
The study of change over time in an economic system. Usually some *exogenous* change is postulated; this disturbs the initial equilibrium; the analysis seeks to trace the process of adjustment as the system moves to a new equilibrium.

Economic efficiency
A production arrangement is efficient if, for the given amounts of inputs used, it is not possible to produce more of one output without reducing the production of some other output *and* if, for the given output levels, it is not possible to reduce the utilisation of one input without increasing that of another input.

(There is a corresponding definition for allocative efficiency, which is equivalent to *Pareto optimality.*)

Economies of scale
These exist when total production costs increase less than proportionately with output as the scale of production of a good is increased.

Endogenous
Describes anything that is not taken as given, but is determined within (explained by) a particular economic model.

Equilibrium
A state in which none of the agents in an economic system have any incentive to change their behaviour; hence the system's condition is unchanging over time. Such an equilibrium is disturbed only by an *exogenous* change (e.g. bad weather that may reduce crop yields and lead to higher prices for agricultural products).

Exogenous
Describes anything that is considered (within a particular economic model) to be predetermined or given. An exogenous variable is not explained by the model; rather it is simply accepted as one of the ingredients of the analysis.

Historical dynamic analysis
In contrast to *economic dynamics* (which generally starts with a supposed *equilibrium*), historical dynamics studies the evolution of an economic system whose initial state is specified in full historical detail.

Neoclassical economics
A school of economic thought that seeks to analyse and explain economic phenomena in terms of choices made by individual agents, who are presumed to have complete information about the choices open to them.

Normative economics
The study of what ought to be. Usually deploys (implicitly or explicitly) value judgments favoured by the study's author, and hence constitutes political advocacy.

Pareto optimality (Pareto welfare-maximisation)
Vilfredo Pareto (1848–1923) defined an optimal (welfare-maximising) situation of exchange as one from which it is not possible to effect a change that makes some people better off, except by making others worse off. For any given economy, a Pareto optimum is not unique; each alternative optimum implies a different distribution of income and wealth.

Perfect competition
A situation in a market (for a homogeneous good) in which there are large numbers of both buyers and sellers (all of whom have complete information about the market's transactions), and such that the quantity traded by any one buyer or seller is so small (relative to the total market) that any conceivable change in such a quantity leaves the market price virtually unaffected. Hence sellers (buyers) in such a market regard the price as given, and not susceptible to influence by the individual seller (buyer).

Positive economics
The study of what is (in contrast to *normative* and *prescriptive* economics).

Prescriptive economics
Analysis designed to find the optimal policy, given a stated objective. That objective can take any form, and (in contrast to *normative economics*) the objective is specified by the decision-maker for whom the analysis is undertaken.

Production function
A function that links input and output levels and traces all the *efficient* production arrangements.

Ricardian economy
David Ricardo (1772–1823) analysed an economic model with a number of distinctive features. One of the most significant (and this is the only feature emphasised in this book) is the assumption that the total supply of land is fixed; land plots of differing qualities have different scarcity values (dual values, rents) in a *competitive equilibrium,* and these rents influence the distribution of income in the economy.

Bibliography

Abadie, J., ed. (1967) *Nonlinear Programming,* Amsterdam: North-Holland

Arrow, K. J. and Enthoven, A. C. (1961) 'Quasi-concave programming', *Econometrica*, vol. 29, pp. 779–800

Arrow, K. J., Karlin, S. and Scarf, H. (1958) *Studies in the Mathematical Theory of Inventory and Production,* Stanford, Calif.: Stanford University Press

Averch, H. and Johnson, L. L. (1962) 'Behavior of the firm under regulatory constraint', *American Economic Review*, vol. 52, pp. 1052–1069

Baumol, W. J. (1967) *Business Behavior, Value and Growth,* rev. edn, New York: Harcourt, Brace and World

Beale, E. M. L. (1968) *Mathematical Programming in Practice*, London: Pitman

Beckmann, M. J. (1968) *Dynamic Programming of Economic Decisions*, Berlin: Springer-Verlag

Bellman, R. E. (1957) *Dynamic Programming*, Princeton, NJ: Princeton University Press

Bellman, R. E. and Dreyfus, S. E. (1962) *Applied Dynamic Programming*, Princeton, NJ: Princeton University Press

Benavie A. (1972) *Mathematical Techniques for Economic Analysis*, Englewood Cliffs, NJ: Prentice-Hall

Day, R. H. (1963) *Recursive Programming and Production Response*, Amsterdam: North-Holland

Dimopoulos, D. (1981) 'Pricing schemes for regulated enterprises and their welfare implications in the case of electricity', *Bell Journal of Economics*, vol. 12, pp. 185–200.

Dixit, A. K. (1976) *Optimisation in Economic Theory,* London: Oxford University Press

Dixon, P. B., Bowles, S. and Kendrick, D. (1980) *Notes and Problems in Microeconomic Theory*, Amsterdam: North-Holland

Dorfman, R. (1969) 'An economic interpretation of optimal control theory', *American Economic Review*, vol. 59, pp. 817–31

Dorfman, R., Samuelson, P. A. and Solow, R. M. (1958) *Linear Programming and Economic Analysis,* New York: McGraw-Hill

Epple, D. and Lave, L. (1980) 'Helium: investments in the future', *Bell Journal of Economics,* vol. 11, pp. 617–30

Flemming, J. S. (1969) 'The utility of wealth and the utility of windfalls', *Review of Economic Studies*, vol. 36, pp. 55–66

Frank, C. R. (1969) *Production Theory and Indivisible Commodities*, Princeton, NJ: Princeton University Press

Freidenfelds, J. (1981) *Capacity Expansion*, Amsterdam: Elsevier

Frey, S. C. and Nemhauser, G. L. (1972) 'Temporal expansion of a transportation network', *Transportation Science*, vol. 6, pp. 306–23

Gill, P. E., Murray, W. and Wright, M. H. (1981) *Practical Optimization*, London: Academic Press

Glaister, S. (1976) 'Peak load pricing and the Channel tunnel', *Journal of Transport Economics and Policy,* vol. 10, pp. 99–112

Gomory, R. E. and Baumol, W. J. (1960) 'Integer programming and pricing', *Econometrica*, vol. 28, pp. 521–50

Green, H. A. J. (1971) *Consumer Theory*, Harmondsworth, Middx: Penguin (rev. edn, 1976, London: Macmillan)

Hadley, G. (1964) *Nonlinear and Dynamic Programming*, Reading, Mass.: Addison-Wesley

Hammond, P. J. (1976) 'Changing tastes and coherent dynamic choice', *Review of Economic Studies*, vol. 43, pp. 159–73

Heady, E. O. and Dillon, J. L., eds (1961) *Agricultural Production Functions*, Ames: Iowa State University Press

Henderson, J. M. (1958) *The Efficiency of the Coal Industry: an Application of Linear Programming*, Cambridge, Mass.: Harvard University Press

Intriligator, M. D. (1971) *Mathematical Optimisation and Economic Theory*, Englewood Cliffs, NJ: Prentice-Hall

Jacobs, D., ed. (1977) *The State of the Art in Numerical Analysis*, London: Academic Press

Jacobs, L. R. (1967) *An Introduction to Dynamic Programming*, London: Chapman and Hall

Kamien, M. and Schwartz, N. L. (1981) *Dynamic Optimisation: The Calculus of Variations and Optimal Control in Economics and Management*, New York: North-Holland

Kendrick, D. A. (1967) *Programming Investment in the Process Industries*, Cambridge, Mass.: MIT Press

Kennedy, M. (1974) 'An economic model of the world oil market', *Bell Journal of Economics*, vol. 5, pp. 540–77

Kogiku, K. C. (1971) *Microeconomic Models*, New York: Harper and Row

Kydland, F. E. and Prescott, E. C. (1977) 'Rules rather than discretion: the inconsistency of optimal plans', *Journal of Political Economy*, vol. 85, pp. 473–91

Lancaster, K. (1968) *Mathematical Economics*, New York: Macmillan

Land, A. H. and Doig, A. G. (1960) 'An automatic method of solving discrete programming problems', *Econometrica*, vol. 28, pp. 497–520

Layard, P. R. G. and Walters, A. A. (1978) *Microeconomic Theory*, New York: McGraw-Hill

Maass, A. and others (1962) *Design of Water-Resource Systems*, Cambridge, Mass.: Harvard University Press

Manne, A. S. (1957) 'A note on the Modigliani–Hohn smoothing model', *Management Science*, vol. 3, pp. 371–9

Manne, A. S. (1958) 'A linear programming model of the U.S. petroleum refining industry', *Econometrica*, vol. 26, pp. 67–106

Manne, A. S., ed. (1967) *Investments for Capacity Expansion*, London: Allen & Unwin

Manne, A. S. (1970) 'Sufficient conditions for optimality in an infinite horizon development plan', *Econometrica*, vol. 38, pp. 18–38

Manne, A. S. (1976) 'ETA: a model for energy technology assessment', *Bell Journal of Economics*, vol. 7, pp. 379–406

Marani, A. and Fuchs, Y. (1964) 'Effect of the amount of water applied as a single irrigation on cotton grown under dryland conditions', *Agronomy Journal*, vol. 56, pp. 281–2

Mills, G. and Coleman, W. (1982) 'Peak load pricing and the Channel tunnel: a re-examination', *Journal of Transport Economics and Policy*, vol. 16, pp. 267–76

Modiano, E. M. and Shapiro, J. F. (1980) 'A dynamic optimisation model of depletable resources', *Bell Journal of Economics*, vol. 11, pp. 212–36

Modigliani, F. and Hohn, F. E. (1955) 'Production planning over time', *Econometrica*, vol. 23, pp. 46–66

Moore, P. G. and Hodges, S. D., eds (1970) *Programming for Optimal Decisions*, Harmondsworth, Middx: Penguin

Naylor, T. H. and Byrne, E. T. (1963) *Linear Programming Methods and Cases*, Belmont, Calif.: Wadsworth

Nordhaus, W. D. (1973) 'The allocation of energy resources', *Brookings Papers in Economic Activity*, vol. 3, pp. 529–76

Pollak, R. A. (1968) 'Consistent planning', *Review of Economic Studies*, vol. 35, pp. 201–8

Quirk, J. P. (1982) *Intermediate Microeconomics*, 2nd edn; Chicago: Science Research Associates (1st edn, 1976)

Scherer, C. R. (1976) 'Estimating peak and off-peak marginal costs for an electric power system: an ex ante approach', *Bell Journal of Economics*, vol. 7, pp. 575–60

Shone, R. (1981) *Applications in Intermediate Microeconomics*, New York: Wiley

Smith, V. L. (1961) *Investment and Production*, Cambridge, Mass.: Harvard University Press

Sternberger, A. P. (1959) 'Evaluating the competitive position of North Carolina eggs by use of the transportation model', *Journal of Farm Economics*, vol. 41, pp. 790–8

Strotz, R. H. (1955/6) 'Myopia and inconsistency in dynamic utility maximisation', *Review of Economic Studies*, vol. 23, pp. 165–80

Takayama, T. and Judge, G. G. (1971) *Spatial and Temporal Price and Allocation Models*, Amsterdam: North-Holland

Vandermeulen, D. C. (1971) *Linear Economic Theory*, Englewood Cliffs, NJ: Prentice-Hall

Varian, H. R. (1978) *Microeconomic Analysis*, New York: Norton

Wein, H. H. and Sreedharan, V. P. (1968) *The Optimal Staging and Phasing of Multi-Product Capacity*, East Lansing: Michigan State University

White, D. J. (1969) *Dynamic Programming*, Edinburgh: Oliver and Boyd

Whitin, T. M. (1953) 'Classical theory, Graham's theory and linear programming in international trade', *Quarterly Journal of Economics*, vol. 67, pp. 520–44

Index

(An italicised page number indicates a formal definition or a fairly full explanation of the term.)